DICTIONARY
OF MIND,
MATTER AND MORALS

Bertrand Russell:

~ Dictionary of Mind, Matter & Morals ~

Edited, with an Introduction, by
LESTER E. DENONN

A CITADEL PRESS BOOK
Published by Carol Publishing Group

PREFACE

I feel considerably honoured that my philosophy should have been thought worthy to be alphabetically anatomized in this dictionary. I have been accused of a habit of changing my opinions in philosophy and, in so far as this is true, the dictionary will enable readers to find it out. I am not myself in any degree ashamed of having changed my opinions. What physicist who was already active in 1900 would dream of boasting that his opinions had not changed during the last half century? In science men change their opinions when new knowledge becomes available, but philosophy in the minds of many is assimilated rather to theology than to science. A theologian proclaims eternal truths, the creeds remain unchanged since the Council of Nicaea. Where nobody knows anything, there is no point in changing your mind. But the kind of philosophy that I value and have endeavoured to pursue is scientific in the sense that there is some definite knowledge to be obtained and that new discoveries can make the admission of former error inevitable to any candid mind. For what I have said, whether early or late, I do not claim the kind of truth which theologians claim for their creeds. I claim only, at best, that the opinion expressed was a sensible one to hold at the time when it was expressed. I should be much surprised if subsequent research did not show that it needed to be modified. I hope, therefore, that whoever uses this dictionary will not suppose the remarks which it quotes to be intended as pontifical pronouncements, but only as the best that I could do at the time towards the promotion of clear and accurate thinking. Clarity, above all, has been my aim. I prefer a clear statement subsequently disproved to a misty dictum capable of some profound interpretation which can be welcomed as a "great thought." It is not by "great thoughts," but by careful and detailed analysis, that the kind of technical philosophy which I value can be advanced.

I will not deny, however, that there are regions as yet inaccessible to exact knowledge and yet of such practical importance that we cannot be content merely to suspend judgment. The reader will find that on such matters, also, I have spoken copiously, perhaps too copiously. But I make always in my thought a sharp distinction between the doubtful problems in which the emotion must have its place and the happy realms of exactness where pure thought can disport itself in freedom. I hope that readers will bear this difference in mind.

BERTRAND RUSSELL

INTRODUCTION

On May 18, 1872, there was born to Lord and Lady Amberley, a son named Bertrand Arthur William Russell. He was orphaned at an early age and therefore brought up at the home of his grandfather, the famous English Liberal Prime Minister, Lord John Russell. He was taught by private tutors until old enough to enter Cambridge University, where he early displayed his brilliance in mathematics and philosophy.

Upon graduation, he entered the diplomatic service, but disliked it. Following observation and study on the Continent, leading to his earliest works on "German Social Democracy" and "The Foundations of Geometry," he returned to Cambridge where he lectured. Chance enabled him to give a course on the philosophy of Leibniz, the essence of which he embodied in a definitive work on the subject.

The next ten years were devoted primarily to his work in mathematical philosophy. His "Principles of Mathematics" was followed by the three volumes of a pioneering work in mathematical or symbolic logic, "The Principia Mathematica," in the preparation of which he collaborated with Alfred North Whitehead.

World War I found him still busily engaged in writing and lecturing on topics in the advanced fields of technical philosophy, but the impact of the world conflict turned his attention anew to social, political and international problems. A succession of trenchant works followed, including his most provocative "Principles of Social Reconstruction." During this period he wrote a number of pamphlets and articles on the war, one of which led to a fine and another to six months' imprisonment. He was fortunately allowed to use this term to advantage and wrote "Introduction to Mathematical Philosophy" while incarcerated.

He was deprived of his Lectureship at Cambridge because of his difficulties during the war, so that he turned exclusively to writing, lecturing and travelling during the decades between the two world wars. His visits to China and Russia led to volumes on the conditions in these countries. He expressed high regard for the ancient civilization of China and, in the early twenties, he was among the first to decry the theory and practice of Communism, a view he has staunchly maintained through the years.

He made a number of short lecture tours to the United States and also spent a number of years here lecturing at some of our largest universities. Rancorous bigotry prevented his taking a post at The City College of New York. After this distasteful incident, he accepted a position at The Barnes Foundation, but found himself once again in litigation when he had to sue for dismissal without legal cause. The lectures he gave at The Barnes Foundation were part of his preparation for his monumental "A History of Western Philosophy."

Following these events in America, he returned to Cambridge where he had been restored to favor. World War II found him an outspoken opponent of totalitarianism and, in contradistinction to his views during World War I, he felt the war to oppose Nazi, Fascist and Japanese aggression to be entirely justifiable. He continues as a vigorous antagonist of Communist imperialism.

After World War II, he felt more at home with the advent of the Labor Government and its socialist aims. He even took the opportunity on a few occasions of taking his seat in the House of Lords. He had fallen heir to the title of Lord Russell upon the untimely death of an elder brother, but had scarcely bothered to employ the title much less enjoy any of its privileges until the Labor Government's rule. His voice then as a leading exponent of democratic and liberal traditions was widely hearkened to and his labors duly rewarded by the Order of Merit.

Despite advancing age, he still astounds the world with volumes of penetrating analysis on a wide variety of subjects and still fascinates large, clamoring audiences with his sharp wit and his abundant wisdom.

II.

This volume contains more than 1000 selections from over 100 of Lord Russell's books and articles. The fact of English and American editions reveals a variance in spelling and in punctuation. No attempt has been made to attain any consistency. It is hoped that this will not be disconcerting to the reader.

Here are but samples and they cannot—and should not—be permitted to take the place of careful reading of the works themselves, but these selections, as here set forth, lend themselves to a variety of uses through either casual or intensive study of their import.

In the first place, this volume can serve as an introduction to Russell for the Russell flavor abounds and the Russell brilliance in analysis, argument and exposition is everywhere in evidence in the pages that follow. One can gain a clear notion of his method of approach, his fundamental principles and many of his leading ideas, all of which make him recognized as one of the twentieth century's foremost philosophers.

Secondly, as the title indicates, this volume is a Dictionary of Matter, Mind and Morals and can be used as a dictionary of terms related to these categories. Here will be found definitions and opinions of Lord Russell on a great many topics and a great many terms that crop up in current studies and in contemporary controversies.

In addition to the light these selections throw upon particular terms, the cross references enable the reader to follow Lord Russell into many facets of contemporary thought in a wide and astonishing variety of fields in which he speaks authoritatively. He is alive to the reigning controversies in these fields and, whether one agrees or disagrees with his views, his exposition can be used as an encyclopaedic introduction to current speculation. A mere listing of some of the subjects sounds pretty much like a college curriculum for here we have a treatment of concepts and contending principles—all treated with a typical Russell touch and with unmistakable evidence of where Russell stands—in such important fields as ethics, politics, metaphysics, religion, theology, epistemology, traditional and modern logic, semantics, psychology, philosophy of history, history of philosophy, the sciences and, in particular, mathematics and physics, to mention but some of the more outstanding divisions of thought in which he has allowed his fertile mind to roam creatively.

Especial reference should be made to one field in which Lord Russell has been outspoken and regarding which the selections given here will reveal his important pronouncements and that is the subject of international relations. In these pages will be found an informative review of problems of international concern as Lord Russell has formulated them.

The last, and by far not the least important, of the advantages flowing from a reading of these pages is the samples they furnish from the pen of one of the best of contemporary English prose stylists. There is charm, balance, clarity, penetration and abundant stimulating turn of phrase. There is ample evidence here of why there was conferred upon Lord Russell the 1950 Nobel Prize—not for philosophy—but for literature.

KEY TO SYMBOLS

AA	Americans Are. . .The Impact of America upon European Culture (1950)
AAI	Authority and the Individual (1949)
ABCA	The ABC of Atoms (1923)
ABCR	The ABC of Relativity (1925)
AM	The Analysis of Mind (1921)
AOM	The Analysis of Matter (1927)
APFY	A Philosophy for You in These Times (1941)
API	The Amberley Papers, Volume I. (1937)
AWF	A World Federation (1941)
BOD	Boredom or Doom in a Scientific World (1948)
BW	Bolshevism and the West (1924)
CAB	Can America and Britain be Friends? (1944)
CAN	If War Comes Can America Stay Neutral? (1939)
CAW	Carroll's Alice in Wonderland (1942)
CGS	Citizenship in a Great State (1943)
CH	The Conquest of Happiness (1930)
CTR	Came the Revolution. . .(1950)
CWA	Can We Afford to Keep Open Minds? (1950)
DAE	Democracy and Economics (1939)
DDM	Descartes' Discourse on Method (1942)
DMC	Divorce by Mutual Consent (1930)
DNL	Dewey's New Logic (1939)
EAW	Education after the War (1943)
EDTF	On the Evils Due to Fear (1929)
EEC	On Education Especially in Early Childhood (1926)
EIU	Education in International Understanding (1944)
ER	The Essence of Religion (1912)
ESO	Education and the Social Order (1932)
FAC	Freedom and the Colleges (1940)

FAG	Freedom and Government (1940)
FAH	How to be Free and Happy (1924)
FAR	The Faith of a Rationalist (1947)
FIE	Freedom in Education (1923)
FO	Freedom and Organization (1934)
FOD	The Future of Democracy (1937)
FOP	Future of Pacifism (1944)
FT	Free Thought and Official Propaganda (1922)
GAT	A Guide for Living in the Atomic Age (1949)
GBP	Government by Propaganda (1924)
HCS	The High Cost of Survival (1949)
HFA	Hopes and Fears as Regards America (1922)
HK	Human Knowledge: Its Scope and Limits (1948)
HPH	Hegel's Philosophy of History (1941)
HWP	A History of Western Philosophy (1945)
I	Icarus, or the Future of Science (1924)
IMP	Introduction to Mathematical Philosophy (1919)
IMT	An Inquiry into Meaning and Truth (1940)
ING	Introduction to The New Generation (1930)
IPI	In Praise of Idleness (1935)
ISI	Is Security Increasing? (1939)
ISIP	The International Significance of the Indian Problem (1943)
ISOS	The Impact of Science on Society (1951)
ISP	Introduction to Selected Papers of Bertrand Russell (1927)
IWS	If We are to Survive this Time (1950)
JWT	Justice in War-Time (1916)
KEW	Our Knowledge of the External World (1914)
KF	The Kind of Fear We Sorely Need (1950)
LA	Logical Atomism (1924)
LAM	Leisure and Mechanism (1923)
LBRC	Letter on the Bertrand Russell Case (1940)
LC	Last Chance (1948)
LIWB	Letter in The World's Best (1950)
LMA	Life in the Middle Ages (1925)
LPR	Living Philosophy Revised (1939)

ML	Mysticism and Logic (1918)
MM	Marriage and Morals (1929)
MMD	My Mental Development (1944)
MPQ	Marriage and the Population Question (1916)
MRR	My Religious Reminiscences (1938)
MRW	Munich Rather than War (1939)
OH	On History (1904)
OP	An Outline of Philosophy (1927)
OSE	Our Sexual Ethics (1936)
P	Power (1938)
PC	The Problem of China (1922)
PCI	The Political and Cultural Interest (1951)
PI	Political Ideals (1917)
PIC	The Prospects of Industrial Civilization (1923)
PL	A Critical Exposition of the Philosophy of Leibniz (1900)
PNW	If We are to Prevent the Next War (1924)
POS	The Philosophy of Santayana (1940)
PP	The Problems of Philosophy (1912)
PPW	Some Problems of the Post-War World (1943)
PSR	Principles of Social Reconstruction (1916)
PTB	The Practice and Theory of Bolshevism (1920)
RAS	Religion and Science (1935)
RF	Roads to Freedom (1917)
RTC	Reply to Criticisms (1944)
RUC	Has Religion Made Useful Contributions to Civilization? (1930)
S	Science (1928)
SAE	Science and Education (1928)
SC	Social Cohesion and Human Nature (1948)
SE	Sceptical Essays (1928)
SIE	Styles in Ethics (1924)
SO	The Scientific Outlook (1931)
SPE	Spinoza's Ethics (1942)
SSI	Science and Social Institutions (1938)
STGS	Still Time for Good Sense (1947)
STS	The Science to Save Us from Science (1950)
TEP	Taming Economic Power (1938)
TFD	To Face Danger without Hysteria (1951)

TRF	To Replace Our Fears with Hope (1950)
TWI	Is a Third War Inevitable? (1950)
TWW	Three Ways to the World (1922)
UE	Unpopular Essays (1951)
WIB	What I Believe (1925)
WIBII	What I Believe (1929)
WIG	Where is Industrialism Going? (1923)
WIH	What is Happiness? (1939)
WMD	When Should Marriage be Dissolved? (1912)
WNC	Why I am Not a Christian (1927)
WNCO	Why I am Not a Communist (1934)
WRU	Why Radicals are Unpopular (1936)
WWP	Which Way to Peace? (1936)
ZPS	Zionism and the Peace Settlement (1943)

DICTIONARY
OF MIND,
MATTER AND MORALS

A

A
see ALL

ABELARD

Abelard's view, that (apart from Scripture) dialectic is the sole road to truth, while no empiricist can accept it, had, at the time, a valuable effect as a solvent of prejudices and an encouragement to the fearless use of the intellect. Nothing outside the Scriptures, he said, is infallible; even Apostles and Fathers may err. (HWP 437)

ABSTRACT

We may thus say that the world of elementary physics is semi-abstract, while that of deductive relativity-theory is wholly abstract. The appearance of deducing actual phenomena from mathematics is delusive; what really happens is that the phenomena afford inductive verification of the general principles from which our mathematics starts. Every observed fact retains its full evidential value; but now it confirms not merely some particular law, but the general law from which the deductive system starts. (AOM 88)

ABSTRACTION
see PHYSICS, MODERN

ACADEMIC FREEDOM

Thus the interlocking power of stupidity below and love of power above paralyses the efforts of rational men. Only through a greater measure of academic freedom than has yet been achieved in the public educational institutions of this country can this evil be averted. (FAC 30)

ACCELERATION
see GALILEO

ACCURACY
see VAGUENESS

ACTION

The word "action" is used to denote energy multiplied by time. That is to say, if there is one unit of energy in a system, it will exert one unit of action in a second, 100 units of action in 100 seconds, and so on; a system which has 100 units of energy will exert 100 units of action in a second, and 10,000 in 100 seconds, and so on. "Action" is thus, in a loose sense, a measure of how much has been accomplished: it is increased both by displaying more energy and by working for a longer time. (ABCR 161)

ADMINISTRATOR'S FALLACY

Our political and social thinking is prone to what may be called the "administrator's fallacy," by which I mean the habit of looking upon a society as a systematic whole, of a sort that is thought good if it is pleasant to contemplate as a model of order, a planned organism with parts neatly dovetailed into each other. But a society does not, or at least should not, exist to satisfy an external survey, but to bring a good life to the individuals who compose it. (AAI 116)

ADULTERY, OFFICIAL

The official adultery to which men have to submit in order that their wives may divorce them is a sordid business, and not the sort of thing that the law ought to demand and promote as it does when adultery is the sole ground for divorce. (DMC 15)

ADVENTURE

A life without adventure is likely to be unsatisfying, but a life in which adventure is allowed to take whatever form it will is sure to be short. (SC 1010)

ADVENTURE, OUTLETS FOR LOVE OF

If mankind succeeds in abolishing war, it should not be difficult to find other outlets for the love of adventure and risk. The old outlets, which at one time served a biological purpose, do so no longer, and therefore new outlets are necessary. But there is nothing in human nature that compels us to acquiesce in continued savagery. Our less orderly impulses are dangerous only when they are denied or misunderstood. When this mistake is avoided, the problem of fitting them into a good social system can be solved by the help of intelligence and goodwill. (AAI 45)

ADVERTISING
see PROPAGANDA; PROPAGANDA, TECHNIQUE OF

AFFECTION
Affection in the sense of a genuine reciprocal interest of two persons in each other, not solely as means to each other's good but rather as a combination having a common good, is one of the most important elements of real happiness, and the man whose ego is so enclosed within steel walls that this enlargement of it is impossible misses the best that life has to offer, however successful he may be in his career. (CH 184-5)

AFFECTIONATENESS
Affectionateness is an emotional habit which is good in moderation, but can easily be carried too far. When carried too far, it involves a lack of self-dependence, which may have very undesirable effects upon character. Some people who are moralists rather than psychologists confound affection with benevolence, and imagine that it consists in a desire for the happiness of the beloved object. This is only very partially the case; in fact, affection in its instinctive manifestations is bound up with jealousy, and is not in all its forms a desirable emotion. (SAE 92)

AFFERENT
The nerve fibers which carry messages to the brain are called "afferent"; those which carry messages from the brain are called "efferent." Broadly speaking, the afferent fibers start from sense organs and the efferent fibers end in muscles. (HK 38)

AGGRESSION
"Aggression" may be defined as any act of war not sanctioned by the international authority. (STGS 57)

There is first the difficulty of defining an "aggressor" . . . . It is enough to say that no definition has yet been proposed which has seemed satisfactory to authorities on international law, and that every imaginable definition would lend itself to deceit and trickery at the outbreak of a war. Perhaps in time the inculcation of a warlike spirit may come to be considered a form of aggression; schools may be forbidden to teach excessive nationalism; and newspapers may be prevented from publishing incitements to national hatred. (WWP 75-6)

AIMS OF THE ECONOMIC SYSTEM
We may distinguish four purposes at which an economic system

may aim: first, it may aim at the greatest possible production of goods and at facilitating technical progress; second, it may aim at securing distributive justice; third, it may aim at giving security against destitution; and, fourth, it may aim at liberating impulses and diminishing possessive impulses. (PI 43)

AIRPLANES, EFFECT OF

The aeroplane, however, by the preponderance which it has given to the attack, has altered completely the strategy and even the politics of war. There are those, among the older Generals and Admirals, who refuse to admit this, and who cling desperately to traditional conceptions. (WWP 18)

ALIORELATIVE

A relation is said to be an aliorelative or to *be contained in* or *imply diversity*, if no term has this relation to itself. Thus, for example, "greater," "different in size," "brother," "husband," "father" are aliorelatives; but "equal," "born of the same parents," "dear friend" are not. (IMP 32)

ALL

Empirical evidence can prove propositions containing "a" or "some," and can disprove propositions containing "the", "all," or "none." It cannot disprove propositions containing "a" or "some," and cannot prove propositions containing "the," "all," or "none." (IMT 55)

Propositions containing "all" or "none" can be disproved by empirical data, but not proved except in logic and mathematics. We can prove "all primes except 2 are odd," because this follows from definitions; but we cannot prove "all men are mortal," because we cannot prove that we have overlooked no one. (IMT 55)

ALLIANCES

So far, I have considered alliances only from the standpoint of the prevention of war. But in the minds of statesmen the chief motive for concluding them has always been not peace, but victory. The two are, however, connected, since wars do not occur, as a rule, when one side is *sure* of victory. (WWP 98)

ALOOFNESS
see ARISTOCRACY

AMBERLEY
see INTELLECTUAL INTEGRITY

AMERICA AND IMPERIALISM

In international affairs the record of America compares very favourably with that of other Great Powers. There have been, it is true, two short periods of imperialism, one connected with the Mexican war of 1846, the other with the Spanish-American war of 1898, but in each case a change of policy came very soon. In China, where the record of Britain, France, Germany, and Russia is shameful, that of the United States has always been generous and liberal. No territorial concessions were ever demanded, and the Boxer indemnity money was spent on Chinese education. Since 1945, American policy, both as regards control of atomic power and as regards the Marshall Plan, has been generous and farsighted. Western Union economic and political, which America urges is obviously to the interest of western Europe; in fact, American authorities have shown more awareness of what western Europe needs than western Europe itself has shown. (AA 164)

AMERICA AND MATERIALISM

A great deal of nonsense is talked about American so-called "materialism" and what its detractors call "bathroom civilization." I do not think Americans are, in any degree more "materialistic," in the popular sense of that word, than people of other nations. We think they worship the "almighty dollar" because they succeed in getting it. But a needy aristocrat or a French peasant will do things for the sake of money that shock every decent American. Very few Americans marry for mercenary motives. (AA 211)

AMERICA AND TYRANNY OF THE HERD

There is one aspect of American life which I have not yet touched on, and which I think wholly undesirable—I mean, the tyranny of the herd. Eccentricity is frowned upon, and unusual opinions bring social penalties upon those who hold them. It is not a new thing: it was noted by De Tocqueville in his book on American democracy: it was rampant in the time of Washington; and it goes back to the early Puritan colonies of the seventeenth century. It is, I think, the worst feature of America. I earnestly hope that fear of Russia will not cause us to imitate it. (AA 211)

AMERICAN LANGUAGE

There is something in this, but, for my own part, it is not the American modifications of the English language which annoy me. I find much American speech very pleasant to listen to, and much of the slang refreshingly expressive. But I wish they would frankly call it American, and not English. I should not mind being told that I do not talk American very well. I don't. (CAB 57)

ANALYSIS

The operation by which, from examination of a whole W, we arrive at "P is part of W," is called "analysis." It has two forms: logical analysis, and analysis into spatio-temporal parts. (IMT 411)

ANALYTIC

We must therefore suppose that natural processes have the character attributed to them by the analyst, rather than the holistic character which the enemies of analysis take for granted. I do not contend that the holistic world is logically impossible, but I do contend that it could not give rise to science or to any empirical knowledge. (DNL 142)

ANALYTICAL PHILOSOPHY
see EMPIRICISM, MODERN ANALYTIC

ANARCHISM

Anarchism, as its derivation indicates, is the theory which is opposed to every kind of forcible government. It is opposed to the State as the embodiment of the force employed in the government of the community. Such government as Anarchism can tolerate must be free government, not merely in the sense that it is that of a majority, but in the sense that it is that assented to by all. (RF 33)

Anarchism, however attractive, is rejected as a method of regulating the internal affairs of a State except by a few idealistic dreamers. Per contra, except by a few idealistic dreamers it is accepted as the only method of regulating international affairs. The same mentality that insists most strongly on the necessity of subjecting the individual to the State insists simultaneously on the complete independence of the sovereign State from all external control. Logically, such a view is untenable. If anarchy is bad nationally, it is bad internationally; if it is good internationally, it must be good nationally. For my part, I cannot believe it to be good in either sphere. (FAG 249)

ANAXAGORAS

The philosopher Anaxagoras, though not the equal of Pythagoras, Heraclitus, or Parmenides, has nevertheless a considerable historical importance. He was an Ionian, and carried on the scientific, rationalist tradition of Ionia. He was the first to introduce philosophy to the Athenians, and the first to suggest mind as the primary cause of physical changes. (HWP 61)

ANIMAL FAITH
see LEARNED REACTION

ANSELM

Saint Anselm was, like Lanfranc, an Italian, a monk at Bec, and archbishop of Canterbury (1093-1109), in which capacity he followed the principles of Gregory VII and quarreled with the king. He is chiefly known to fame as the inventor of the "ontological argument" for the existence of God. As he put it, the argument is as follows: We define "God" as the greatest possible object of thought. Now if an object of thought does not exist, another, exactly like it, which does exist, is greater. Therefore the greatest of all objects of thought must exist, since, otherwise, another, still greater, would be possible. Therefore God exists. (HWP 417)

ANTI-SEMITISM

Anti-Semitism is not only an abomination towards the Jews but a serious loss to the nations which, by practicing it, lose the advantages that they could derive from Jewish ability and industry. It is to be hoped—I speak as one who is not a Jew—that mankind will not continue thus to waste the by no means excessive capital of human merit. (ZPS 23)

APPEASEMENT

But the moral effect of yielding, which would have been admirable while German force was lacking, is quite different now, and is no longer capable of producing a peaceful atmosphere, since, if fear is supposed to be its motive, it encourages the habit of threatening and bullying. (WWP 13)

APPROXIMATION

Although this may seem a paradox, all exact science is dominated by the idea of approximation. When a man tells you that he knows the exact truth about anything, you are safe in inferring that he is an in-exact man. Every careful measurement in science is always given with the probable error, which is a technical term, conveying a precise meaning. It means: that amount of error which is just as likely to be greater than the actual error as to be less. (SO 63-4)

A PRIORI KNOWLEDGE

Knowledge is said to be *a priori* when it can be acquired without requiring any fact of experience as a premiss; in the contrary case, it is said to be empirical. (AOM 173)

AQUINAS

He succeeded in persuading the Church that Aristotle's system was to be preferred to Plato's as the basis of Christian philosophy, and that Mohammedans and Christian Averroists had misinterpreted Aristotle. For my part, I should say that the *De Anima* leads much more naturally to the view of Averroes than to that of Aquinas; however, the Church, since Saint Thomas, has thought otherwise. I should say, further, that Aristotle's views on most questions of logic and philosophy were not final, and have since been proved to be largely erroneous; this opinion, also, is not allowed to be professed by any Catholic philosopher or teacher of philosophy. (HWP 453)

ARABIAN PHILOSOPHY

In philosophy, the Arabs were better as commentators than as original thinkers. Their importance, for us, is that they, and not the Christians, were the immediate inheritors of those parts of the Greek tradition which only the Eastern Empire had kept alive. (HWP 283)

Arabic philosophy is not important as original thought. Men like Avicenna and Averroes are essentially commentators. Speaking generally, the views of the more scientific philosophers come from Aristotle and the Neoplatonists in logic and metaphysics, from Galen in medicine, from Greek and Indian sources in mathematics and astronomy, and among mystics religious philosophy has also an admixture of old Persian beliefs. Writers in Arabic showed some originality in mathematics and in chemistry—in the latter case, as an incidental result of alchemical researches. Mohammedan civilization in its great days was admirable in the arts and in many technical ways, but it showed no capacity for independent speculation in theoretical matters. Its importance, which must not be underrated, is as a transmitter. (HWP 427)

ARCHITECTURE, PLANNED

But although we take the hideousness of surburbs for granted, like March winds and November fogs, it has not, in fact, the same inevitability. If they were constructed by municipal instead of private enterprise, with planned streets, and houses like the Courts of Colleges, there is no reason why they should not be a delight to the eye. Hideousness, as much as worry and poverty, is part of the price we pay for our slavery to the motive of private profit. (IPI 70)

ARIANISM

Arius, a cultivated Alexandrian priest, maintained that the Son is not the equal of the Father, but was created by Him. At an earlier period, this view might not have aroused much antagonism, but in the fourth century most theologians rejected it. (HWP 333)

ARISTOCRACY

... but I shrink—perhaps irrationally—from the admission that, not only here and now, but always and everywhere, what is best worth having can only be enjoyed by a cultural aristocracy. Those who take this view have the advantage of avoiding conflict with the mob, but I would rather rouse its hostility in attempting to serve it than secure its tolerance by concealing a contemptuous aloofness. From a personal point of view, aloofness may be wiser philosophically and practically, but the opposite attitude is a heritage of Christianity, and one which is essential to the survival of intelligence as a social force. (POS 474)
see HUMAN EXCELLENCE

ARISTOTLE'S ETHICS

The views of Aristotle on ethics represent, in the main, the prevailing opinions of educated and experienced men of his day. They are not, like Plato, impregnated with mystical religion; nor do they countenance such unorthodox theories as are to be found in the *Republic* concerning property and the family. Those who neither fall below nor rise above the level of decent, well-behaved citizens will find in the *Ethics* a systematic account of the principles by which they hold that their conduct should be regulated. Those who demand anything more will be disappointed. The book appeals to the respectable middle-aged, and has been used by them, especially since the seventeenth century, to repress the ardours and enthusiasms of the young. But to a man with any depth of feeling it cannot but be repulsive. (HWP 172-173)

ARISTOTLE'S LOGIC

Even at the present day, all Catholic teachers of philosophy and many others still obstinately reject the discoveries of modern logic, and adhere with a strange tenacity to a system which is as definitely antiquated as Ptolemaic astronomy. This makes it difficult to do historical justice to Aristotle. His present-day influence is so inimical to clear thinking that it is hard to remember how great an advance he made upon all his predecessors (including Plato), or how admirable his logical work would still seem if it had been a stage in a continual progress, instead of being (as in fact it was) a dead end, followed by over two thousand years of stagnation. (HWP 195)

ARISTOTLE'S SCIENCE
see BRAHE, TYCHO

ARISTOTLE'S VIEW OF IMMORTALITY

It does not appear that Aristotle believed in *personal* immortality, in the sense in which it was taught by Plato and afterwards by Christianity. He believed only that, in so far as men are rational, they partake of the divine, which is immortal. It is open to man to increase the element of the divine in his nature, and to do so is the highest virtue. But if he succeeded completely, he would have ceased to exist as a separate person. This is perhaps not the only possible interpretation of Aristotle's words, but I think it is the most natural. (HWP 172)

ARITHMETIC

No one before the non-Euclideans perceived that arithmetic and geometry stand on a quite different footing, the former being continuous with pure logic and independent of experience, the latter being continuous with physics and dependent upon physical data. (AOM 21)

Thus to return to Arithmetic, even if $2 + 1$ be indeed the *meaning* of 3, still the proposition that $2 + 1$ is possible is necessarily synthetic. A possible idea cannot, in the last analysis, be *merely* an idea which is not contradictory; for the contradiction itself must always be deduced from synthetic propositions. And hence the propositions of Arithmetic, as Kant discovered, are one and all synthetic. (PL 21)

ART

All great art and all great science springs from the passionate desire to embody what was at first an unsubstantial phantom, a beckoning beauty luring men away from safety and ease to a glorious torment. The men in whom this passion exists must not be fettered by the shackles of a utilitarian philosophy, for to their ardour we owe all that makes man great. (EEC 312-3)
see ASCETIC

ASCETIC

The man who is enjoying a good dinner or carving a statue out of marble is not thinking of matter as his enemy, but as his opportunity. The ascetic, on the contrary—who, if he is logical, is a Manichaean—condemns all pleasures that depend on matter, and regards them as due to the material part of himself, from which he strives to be liberated. This condemnation applies not only to the pleasures commonly called sensual, but to the whole realm of art, since art is bound up with sense. Such a morality is an outcome of despair, and arises only when the primitive zest for life is extinct. (POS 463)

ASIATICS
see FOREIGNERS, EDUCATION ABOUT

ASSOCIATION

The broad fact of association, on the mental side, is that when we experience something which we have experienced before, it tends to call up the context of the former experience. The smell of peat-smoke recalling a former scene is an instance which we discussed a moment ago. (AM 80)

ASYMMETRY

Asymmetry, i.e. the property of being incompatible with the converse, is a characteristic of the very greatest interest and importance. In order to develop its functions, we will consider various examples. The relation *husband* is asymmetrical, and so is the relation *wife;* i.e. if a is husband of b, b cannot be husband of a, and similarly in the case of *wife.* On the other hand, the relation "spouse" is symmetrical: if a is spouse of b, then b is spouse of a. Suppose now we are given the relation *spouse,* and we wish to derive the relation *husband. Husband* is the same as *male spouse* or *spouse of a female;* thus the relation *husband* can be derived from *spouse* either by limiting the domain to males or by limiting the converse to females. (IMP 42-43)

ATHENS

The achievements of Athens in the time of Pericles are perhaps the most astonishing thing in all history. Until that time, Athens had lagged behind many other Greek cities; neither in art nor in literature had it produced any great man (except Solon, who was primarily a lawgiver). Suddenly, under the stimulus of victory and wealth and the need of reconstruction, architects, sculptors, and dramatists, who remain unsurpassed to the present day, produced works which dominated the future down to modern times. (HWP 59)

AUGUSTINE

The theory that time is only an aspect of our thoughts is one of the most extreme forms of that subjectivism which, as we have seen, gradually increased in antiquity from the time of Protagoras and Socrates onwards. Its emotional aspect is obsession with sin, which came later than its intellectual aspects. Saint Augustine exhibits both kinds of subjectivism. Subjectivism led him to anticipate not only Kant's theory of time, but Descartes' *cogito*. In his *Soliloquia* he says: "You, who wish to know, do you know you are? I know it. Whence are you? I know not. Do you feel yourself single or multiple? I know not. Do you feel yourself moved? I know not. Do you know that you think? I do." This contains not only Descartes' *cogito*, but his reply to Gassendi's *ambulo ergo sum*. As a philosopher, therefore, Augustine deserves a high place. (HWP 354-5)

AUTHORITY

As soon as we abandon our own reason, and are content to rely upon authority, there is no end to our troubles. Whose authority? The Old Testament? The New Testament? The Koran? In practice, people choose the book considered sacred by the community in which they are born, and out of that book they choose the parts they like, ignoring the others. At one time, the most influential text in the Bible was: "Thou shalt not suffer a witch to live." Nowadays, people pass over this text, in silence if possible; if not, with an apology. And so, even when we have a sacred book, we still choose as truth whatever suits our own prejudices. No Catholic, for instance, takes seriously the text which says that a Bishop should be the husband of one wife. (UE 81-2)

AVERROES

Averroes was concerned to improve the Arabic interpretation

of Aristotle, which had been unduly influenced by Neoplatonism. He gave to Aristotle the sort of reverence that is given to the founder of a religion—much more than was given even by Avicenna. He holds that the existence of God can be proved by reason independently of revelation, a view also held by Thomas Aquinas. As regards immortality, he seems to have adhered closely to Aristotle, maintaining that the soul is not immortal, but intellect *(nous)* is. This, however, does not secure *personal* immortality, since intellect is one and the same when manifested in different persons. This view, naturally, was combated by Christian philosophers. (HWP 426)

AVICENNA

Avicenna invented a formula, which was repeated by Averroes and Albertus Magnus: "Thought brings about the generality in forms." From this it might be supposed that he did not believe in universals apart from thought. This, however, would be an unduly simple view. Genera—that is, universals—are, he says, at once before things, in things, and after things. He explains this as follows: They are *before* things in God's understanding. (God decides, for instance, to create cats. This requires that He should have the idea "cat," which is thus, in this respect anterior to particular cats.) Genera are *in* things in natural objects. (When cats have been created, felinity is in each of them.) Genera are *after* things in our thought. (When we have seen many cats, we notice their likeness to each other, and arrive at the general idea "cat".) This view is obviously intended to reconcile different theories. (HWT 425)

B

BACON

Bacon's most important book, *The Advancement of Learning,* is in many ways remarkably modern. He is commonly regarded as the originator of the saying, "Knowledge is power," and though he may have had predecessors who said the same thing, he said it with new emphasis. The whole basis of his philosophy was practical: to give mankind mastery over the forces of nature by means of scientific discoveries and inventions. He held that philosophy should be kept separate from theology, not intimately blended with it as in scholasticism. He accepted orthodox religion; he was not the man to quarrel with the government on such a matter. (HWP 542)
see INDUCTION BY SIMPLE ENUMERATION

BALANCE-OF-POWER POLITICS
see FOREIGN NATIONS, ATTITUDE TOWARD

BEHAVIOR-CYCLE

A "behaviour-cycle" is a series of voluntary or reflex movements of an animal, tending to cause a certain result, and continuing until that result is caused, unless they are interrupted by death, accident, or some new behaviour-cycle. (Here "accident" may be defined as the intervention of purely physical laws causing mechanical movements.) (AM 65)

BEHAVIOR-CYCLE, PURPOSE OF A

The "purpose" of a behaviour-cycle is the result which brings it to an end, normally by a condition of temporary quiescence—provided there is no interruption. (AM 65)

BEHAVIORISM

The view of the "behaviourists" is that nothing can be known except by external observation. They deny altogether that there is a separate source of knowledge called "introspection," by which we can know things about ourselves which we could never observe in others. They do not by any means deny that all sorts of things *may* go on in our minds: they only say that such things, if they occur, are not susceptible of scientific observation, and do not therefore concern psychology as a science. (AM 26)

And perhaps it may be as well, at this point, to state my own view of the question of "behaviourism." This philosophy, of which the chief protagonist is Dr. John B. Watson, holds that everything that can be known about man is discoverable by the method of external observation, i.e. that none of our knowledge depends, essentially and necessarily, upon data in which the observer and the observed are the same person. I do not fundamentally agree with this view, but I think it contains much more truth than most people suppose, and I regard it as desirable to develop the behaviourist method to the fullest possible extent. I believe that the knowledge to be obtained by this method, so long as we take physics for granted, is self-contained, and need not, at any point, appeal to data derived from introspection, i.e. from observations which a man can make upon himself but not upon anyone else. Nevertheless, I hold that there are such observations and that there is knowledge which depends upon introspection. (OP 70)

BELIEF

"Belief," as I wish to use the word, denotes a state of mind or body, or both, in which an animal acts with reference to something not sensibly present. When I go to the station in expectation of finding a train, my action expresses a belief. (HK 113)

I propose, therefore, to treat belief as something that can be pre-intellectual, and can be displayed in the behavior of animals. I incline to think that, on occasion, a purely bodily state may deserve to be called a "belief." For example, if you walk into your room in the dark and someone has put a chair in an unusual place, you may bump into it, because your body believed there was no chair there. But the parts played by mind and body respectively in belief are not very important to separate for our present purposes. A belief, as I understand the term, is a certain kind of state of body or mind or both. To avoid verbiage, I shall call it a state of an organism, and ignore the distinction of bodily and mental factors. (HK 144-5)

Belief, however, as modern psychologists are never weary of telling us, is seldom determined by rational motives, and the same is true of disbelief, though skeptics often overlook this fact. (IPI 213)

The fact that an opinion has been widely held is no evidence whatever that it is not utterly absurd; indeed in view of the silliness of the majority of mankind, a widespread belief is more likely to be foolish than sensible. (MM 58)

We may end our preliminary catalogue with *belief*, by which I mean that way of being conscious which may be either true or false. We say that a man is "conscious of looking a fool," by which we mean that he believes he looks like a fool, and is not mistaken in this belief. (AM 13)

But there is a further point which needs emphasizing, namely, that a belief that something is desired has often a tendency to cause the very desire that is believed in. It is this fact that makes the effect of "consciousness" on desire so complicated. (AM 72)

see REACTIONS, SUSPENDED

BELIEF, AFFIRMATIVE AND NEGATIVE

A belief is affirmative when what is considered is accepted, and is negative when what is considered is rejected. Thus "all men are mortal," when affirmative, will involve some connection between the predicates "man" and "mortal," but when negative may be represented by the question "An immortal man?" followed by the answer "no." The psychology is somewhat different in these two cases. (IMT 316)

BELIEF, TRUE

What makes a belief true or false I call a "fact." The particular fact that makes a given belief true or false I call its "objective," and the relation of the belief to its objective I call the "reference" or the "objective reference" of the belief. (AM 232)

BELIEFS, GENERAL

General beliefs—by which I mean such as, in their verbal expression, involve "all" or "none" or some synonym—have their pre-intellectual origin in habits of a certain kind. In those who possess language, such habits may be purely verbal. (IMT 310)

BELIEFS, HARMFUL

But although passions have had more to do than beliefs with what is amiss in human life, yet beliefs, especially where they are ancient and systematic and embodied in organizations, have a great power of delaying desirable changes of opinion and of influencing in the wrong direction people who otherwise would have no strong feeling either way. (UE 148-9)

BENTHAM

Bentham did not distinguish between pleasure and happiness, and resolutely refused to assign a qualitative superiority to what are called "higher" pleasures. As he put it, "quantity of pleasure being equal, pushpin is as good as poetry." None the less, his doctrine was, in practice, almost ascetic. He held that self-approbation is the greatest of pleasures. Since men tend to value present pleasures more than pleasures in the future, the wise man will exercise prudence and self-restraint. On the whole, he and his disciples sought happiness in hard work and an almost complete indifference to all pleasures of sense. This, no doubt, was a matter of temperament, not to be explained as a deduction from the doctrine; but the result was that their morality was quite as severe as that of their orthodox opponents. (FO 92-3)

There is an obvious lacuna in Bentham's system. If every man always pursues his own pleasure, how are we to secure that the legislator shall pursue the pleasure of mankind in general? Bentham's own instinctive benevolence (which his psychological theories prevented him from noticing) concealed the problem from him. If he had been employed to draw up a code of laws for some country, he would have framed his proposals in what he conceived to be the public interest, not so as to further his own interests or (consciously) the interests of his class. But if he had recognized this fact, he would have had to modify his psychological doctrines. (HWP 777-8)
see SELF-INTEREST

BERGSON

A great part of Bergson's philosophy is merely traditional mysticism expressed in slightly novel language. The doctrine of interpenetration, according to which different things are not really separate, but are merely so conceived by the analytic intellect, is to be found in every mystic, eastern or western, from Parmenides to Mr. Bradley. (SE 66)

There is no room in this philosophy for the moment of contemplative insight when, rising above the animal life, we become conscious of the greater ends that redeem man from the life of the brutes. Those to whom activity without purpose seems a sufficient good will find in Bergson's books a pleasing picture of the universe. But those to whom action, if it is to be of any value, must be inspired by some vision, by some imaginative foreshadowing of a world less painful, less unjust, less full of strife than the world of our everyday life, those, in a word, whose action is built on contemplation, will find in this philosophy nothing of what they seek, and will not regret that there is no reason to think it true. (HWP 810)

BERKELEY

George Berkeley (1658-1753) is important in philosophy through his denial of the existence of matter—a denial which he supported by a number of ingenious arguments. He maintained that material objects only exist through being perceived. To the objection that, in that case, a tree, for instance, would cease to exist if no one was looking at it, he replied that God always perceives everything; if there were no God, what we take to be material objects would have a jerky life, suddenly leaping into being when we look at them; but as it is, owing to God's perceptions, trees and rocks and stones have an existence as continuous as common sense supposes. This is, in his opinion, a weighty argument for the existence of God. (HWP 647)

BETWEEN

There are many ways in which series may be generated, but all depend upon the finding or construction of an asymmetrical transitive connected relation. Some of these ways have considerable importance. We may take as illustration the generation of series by means of a three-term relation which we may call "between." (IMP 38)

BIOLOGIC NEEDS
see ECONOMIC ASPECTS OF LIFE

BIRTH CONTROL

If either of the parents has venereal disease, the child is likely to inherit it. If they already have too many children for the family income, there will be poverty, underfeeding, overcrowding, very likely incest. Yet the great majority of moralists agree that the parents had better not know how to prevent this misery by pre-

venting conception. To please these moralists, a life of torture is
inflicted upon millions of human beings who ought never to have
existed, merely because it is supposed that sexual intercourse is
wicked unless accompanied by desire for offspring, but not wicked
when this desire is present, even though the offspring is humanly
certain to be wretched. (WIB 42-3)

BOETHIUS

During the two centuries before his time and the ten centuries
after it, I cannot think of any European man of learning so free
from superstition and fanaticism. Nor are his merits merely negative;
his survey is lofty, disinterested, and sublime. He would have been
remarkable in any age; in the age in which he lived, he is utterly
amazing. (HWP 373)

Boethius is a singular figure. Throughout the Middle Ages he
was read and admired, regarded always as a devout Christian, and
treated almost as if he had been one of the Fathers. Yet his *Consolations of Philosophy*, written in 524 while he was awaiting execution,
is purely Platonic; it does not prove that he was not a Christian,
but it does show that pagan philosophy had a much stronger hold
on him than Christian theology. (HWP 370)

BOLSHEVISM
see RELIGION

BOMB, HYDROGEN

I do not agree with those who object to the manufacture of
the hydrogen bomb. All arguments for a unilateral limitation of
weapons of war are only logically defensible if carried to the length
of absolute pacifism, for a war cannot be worth fighting unless it is
worth winning. I think also, for the reasons given above, that every
increase of Western strength makes war less likely. (TWI 13)

BOOK CLUBS
see READING

BOREDOM, AVOIDANCE OF
see SOCIETY, SCIENTIFIC

BRAHE, TYCHO

The next astronomer of importance was Tycho Brahe (1546-
1601), who adopted an intermediate position: he held that the sun
and moon go round the earth, but the planets go round the sun.

As regards theory he was not very original. He gave, however, two good reasons against Aristotle's view that everything above the moon is unchanging. One of these was the appearance of a new star in 1572, which was found to have daily parallax, and must therefore be more distant than the moon. The other reason was derived from observation of comets, which were also found to be distant. The reader will remember Aristotle's doctrine that change and decay are confined to the sublunary sphere; this, like everything else that Aristotle said on scientific subjects, proved an obstacle to progress. The importance of Tycho Brahe was not as a theorist, but as an observer, first under the patronage of the king of Denmark, then under the Emperor Rudolf II. (HWP 529)

BRAIN
see MIND

BUDDHISM

Buddhism, on the contrary, in spite of the fact that in its early days it was the religion of princes, is essentially non-political. I do not mean that it has always remained so. In Tibet it is as political as the papacy, and in Japan I have met high Buddhist dignitaries who reminded me of English archdeacons. Nevertheless, the Buddhist, in his more religious moments, considers himself essentially as a solitary being. (ESO 16)

BUREAUCRATS
see COMMUNISM AND LIBERTY

C

CAPITAL, LAW OF THE CONCENTRATION OF

Marx pointed out that capitalist undertakings tend to grow larger and larger. He foresaw the substitution of trusts for free competition, and predicted that the number of capitalist enterprises must diminish as the number of single enterprises increased. (RF 8)

CAPITALISM, STATE

The term "state capitalism" occurs frequently in this article, as well as in others of his writings. It seems to mean the running of enterprises by the state for profit, i.e., in the same way as they would be run by private capitalists. (PIC 103)

CARDINALS

The definition of cardinals as classes of classes, and the discovery that class-symbols could be "incomplete symbols," persuaded me that cardinals as entities are unnecessary. But what had really been demonstrated was something quite independent of metaphysics, which is best stated in terms of "minimum vocabularies." I mean by a "minimum vocabulary" one in which no word can be defined in terms of the others. All definitions are theoretically superfluous, and therefore the whole of any science can be expressed by means of a minimum vocabulary for that science. (MMD 14)

CASUISTRY

As a provisional definition, we may take ethics to consist of general principles which help to determine rules of conduct. It is not the business of ethics to say how a person should act in such and such specific circumstances; that is the province of casuistry. (OP 225)

CATHOLIC PHILOSOPHY

The first great period of Catholic philosophy was dominated by Saint Augustine, and by Plato among the pagans. The second period culminates in Saint Thomas Aquinas, for whom, and for his successors, Aristotle far outweighs Plato. The dualism of *The City of God*, however, survives in full force. The church represents the City of God, and politically philosophers stand for the interests of the Church. (HWP 303)

CAUSAL LAW

A "causal law," as I shall use the term, may be defined as a general principle in virtue of which, given sufficient data about certain regions of space-time, it is possible to infer something about certain other regions of space-time. The inference may be only probable, but the probability must be considerably more than a half if the principle in question is to be considered worthy to be called a "causal law." (HK 308)

CAUSAL LAWS

I think we may lay down the following universal characteristics of causal laws in an advanced science. Given any event, there are other events at neighboring places in space-time which will occur slightly later if no other factors intervene; but in practice other factors almost always do intervene, and, in that case, the event which actually occurs at any point of space-time is a mathematical resultant of those which would have followed the various neighbouring events if they had been alone concerned. The equations of physics give the rules according to which events are connected, but all are of the above sort. (OP 149)

CAUSE

No doubt the reason why the old "law of causality" has so long continued to pervade the books of philosophers is simply that the idea of function is unfamiliar to most of them, and therefore they seek an unduly simplified statement. There is no question of repetitions of the "same" cause producing the "same" effect; it is not in any sameness of causes and effects that the constancy of scientific law consists, but in sameness of relations. And even "sameness of relations" is too simple a phrase; "sameness of differential equations" is the only correct phrase. It is impossible to state this accurately in non-mathematical language; the nearest approach would be as follows: "There is a constant relation between the state of the universe at any constant and the rate of change in the rate at which any part of the universe is changing at that instant, and this relation is many-one, i.e. such that the rate of change in the rate of change is determinate when the state of the universe is given." If the "law of causality" is to be something actually discoverable in the practice of science, the above proposition has a better right to the name than any "law of causality" to be found in the books of philosophers. (ML 194-5)

CENSORSHIP

When power is confined to the members of one sect, there is inevitably a severe ideological censorship. Sincere believers will be anxious to spread the true faith; others will be content with outward conformity. The former attitude kills the free exercise of intelligence; the latter promotes hypocrisy. Education and literature must be stereotyped, and designed to produce credulity rather than initiative and criticism. (P 189)

CENTRALIZATION

A considerable degree of centralization is indispensable, if only for the reasons that we considered at the beginning of this lecture. But to the utmost extent compatible with this requisite, there should be devolution of the powers of the State to various kinds of bodies—geographical, industrial, cultural, according to their functions. The powers of these bodies should be sufficient to make them interesting, and to cause energetic men to find satisfaction in influencing them. They would need, if they were to fulfil their purpose, a considerable measure of financial autonomy. (AAI 98-9)

CERTAINTY, EPISTEMOLOGICAL

A proposition is certain when it has the highest degree of credibility, either intrinsically or as a result of argument. Perhaps no proposition is certain in this sense; i.e., however certain it may be in relation to a given person's knowledge, further knowledge might increase its degree of credibility. We will call this kind of certainty "epistemological." (HK 396)

CERTAINTY, LOGICAL

A propositional function is certain with respect to another when the class of terms satisfying the second is part of the class of terms satisfying the first. E.g., "x is an animal" is certain in relation to "x is a rational animal." This meaning of certainty belongs to mathematical probability. We will call this kind of certainty "logical." (HK 396)

CERTAINTY, PSYCHOLOGICAL

A person is certain of a proposition when he feels no doubt whatever of its truth. This is a purely psychological concept, and we will call it "psychological certainty." (HK 396)

CHANCE

"Chance" decides whether an expected child turns out to be a boy or a girl, and "chance" decides which of the hereditary possibilities that Mendelian principles allow will be realized. But when we deal with large groups, "chance" no longer decides: there will be about twenty-one boys to twenty girls, if I remember aright. In this sense I should regard the birth of Napoleon as a "chance" event. We do not know why a man of supreme military genius was born in Corsica at that time. (RTC 738)

CHANGE

Change is one thing, progress is another. "Change" is scientific, "progress" is ethical; change is indubitable, whereas progress is a matter of controversy. (UE 8)

CHARITY

The world at the present day stands in need of two kinds of things. On the one hand, organization—political organization for the elimination of wars, economic organization to enable men to work productively, especially in the countries that have been devastated by war, educational organization to generate a sane internationalism. On the other hand it needs certain moral qualities—the qualities which have been advocated by moralists for many ages, but hitherto with little success. The qualities most needed are charity and tolerance, not some form of fanatical faith such as is offered to us by the various rampant isms. I think these two aims, the organizational and the ethical, are closely interwoven; given either the other would soon follow. (UE 165)

CHILD, RESPECT FOR THE

Treat even the youngest baby with respect, as a person who will have to take his place in the world. Do not sacrifice his future to your present convenience, or to your pleasure in making much of him: the one is as harmful as the other. Here—as elsewhere, a combination of love and knowledge is necessary if the right way is to be followed. (EEC 100)

CHRISTIANITY

One thing more was necessary to complete Western civilization as it existed before modern times, and that was the peculiar relation between government and religion which came through Christianity. Christianity was originally quite non-political, since it grew up in the Roman Empire as a consolation to those who had lost national and personal liberty; and it took over from Judaism an attitude of moral condemnation towards the rulers of the world. In the years before Constantine, Christianity developed an organization to which the Christian owed a loyalty even greater than that which he owed to the State. When Rome fell, the Church preserved in a singular synthesis what had proved most vital in the civilizations of the Jews, the Greeks, and the Romans. (IPI 187)

see ISLAM

CHRONO-GEOGRAPHY

Let us coin a word, "chrono-geography," for the science which begins with events having space-time relations and does not assume at the outset that certain strings of them can be treated as persistent material units or as minds. (OP 283)

CHURCH, THE MEDIEVAL

In the general decay of civilization that came about during the incessant wars of the sixth and succeeding centuries, it was above all the Church that preserved whatever survived of the culture of ancient Rome. The Church performed this work very imperfectly, because fanaticism and superstition prevailed among even the greatest ecclesiastics of the time, and secular learning was thought wicked. Nevertheless, ecclesiastical institutions created a solid framework, within which, in later times, a revival of learning and civilized arts became possible. (HWP 375)

CITIZENSHIP, WORLD

We come up here against the fundamental trouble of all times. The world has been unified technically, but not emotionally. What happens in one region affects what happens in another much more than it did in former times, but our feelings remain parochial. In antiquity, the loyalty and benevolence of Greeks and Italians were confined to their own city state until Rome unified the Mediterranean world, when first the Stoics and then the Christians taught the doctrine of world citizenship and loyalty to mankind as a whole. But the Roman Empire broke up, and the Christian teaching became merely an ideal with little practiçal efficacy. Now, when technique has made a more effective unification of some sort a practical necessity, it is time to revive the doctrine of world citizenship. (CGS 180)

CIVILIZATION

First of all, what is civilization? Its first essential character, I should say, is *forethought*. This, indeed, is what mainly distinguishes men from brutes and adults from children. But forethought being a matter of degree, we can distinguish more or less civilized nations and epochs according to the amount of it that they display. (IPI 182)

This brings me to another element which is essential to civilization, namely, *knowledge*. Forethought based upon superstition cannot count as fully civilized, although it may bring habits of mind essential to the growth of true civilization. For instance, the Puritan habit of postponing pleasures to the next life undoubtedly facilitated the accumulation of capital required for industrialism. We may then define civilization as: *A manner of life due to the combination of knowledge and forethought.* (IPI 183-4)

What is called civilization may be defined as the pursuit of objects not biologically necessary for survival. It first arose through the introduction of agriculture in the fertile deltas of great rivers, more particularly in Egypt and Babylonia. Everywhere else primitive agriculture exhausts the soil and compels frequent migrations, but this was not the case in the deltas. Here the surplus food produced by one man's labor above one man's needs was sufficient to make possible the creation of a small leisure class, and it was this small leisure class that invented writing, architecture, mathematics, astronomy, and other arts essential to all subsequent civilization. (WIG 143)

Civilization in the more important sense, is a thing of the mind, not of material adjuncts to the physical side of living. It is a matter partly of knowledge, partly of emotion. So far as knowledge is concerned, a man should be aware of the minuteness of himself and his immediate environment in relation to the world in time and space. He should see his own country not *only* as home, but as one among the countries of the world all with an equal right to live and think and feel. He should see his own age in relation to the past and the future, and be aware that its own controversies will seem as strange to future ages as those of the past seem to us now. (UE 117)

CIVILIZATION, BATHROOM

As for "bathroom civilization," it is altogether to the good, unless it is thought to be all-sufficient. Every traveler owes a debt of gratitude to American tourists for the improvement in hotels that has been brought about by their grumbling. (PCI 16)

CIVILIZATION, CHINESE

There are certain broad features of the traditional Chinese civilization which give it its distinctive character. I should be inclined to select as the most important: (1) the use of ideograms instead of an alphabet in writing; (2) the substitution of the Confucian ethic for religion among the educated classes; (3) government by literati chosen by examination instead of a hereditary aristocracy. (PC 30)

CLASS

A class or collection may be defined in two ways that at first sight might seem quite distinct. We may enumerate its members, as when we say, "The collection I mean is Brown, Jones, and Robinson." Or we may mention a defining property, as when we speak of "mankind" or "the inhabitants of London." The definition which enumerates is called a definition by "extension," and the one which mentions a defining property is called a definition by "intension." Of these two kinds of definition, the one by intension is logically the more fundamental. (IMP 12)

CLASS, LEISURE
see CIVILIZATION

CLASS, THE NUMBER OF A

The number of a class is the class of all those classes that are similar to it. (IMP 18)

CLASS WAR

Marx conceives the wage-earner and the capitalist in a sharp antithesis. He imagines that every man is, or must soon become, wholly the one or wholly the other. (RF 9)

Marx, by his teaching, created the class war which he prophesied, but by his excessive glorification of manual labor he caused the division of classes to come at a lower point in the social scale than was necessary, and thereby made enemies of the most important class in the modern economic world, the men who do the skilled work of industrialism. (FO 218)

CLASSICAL TRADITION

The first of these, which I shall call the classical tradition, descends in the main from Kant and Hegel; it represents the attempt to adapt to present needs the methods and results of the great constructive philosophers from Plato downwards. (KEW 4)

COLONISATION, WAR OF

By a "war of colonization" I mean a war whose purpose is to drive out the whole population of some territory and replace it by an invading population of a different race. (JWT 28)

COMMUNISM

Communism, as it has developed in Russia, is a political religion analogous to Islam. It is, however, unavoidably influenced by Byzantine tradition; and there is a possibility that the Communist party may take the place of the Church, leaving the secular government to that degree of independence of ecclesiastical authority which it possessed before the Revolution. In this, as in other matters, Russia is divided between an Eastern and a Western mentality. In so far as Russia is Asiatic, the Communist party takes the place of the caliphate; while in so far as Russia is European, the Communist party takes the place of the Church. (ESO 17)

COMMUNISM AND DEMOCRACY

Communism is not democratic. What it calls the "dictatorship of the proletariat" is in fact the dictatorship of a small minority, who become an oligarchic governing class. All history shows that government is always conducted in the interests of the governing class, except in so far as it is influenced by fear of losing its power. This is the teaching, not only of history, but of Marx. (WNCO 133-4)

COMMUNISM AND LIBERTY

Communism restricts liberty, particularly intellectual liberty, more than any other system except Fascism. The complete unification of both economic and political power produces a terrifying engine of oppression, in which there are no loopholes for exceptions. Under such a system, progress would soon become impossible, since it is the nature of bureaucrats to object to all change except increase in their own power. (WNCO 134)

COMPETITION

Competition, formerly between individual firms, is now mainly between nations, and is therefore conducted by methods quite different from those contemplated by the classical economists. . . . Modern industrialism is a struggle between nations for two things, markets and raw materials, as well as for the sheer pleasure of dominion. (I 17)

I do not think that ordinary human beings can be happy without competition, for competition has been, ever since the origin of Man, the spur to most serious activities. We should not, therefore, attempt to abolish competition, but only to see to it that it takes forms which are not too injurious. Primitive competition was a conflict as to which should murder the other man and his wife and children; modern competition in the shape of war still takes this form. But in sport, in literary and artistic rivalry, and in constitutional polities it takes forms which do very little harm and yet offer a fairly adequate outlet for our combative instinct. What is wrong in this respect is not that such forms of competition are bad, but that they form too small a part of the lives of ordinary men and women. . . . Apart from war, modern civilization has aimed increasingly at security, but I am not at all sure that the elimination of all danger makes for happiness. (AAI 22)

COMPETITIVENESS

Competitiveness is by no means wholly an evil. When it takes the form of emulation in the service of the public, or in discovery or the production of works of art, it may become a very useful stimulus, urging men to profitable effort beyond what they would otherwise make. It is only harmful when it aims at the acquisition of goods which are limited in amount, so that what one man possesses he holds at the expense of another. When competitiveness takes this form it is necessarily attended by fear, and out of fear cruelty is almost inevitably developed. (RF 160)

COMPRESENCE

Every event has to a certain number of others a relation which may be called "compresence"; from the point of view of physics, a collection of compresent events all occupy one small region in space-time. One example of a set of compresent events is what would be called the contents of one man's mind at one time—i.e. all his sensations, images, memories, thoughts, etc., which can coexist temporally. (LA 380)

There is a relation, which I call "compresence," which holds between two or more qualities when one person experiences them simultaneously—for example, between high C and vermilion when you hear one and see the other. We can form groups of qualities having the following two properties: (a) all members of the group are compresent; (b) given anything not a member of the group, there is at least one member of the group with which it is not compresent. (HK 297)

COMTE
see DETERMINISM, ECONOMIC

CONDITIONING

I come now to the question of the object toward which emotions are directed. This is the question of "conditioning" which has been stressed by the behaviourists. It is undoubtedly very important, but I do not agree with them in thinking that it constitutes practically the whole of education. There are not only good and bad objects for emotions, there are also, speaking broadly, good and bad emotions. The cultivation of good emotions and the elimination of bad ones is not in the main a question of conditioning, which is concerned with the objects to which the emotions are attached. (SAE 93)

CONFESSIONS

The desire to obtain a confession was the basis of the tortures of the Inquisition. In Old China, torture of suspected persons was habitual, because a humanitarian Emperor had decreed that no man should be condemned except on his own confession. For the taming of the power of the police, one essential is that a confession shall never, in any circumstances, be accepted as evidence. (P 282-3)

CONFUCIANISM

Confucianism is a political religion: Confucius, as he wandered from court to court, became concerned with the problem of government, and with the instilling of such virtues as to make good government easy. (ESO 16)

CONFUCIUS

Confucius (B. C. 551-479) must be reckoned, as regards his social influence, with the founders of religions. His effect on institutions and on men's thoughts has been of the same kind of magnitude as that of Buddha, Christ, or Mohammed, but curiously different in its nature. Unlike Buddha and Christ, he is a completely historical character, about whose life a great deal is known, and with whom legend and myth have been less busy than with most men of his kind. What most distinguishes him from other founders is that he inculcated a strict code of ethics, which has been respected ever since, but associated it with very little religious dogma, which gave place to complete theological skepticism in the countless generations of Chinese literati who revered his memory and administered the empire. (PC 34-35)

CONJUNCTION

Next we may take *conjunction*, "p and q." This has truth for its truth-value when p and q are both true; otherwise it has falsehood for its truth-value. (IMP 147)

CONSCIOUSNESS

Man has developed out of the animals, and there is no serious gap between him and the amoeba. Something closely analogous to knowledge and desire, as regards its effects on behaviour, exists among animals, even where what we call "consciousness" is hard to believe in; something equally analogous exists in ourselves in cases where no trace of "consciousness" can be found. It is therefore natural to suppose that, whatever may be the correct definition of "consciousness," "consciousness" is not the essence of life or mind. (AM 40)

If this is correct, what really happens when, as common sense would say, we are conscious of a table, is more or less as follows. First there is a physical process external to the body, producing a stimulus to the eye which occurs rarely (not never) in the absence of an actual physical table. Then there is a process in the eye, nerves, and brain, and finally there is the coloured pattern. This coloured pattern, by the law of association, gives rise to tactual and other expectations and images; also, perhaps, to memories and other habits. But everything in this whole series consists of a causally continuous chain of events in space-time, and we have no reason to assert that the events in us are so very different from the events outside us—as to this, we must remain ignorant, since the outside events are only known as to their abstract mathematical characteristics, which do not show whether these events are like "thoughts" or unlike them. (OP 213)

CONSCIOUSNESS, FUNCTION OF
see THOUGHT, FUNCTION OF

CONSEQUENCES OF ACTS
see MOTIVES

CONSISTENCY
No one has yet succeeded in inventing a philosophy at once credible and self-consistent. Locke aimed at credibility, and achieved it at the expense of consistency. Most of the great philosophers have done the opposite. A philosophy which is not self-consistent cannot be wholly true, but a philosophy which is self-consistent can very well be wholly false. (HWP 613)

CONSTRUCTIVENESS, PSYCHOLOGICAL
I am trying in this book to show, in concrete instances, how psychological construction differs from the construction of a machine. The imaginative side of this idea ought to be made familiar in higher education; if it were, I believe that our politics would cease to be angular and sharp and destructive, becoming instead supple and truly scientific, with the development of splendid men and women as its goal. (EEC 146)

CONTAIN
One relation is said to *contain* or *be implied by* another if it holds whenever the other holds. (IMP 33)

CONTEMPLATION
A habit of finding pleasure in thought rather than in action is a safeguard against unwisdom and excessive love of power, a means of preserving serenity in misfortune and peace of mind among worries. A life confined to what is personal is likely, sooner or later, to become unbearably painful; it is only by windows into a larger and less fretful cosmos that the more tragic parts of life become endurable. (IPI 49)

CONTEMPLATION AND PRACTICE
I think Plotinus was right in urging contemplation of eternal things, but he was wrong in thinking of this as enough to constitute a good life. Contemplation, if it is to be wholesome and valuable, must be married to practice; it must inspire action and ennoble the

aims of practical statesmanship. While it remains secluded in the cloister it is only a means of escape. (IWS 5)

CONTINUITY

There are three distinct kinds of continuity, all of which Leibniz asserts. None of them, he thinks, has metaphysical necessity, but all are regarded as required by the "order of things." These three kinds are (1) spatio-temporal continuity, (2) what may be called continuity of cases, (3) the continuity of actual existents or of forms. (PL 63)

CONTINUITY, DEDEKINDIAN

A series has "Dedekindian continuity" when it is Dedekindian and compact. (IMP 101)

CONTRADICTION, LAW OF

We may argue generally, from the mere statement of the Law of Contradiction, that no proposition can follow from it alone, except the proposition that there is truth, or that some proposition is true. For the law states simply that any proposition must be true or false, but cannot be both. It gives no indication as to the alternative to be chosen, and cannot of itself decide that any proposition is true. (PL 22)

We must now interpret the law of contradiction. We must not say, " 'This is red' and 'This is not red' cannot both be true," since we are concerned to eliminate "not." We must say, "A disbelief in the sentence 'The belief that this is red and the disbelief that this is red are both true' is always true." It seems that in this way we can replace "not" and "falsehood" by "disbelief" and "the truth of a disbelief." We then reintroduce "not" and "falsehood" by definitions: the words "This is not blue" are defined as expressing disbelief in what is expressed by the words "This is blue." In this way the need of "not" as an indefinable constituent of facts is avoided. (HK 124-5)

see TRUTH-FUNCTION, THEORY OF

CONVERSE

The relation of wife to husband is called the *converse* of the relation of husband to wife. Similarly *less* is the converse of *greater*, *later* is the converse of *earlier*, and so on. Generally, the converse of a given relation is that relation which holds between y and x whenever the given relation holds between x and y. (IMP 16)

COOPERATION

The injustices suffered by Jews in Germany, by "kulaks" in Russia, by nationalists in India, and by colored people in the United States, are all parts of one global system of tyranny; to mitigate any one, we must mitigate all, by the creation of institutions that will foster a new spirit of cooperation. This is a large undertaking, suggesting a program of reform which even the youngest of us can scarcely hope to see fully carried out, but which gives a constant goal towards which our efforts shall be directed. (ZPS 22)

COPERNICUS

What was important in his work was the dethronement of the earth from its geometrical pre-eminence. In the long run, this made it difficult to give to man the cosmic significance assigned to him in the Christian theology, but such consequence would not have been accepted by Copernicus, whose orthodoxy was sincere, and who protested against the view that his theory contradicted the Bible. (HWP 526-7)

COSMIC CONSTANT
see RELATIVITY, GENERAL THEORY OF

COSMIC PURPOSE

There is a different and vaguer conception of Cosmic Purpose as not omnipotent but slowly working its way through a recalcitrant material. This is a more plausible conception than that of a God who, though omnipotent and loving, has deliberately produced beings so subject to suffering and cruelty as the majority of mankind. I do not pretend to know that there is no such Purpose; my knowledge of the universe is too limited. (FAR 4)

With regard to Cosmic Purpose in general, in whichever of its forms, there are two criticisms to be made. In the first place, those who believe in Cosmic Purpose always think that the world will go on evolving in the same direction as hitherto; in the second place, they hold that what has already happened is evidence of the good intentions of the universe. Both these propositions are open to question. (RAS 226)

COSMIC PURPOSE, MAN AND

Man, as a curious accident in a backwater, is intelligible: his mixture of virtues and vices is such as might be expected to result from a fortuitous origin. But only abysmal self-complacency can see in Man a reason which Omniscience could consider adequate as a motive for the Creator. The Copernican revolution will not have done its work until it has taught men more modesty than is to be found among those who think Man sufficient evidence of Cosmic Purpose. (RAS 233)

COSMOLOGICAL ARGUMENT

The cosmological argument is, at first sight, more plausible than the ontological argument, but it is less philosophical, and derives its superior plausibility only from concealing its implications. It has a formal vice, in that it starts from finite existence as its datum, and admitting this to be contingent, it proceeds to infer an existent which is not contingent. But as the premiss is contingent, the conclusion also must be contingent. This is only to be avoided by pointing out that the argument is analytic, that it proceeds from a complex proposition to one which is logically presupposed in it, and that necessary truths may be involved in those that are contingent. But such a procedure is not properly a proof of the presupposition. (PL 175)

COURAGE

But courage in fighting is by no means the only form, nor perhaps even the most important. There is courage in facing poverty, courage in facing derision, courage in facing the hostility of one's own herd. In these, the bravest soldiers are often lamentably deficient. And above all there is the courage to think calmly and rationally in the face of danger, and to control the impulse of panic fear or panic rage. (WIB 74)

CREATION

Dr. Johnson said the devil was the first Whig; I suggest that he was the first Tory. When the Lord decided to create Man, He acted as a revolutionary; to Satan, when he got wind of the project, it seemed a wild and foolish innovation, since the angelic universe was well ordered, had an ancient mellow ritual, and was long since purged of all the crudities that had marred its earlier aeons. The only solution that occurred to him was to bring death into our world;

he did not foresee that death would come too slowly to prevent our first parents from leaving progeny who would perpetuate the legacy of confusion. In all this dislike of rash and chaotic novelty, I feel sure that Santayana would have agreed with Satan; I should have agreed myself if I could have foreseen what Man would make of his planet. (POS 471)

A curious attempt to save orthodoxy in the field of biology was made by Gosse the naturalist, father of Edmund Gosse. He admitted fully all the evidence adduced by geologists in favour of the antiquity of the world, but maintained that, when the Creation took place, everything was constructed *as if* it had a past history. There is no logical possibility of *proving* that this theory is untrue. It has been decided by the theologians that Adam and Eve had navels, just as if they had been born in the ordinary way. Similarly everything else that was created could have been created as if it had grown. The rocks could have been filled with fossils, and have been made just such as they would have become if they had been due to volcanic action or to sedimentary deposits. But if once such possibilities are admitted, there is no reason to place the creation of the world at one point rather than another. (RAS 69-70)

CREATIVE WORK

I think most of the best creative work, in art, in science, in literature, and in philosophy, has been the result of such a moment. Whether it comes to others as to me, I cannot say. For my part, I have found that, when I wish to write a book on some subject, I must first soak myself in detail, until all the separate parts of the subject-matter are familiar; then, some day, if I am fortunate, I perceive the whole, with all its parts duly interrelated. (HWP 123)

CREATIVENESS

The supreme principle, both in politics and in private life, should be to promote all that is creative, and so to diminish the impulses and desires that center round possession. (PSR 258)

For all these reasons, the creative part of a man's activity ought to be as free as possible from all public control, in order that it may remain spontaneous and full of vigor. The only function of the state in regard to this part of the individual life should be to do everything possible toward providing outlets and opportunities. (PI 137-8)

CREATIVITY

That is to say, everything concerned with the creation of life is thought to be abominable, while everything concerned with taking life is exalted as noble. This is the morality of suicide. It springs from the fact that we attach value to power, rather than to fullness of life: we think a man a fine fellow when he can cause others to be miserable rather than when he can achieve happiness for himself. All that is needed is to give men a just conception of what constitutes their own happiness. (ISP xvii)

CREATOR, BENEFICENT

Most of us have been brought up to believe that the universe owes its existence to an all-wise and all-powerful Creator, whose purposes are beneficent even in what to us may seem evil. I do not think it is right to refuse to apply to this belief the kind of tests that we should apply to one that reaches our emotions less intimately and profoundly. Is there any evidence of the existence of such a Being? Undoubtedly belief in Him is comforting and sometimes has some good moral effects on character and behaviour. But this is no evidence that the belief is true. For my part, I think the belief lost whatever rationality it once possessed when it was discovered that the earth is not the centre of the universe. (FAR 3)

CREDULITY

One of the chief obstacles to intelligence is credulity, and credulity could be enormously diminished by instructions as to the prevalent forms of mendacity. Credulity is a greater evil in the present day than it ever was before, because, owing to the growth of education, it is much easier than it used to be to spread misinformation, and, owing to democracy, the spread of misinformation is more important than in former times to the holders of power. (FT 52-3)

CROMWELL
see DICTATORSHIP

CRUELTY AND RELIGION
You find this curious fact, that the more intense has been the religion of any period and the more profound has been the dogmatic belief, the greater has been the cruelty and the worse has been the state of affairs. (WNC 27)

CULTURAL QUESTIONS

For my part, I think the cultural questions are the most important, both for China and for mankind; if these could be solved, I would accept, with more or less equanimity, any political or economic system which ministered to that end. Unfortunately, however, cultural questions have little interest for practical men, who regard money and power as the proper ends for nations as for individuals. (PC 4)

CULTURE
see UTILITY AND CULTURE

CULTURE, GENUINE

Genuine culture consists in being a citizen of the universe, not only of one or two arbitrary fragments of space-time; it helps men to understand human society as a whole, to estimate wisely the ends that communities should pursue, and to see the present in its relation to the past and future. Genuine culture is therefore of great value to those who are to wield power, to whom it is at least as useful as detailed information. The way to make men useful is to make them wise, and an essential part of wisdom is a comprehensive mind. (ESO 82-3)

CUSTOM, AUTHORITY OF
see LAW, AUTHORITY OF

CUSTOMS

We find that every kind of custom has existed, many of them such as we should have supposed repugnant to human nature. We think we can understand polygamy, as a custom forced upon women by male oppressors. But what are we to say of the Tibetan custom, according to which one woman has several husbands? Yet travelers in Tibet assure us that family life there is at least as harmonious as in Europe. (SE 15)

CYNICISM

Popular Cynicism did not teach abstinence from the good things of this world, but only a certain indifference to them. In the case of a borrower, this might take the form of minimizing the obligation to the lender. One can see how the word "cynic" acquired its everyday meaning. (HWP 233)

D

DANTE

Dante (1265-1321), though as a poet he was a great innovator, was, as a thinker, somewhat behind the times. His book *De Monarchia* is Ghibelline in outlook, and would have been more timely a hundred years earlier. He regards Emperor and Pope as independent, and both divinely appointed. In the *Divine Comedy*, his Satan has three mouths, in which he eternally chews Judas Iscariot, Brutus, and Cassius, who are all three equally traitors, the first against Christ, the other two against Caesar. Dante's thought is interesting, not only in itself, but as that of a layman, but it was not influential, and was hopelessly out of date. (HWP 469-70)

DARK AGES

Our use of the phrase the "Dark Ages" to cover the period from 600 to 1000 marks our undue concentration on Western Europe. In China, this period includes the time of the Tang dynasty, the greatest age of Chinese poetry, and in many other ways a most remarkable epoch. From India to Spain, the brilliant civilization of Islam flourished. What was lost to Christendom at this time was not lost to civilization, but quite the contrary. (HWP 399)

DATA

The question of data has been, mistakenly as I think, mixed up with the question of certainty. The essential characteristic of a datum is that it is not inferred. It may not be true, and we may not feel certain that it is true. The most obvious example is memory. We know that memory is fallible, but there are many things that we believe, though not with complete assurance, on the basis of memory alone. (IMT 155)

In every philosophical problem, our investigation starts from what may be called "data," by which I mean matters of common knowledge, vague, complex, inexact, as common knowledge always is, but yet somehow commanding our assent as on the whole and in some interpretation pretty certainly true. (KEW 69-70)

DATUM, PUBLIC AND PRIVATE

Therefore if we were to speak with pedantic accuracy, we should have to say that everything that can be observed is private to one person. There is often, however, such a close similarity between the simultaneous percepts of different people that the minute differences can, for many purposes, be ignored; we then say that they are all perceiving the same occurrence, and we place this occurrence in a public world outside all the observers. Such occurrences are the data of physics, while those that have not this social and public character supply (so I suggest) the data of psychology. (HK 44-5)

DEATH, ATTITUDE TOWARD

At all times, a man should feel that there are matters of importance for which he lives, and that his death, or the death of wife or child, does not put an end to all that interests him in the world. If this attitude is to be genuine and profound in adult life, it is necessary that, in adolescence, a youth should be fired with generous enthusiasms, and that he should build his life and career about them. (IPI 254)

DECENTRALIZATION
see CENTRALIZATION

DEDUCTION

The part played by deduction in science is greater than Bacon supposed. Often, when a hypothesis has to be tested, there is a long deductive journey from the hypothesis to some consequence that can be tested by observation. Usually the deduction is mathematical, and in this respect Bacon underestimated the importance of mathematics in scientific investigation. (HWP 545)

This is why there is real utility in the process of *deduction*, which goes from the general to the general or from the general to the particular, as well as in the process of *induction*, which goes from the particular to the particular, or from the particular to the general. (PP 123)

In deduction, we have one or more propositions called *premisses*, from which we infer a proposition called the *conclusion*. (IMP 145)

DEFINITION

Definition, as is evident, is only possible in respect of complex ideas. It consists, broadly speaking, in the analysis of complex ideas into their simple constituents. Since one idea can only be defined by another, we should incur a vicious circle if we did not admit some indefinable ideas. (PL 18)

DEFINITION BY EXTENSION AND BY INTENSION
see CLASS

DEFINITION, VERBAL AND OSTENSIVE

There are two ways of getting to know what a word means: one is by a definition in terms of other words, which is called *verbal* definition; the other is by frequently hearing the word when the object which it denotes is present, which is called *ostensive* definition. (HK 4)

DEFINITIONS, DENOTATIONAL AND STRUCTURAL

Definitions are of two sorts, which may be called respectively "denotational" and "structural." An example of a denotational definition is "the tallest man in the United States." This is certainly a definition, since there must be one and only one person to whom it applies, but it defines the man merely by his relations. Generally, a "denotational" definition is one which defines an entity as the only one having a certain relation, or certain relations, to one or more known entities. (HK 276)

DEMOCRACY

"Democracy" means the selection of the legislature and the executive by a periodical majority vote. It does not mean the tyranny of a minority enforced by police terrorism, concentration camps and judicial murder. (LC 123)

Democratic education unadulterated has evils which are as great as those of aristocracy, if not greater. Democracy as a sentiment has two sides. When it says "I am as good as you," it is wholesome, but when it says "you are no better than I am," it becomes oppressive and an obstacle to the development of exceptional merit. To put the matter more accurately: democracy is good when it inspires self-respect, and bad when it inspires persecution of exceptional individuals by the herd. (ESO 78-9)

Democracy, as a method of government, is subject to some limitations which are essential, and to others which are, in principle, avoidable. The essential limitations arise chiefly from two sources: some decisions must be speedy, and others require expert knowledge. (P 191)

Democracy may be defined as the equal distribution of ultimate power. Immediate power cannot be equally distributed; there must be an executive government, and there must be judicial authorities. There is no reason to suppose that it would be desirable, even if it were possible, to give executive and judicial power directly into the hands of the electorate. (DAE 76)

Democracy was invented as a device for reconciling government with liberty. It is clear that government is necessary if anything worthy to be called civilization is to exist, but all history shows that any set of men entrusted with power over another set will abuse their power if they can do so with impunity. Democracy is intended to make men's tenure of power temporary and dependent upon popular approval. In so far as it achieves this it prevents the worst abuses of power. (UE 141)

I have referred to Spinoza to show that the view which I am advocating is neither cynical nor novel. The view is that men's purposes, in fact, though often without their own knowledge, are egoistic—not quite invariably, but so preponderantly that the exceptions do not count in dealing with large numbers, as in politics. The belief that this is not so is the cause of hypocrisy, of moral indignation, and also of the theory that a benevolent despotism is possible. If men, with few and rare exceptions, are egoistic, the only way of securing justice is by democracy, since a despot will almost always seek his own advantage. (HFA 163-4)

Democracy is a device—the best so far invented—for diminishing as much as possible the interference of governments with liberty. If a nation is divided into two sections which cannot both have their way, democracy theoretically insures that the majority shall have their way. But democracy is not at all an adequate device unless it is accompanied by a very great amount of devolution. (PI 30-1)

But if government is not to be tyrannical, it must be democratic, and the democracy must feel that the common interests of mankind are more important than the conflicting interests of separate groups. To realize this state of affairs completely would be scarcely possible, but since the problem is quantitative a gradual approach may be hoped for. At present the world is moving away from all that is valued by lovers of freedom, but this movement will not last forever.

The world has oscillated many times between freedom and slavery, and the dark times in which we live are probably no more permanent than the progressive epoch that rejoiced our grandfathers. (FAG 264)

For my part, I retain the tastes and prejudices of an old-fashioned liberal. I like democracy. I like individual liberty, and I like culture. I do not like to see ignorant or despotic officials interfering needlessly with private lives; I do not like to see creative thought crushed by the tyranny of stupid majorities. I do not like persecution, whether by majorities or of minorities. I am suspicious of government and distrustful of politicians; but insofar as there must be government I prefer that it should be democratic. (CGS 185)

see COMMUNISM AND DEMOCRACY; EQUALITY AND DEMOCRACY;
   MAJORITY, POWER OF THE; POWER

DEMOCRACY, FUNCTIONING OF

There are two possible views as to the proper functioning of democracy. According to one view, the opinions of the majority should prevail absolutely in all fields. According to the other view, wherever a common decision is not necessary, different opinions should be represented, as nearly as possible, in proportion to their numerical frequency. (FAC 27)

DEMOCRACY, FUTURE OF

I do not believe that "political democracy is on the wane." There is nothing new about the present anti-democratic movements; there were similar movements after the French Revolution, and after the revolutions of 1848, not to mention the age of Louis XIV. The two Napoleons were closely analogous to modern dictators; they owed their success to French inexperience in working democratic government. (FOD 381)

DEMOCRACY, JEFFERSONIAN

The doctrine of Jeffersonian democracy was thus two-fold. On the one hand, government should be democratic; on the other hand, there should be as little government as possible. Where joint action is necessary, the will of the majority should prevail; but each individual has certain inalienable natural rights, with which no government ought to interfere. (FO 229)

DEMOCRACY, TEACHING AND THE SURVIVAL OF

The thing, above all, that a teacher should endeavor to produce in his pupils, if democracy is to survive, is the kind of tolerance that springs from an endeavor to understand those who are different from ourselves. (UE 121)

DEMOCRITUS

Democritus was a thorough-going materialist; for him, as we have seen, the soul was composed of atoms, and thought was a physical process. There was no purpose in the universe; there were only atoms governed by mechanical laws. He disbelieved in popular religion, and he argued against the *nous* of Anaxagoras. In ethics he considered cheerfulness the goal of life, and regarded moderation and culture as the best means to it. (HWP 72)

DENOTATION
see MEANING

DESCARTES

Rene Descartes (1596-1650) is usually considered the founder of modern philosophy, and I think, rightly. He is the first man of high philosophic capacity whose outlook is profoundly affected by the new physics and astronomy. While it is true that he retains much of scholasticism, he does not accept foundations laid by predecessors, but endeavours to construct a complete philosophic edifice *de novo*. This had not happened since Aristotle. (HWP 557)
see ST. AUGUSTINE

DESCRIPTION

. . . .a *description*, which consists of several words, whose meanings are already fixed, and from which results whatever is to be taken as the "meaning" of the description. (IMP 174)

DESCRIPTION, AMBIGUOUS AND DEFINITE

By a "description" I mean any phrase of the form " a so-and-so" or "the so-and-so." A phrase of the form "a so-and-so" I shall call an "ambiguous" description; a phrase of the form "the so-and-so" (in the singular) I shall call a "definite" description. (PP 82)

DESCRIPTION, INDEFINITE AND DEFINITE

An indefinite description is a phrase of the form "a so-and-so," and a definite description is a phrase of the form "the so-and-so" (in the singular). (IMP 167)

DESCRIPTIONS, THEORY OF
see REALISM, SCHOLASTIC

DESIGN ARGUMENT
see GOD

DESIGN, ARGUMENT FROM

The proof from the pre-established harmony is a particular form of the so-called physico-theological proof, otherwise known as the argument from design. This is the argument of the Bridgewater Treatises, and of popular theology generally. Being more palpably inadequate than any of the others, it has acquired a popularity which they have never enjoyed. The world is so well constructed, we are told, that it must have had a highly skilful Architect. (PL 183).

DESIRE
see BELIEF

DESIRE, ANIMAL

An animal is said to "desire" the purpose of a behaviour-cycle while the behaviour-cycle is in progress. (AM 66)

DESIRE, CONSCIOUS

A desire is called "conscious" when it is accompanied by a true belief as to the state of affairs that will bring quiescence; otherwise it is called "unconscious." (AM 76)

DESIRE, PRIMITIVE

All primitive desire is unconscious, and in human beings beliefs as to the purposes of desires are often mistaken. These mistaken beliefs generate secondary desires, which cause various interesting complications in the psychology of human desire, without fundamentally altering the character which it shares with animal desire. (AM 76)

DESIRE, SECONDARY
see DESIRE, PRIMITIVE

DESIRE, UNCONSCIOUS
see DESIRE, CONSCIOUS

DESIRES

The question of the legislative moralist is, therefore: How shall this system of rewards and punishments be arranged so as to secure the maximum of what is desired by the legislative authority? If I say that the legislative authority has bad desires, I mean merely that its desires conflict with those of some section of the community to which I belong. Outside human desires there is no moral standard. (WIB 32)

DESIRES AND ETHICS

All systems of ethics embody the desires of those who advocate them, but this fact is concealed in a mist of words. Our desires are, in fact, more general and less purely selfish than many moralists imagine; if it were not so, no theory of ethics would make moral improvement possible. It is, in fact not by ethical theory, but by the cultivation of large and generous desires through intelligence, happiness, and freedom from fear, that men can be brought to act more than they do at present in a manner that is consistent with the general happiness of mankind. Whatever our definition of the "Good," and whether we believe it to be subjective or objective, those who do not desire the happiness of mankind will not endeavour to further it, while those who do desire it will do what they can to bring it about. (RAS 254-5)

DESPOT, VIRTUOUS

I do not think you can ever hope to have the virtuous despot because if you do have a man who is virtuous he would soon cease to be so. (TEP 4)

DESPOTISM, BENEVOLENT
see DEMOCRACY

DESTINY
see FATE

DETERMINISM

We can therefore now state the hypothesis of determinism, though I am afraid the statement is rather complicated. The hypothesis is as follows: There are discoverable causal laws such that, given sufficient (but not superhuman) powers of calculation, a man who knows all that is happening within a certain sphere at a certain time can predict all that will happen at the centre of the sphere during the time that it takes light to travel from the circumference of the sphere to the centre. (RAS 157)
see FREEDOM

DETERMINISM, ECONOMIC

Now that is not the way with those who follow Marx on the question of the economic determination of history. There is dogma, a dogma set up in the name of science. It reminds me extremely of the dogma set up by Comte under the name of positivism, also under the name of science. August Comte, as you all know, proved that the whole world would adopt his doctrines before the end of the nineteenth century. Well, as a matter of fact, the nineteenth century was just about finishing when the last of his followers died. (BW 43)

DEWEY

He is a man of the highest character, liberal in outlook, generous and kind in personal relations, indefatigable in work. With most of his opinions I am in almost complete agreement. Owing to my respect and admiration for him, as well as to personal experience of his kindness, I should wish to agree completely, but to my regret I am compelled to dissent from his most distinctive philosophical doctrine, namely the substitution of "inquiry" for "truth" as the fundamental concept of logic and theory of knowledge. (HWP 819) *see* JAMES

DIALECTIC, HEGELIAN

Everything proceeds by thesis, antithesis and synthesis, and what moves it is the self-development of the Idea, and the Idea is what Hegel happened to believe. The whole course of the universe is making it just such as Hegel thought it was. That is the formula. (HPH 411)

DIALECTICAL MATERIALISM

Let us, in the first place, endeavor to be clear as to what the theory of dialectical materialism is. It is a theory which has various elements. Metaphysically it is materialistic; in method it adopts a form of dialectic suggested by Hegel, but differing from his in many important respects. It takes over from Hegel an outlook which is evolutionary, and in which the stages of evolution can be characterized in clear logical terms. These changes are of the nature of development, not so much in an ethical as in a logical sense—that is to say they proceed according to a plan which a man of sufficient intellect could, theoretically, foretell, and which Marx himself professes to have foretold, in its main outlines, up to the moment of the universal establishment of Communism. The materialism of its metaphysics is translated, where human affairs are concerned, into the doctrine that the prime cause of all social phenomena is the method of production and exchange prevailing at any given period. (FO 188)

DIALECTICAL MATERIALISM, CRITICISM OF

To state in advance what I shall be trying to prove, I hold (1) that materialism, in some sense, may be true, though it cannot be known to be so; (2) that the elements of dialectic which Marx took over from Hegel made him regard history as a more rational process than it has in fact been, convincing him that all changes must be in some sense progressive, and giving him a feeling of certainty in regard to the future, for which there is no scientific warrant; (3) that the whole of his theory of economic development may perfectly well be true if his metaphysic is false, and false if his metaphysic is true, and that but for the influence of Hegel it would never have occurred to him that a matter so purely empirical could depend upon abstract metaphysics; (4) with regard to the economic interpretation of history, it seems to me very largely true, and a most important contribution to sociology; I cannot, however, regard it as *wholly* true, or feel any confidence that all great historical changes can be viewed as developments. (FO 190-1)

DICTATORSHIP

History has know many dogmatic dictatorships, and their record is not encouraging. The first historical character to found a government composed of men chosen for their adherence to a certain creed was Pythagoras, who for a time established his authority over the city of Croton, exhorting the inhabitants to study geometry and eschew beans. But, whether from hatred of geometry or from love of beans, the citizens turned against him and he had to fly. A more important example was the medieval Church, which though nominally founded upon a religion of love, endeavored to enforce its tenets by means of the Inquisition. Cromwell's rule of the Saints was in many ways similar to Lenin's system: beginning with advocacy of democracy and freedom, it ended by establishing a hated military tyranny. The French Revolution, starting from the Rights of Man, produced first Robespierre and then Napoleon, neither of whom had any very noticeable respect for human rights. In all these cases the trouble came from dogmatic belief in a panacea so splendid, that any cruelty was thought permissible in bringing about the desired end. (CTR 10)

When a Russian Communist speaks of dictatorship, he means the word literally, but when he speaks of the proletariat, he means the word in a Pickwickian sense. He means the "class-conscious" part of the proletariat, i.e., the Communist Party. He includes people by no means proletarian (such as Lenin and Tchicherin) who have the right opinions, and he excludes such wage-earners as have not the right opinions, whom he classifies as lackeys of the *bourgeoisie*. (PTB 26-7)

DISBELIEF
see BELIEF

DISCIPLINE

The fundamental idea is simple: that the right discipline consists, not in external compulsion, but in habits of mind which lead spontaneously to desirable rather than undesirable activities. (EEC 37)

And you know quite well that it would not do if you followed each whim without a certain amount of discipline, and I don't want you to think that there is not a need of discipline. There is, but it should be that discipline that comes from within, from the realization of one's own needs, from the feeling of something which one wishes to achieve. Nothing of importance is ever achieved without discipline. I feel myself sometimes not wholly in sympathy with some modern educational theorists, because I think that they underestimate the part that discipline plays. But the discipline you have in your life should be one determined by your own desires and your own needs, not put upon you by society or authority. (FAH 32-3)

Apart from actual physical punishment, constant interference with perfectly innocent impulses has almost as bad an effect. Primitive mothers interfere very little with their children, and only when some real danger threatens. But uneducated mothers in civilized communities have none of this primitive calm, and behave very often as if their children were a perpetual irritation to them. "Sit still", "Be quiet", "Don't do that", are constantly recurring phrases, all uttered in an angry voice. The desire for physical activity, which is instinctive in every healthy child, is thwarted, and black thoughts take the place of harmless actions. (WWP 182-3)

DISCOMFORT

"Discomfort" is a property of a sensation or other mental occurrence, consisting in the fact that the occurrence in question stimulates voluntary or reflex movements tending to produce some more or less definite change involving the cessation of the occurrence. (AM 71)

DISCONTINUITY

What, in these circumstances, has science to contribute to metaphysics? Academic philosophers, ever since the time of Parmenides, have believed that the world is a unity. This view has been taken over from them by clergymen and journalists, and its acceptance has been considered the touchstone of wisdom. The most fundamental of my intellectual beliefs is that this is rubbish. I think the universe is all spots and jumps, without unity, without continuity, without coherence or orderliness or any of the other properties that governesses love. (SO 94-5)

DISJUNCTION

A disjunction is the verbal expression of indecision, or, if a question, of the desire to reach a decision. (IMT 104)

We may take next *disjunction*, "p or q." This is a function whose truth-value is truth when p is true and also when q is true, but is falsehood when both p and q are false. (IMP 147)

DISSECTION

Throughout the Middle Ages, as we have seen, the prevention and cure of disease were attempted by methods which were either superstitious or wholly arbitrary. Nothing more scientific was possible without anatomy and physiology, and these, in turn, were not possible without dissection, which the Church opposed. (RAS 105)

DIVORCE

To sum up: Where there are no children, divorce should be obtainable at the request of either party. Where there are children, the usual ground should be mutual consent; other grounds should be insanity, grave crime, habitual drunkenness, and certain other diseases. Adultery *per se* should not be a ground. (DMC 18)

DOGMA

Systems of dogma without empirical foundation, such as those of scholastic theology, Marxism, and fascism, have the advantage of producing a great degree of social coherence among their disciples. But they have the disadvantage of involving persecution

of valuable sections of the population. Spain was ruined by the
expulsion of the Jews and Moors; France suffered by the emigra-
tion of Huguenots after the Revocation of the Edict of Nantes;
Germany would probably have been first in the field with the atomic
bomb but for Hitler's hatred of Jews. (UE 19)
see RELIGION, ELEMENTS OF

DOGMATISM

But if philosophy is to serve a positive purpose, it must not
teach mere skepticism, for, while the dogmatist is harmful, the skep-
tic is useless. Dogmatism and skepticism are both, in a sense, absolute philosophies; one is certain of knowing, the other of not knowing. What philosophy should dissipate is *certainty*, whether of knowledge or of ignorance. (UE 27)

DOGMATISM, CURE FOR

A good way of ridding yourself of certain kinds of dogmatism
is to become aware of opinions held in social circles different from
your own. When I was young, I lived much outside my own country—
in France, Germany, Italy and the United States. I found this very
profitable in diminishing the intensity of insular prejudice. If you
cannot travel, seek out people with whom you disagree, and read
a newspaper belonging to a party that is not yours. (UE 104)

DOMAIN

The class of those terms that have a given relation to something or other is called the *domain* of that relation: thus fathers
are the domain of the relation of father to child, husbands are the
domain of the relation of husband to wife, wives are the domain
of the relation of wife to husband, and husbands and wives together
are the domain of the relation of marriage. (IMP 16)

DOMAIN, CONVERSE

The converse domain of a relation is the domain of its converse:
thus the class of wives is the converse domain of the relation of husband to wife. (IMP 16)

DREAMS
see IMAGES

DREAMS, DAY

Man is essentially a dreamer, wakened sometimes for a moment
by some peculiarly obtrusive element in the outer world, but lapsing

again quickly into the happy somnolence of imagination. Freud has shown how largely our dreams at night are the pictured fulfillment of our wishes; he has, with an equal measure of truth, said the same of day-dreams; and he might have included the day-dreams which we call beliefs. (SE 26)

DUNS SCOTUS

Duns Scotus held that, since there is no difference between being and essence, the "principle of individuation"—i.e., that which makes one thing not identical with another—must be form, not matter. The "principle of individuation" was one of the important problems of the scholastic philosophy. In various forms, it has remained a problem to the present day. (HWP 467)

E

ECONOMIC ASPECTS OF LIFE

The fundamental delusion of our time, in my opinion, is the excessive emphasis upon the economic aspects of life, and I do not expect the strife between Capitalism and Communism as philosophies to cease until it is recognized that both are inadequate through their failure to recognize biological needs. (SE 235-236)

ECONOMIC DEMOCRACY

As I said before, the coalescence of economic and political power is an irresistible tendency in the modern world. It may be effected in an undemocratic manner by the politicians, as has happened in Russia, Italy, and Germany. It may be effected in an undemocratic manner by the plutocrats, in the countries that are nominally democratic. For the believer in democracy, the only practicable course is to advocate its happening in a democratic way, by the transference of ultimate economic power into the hands of the democratic state. (DAE 78)

ECONOMIC POWER

Let us first consider what economic power is. In former days it consisted in ownership of land or capital, but in a developed industrial community ownership does not, as a rule, confer any appreciable share of power. Economic power belongs to large corporations, in which, by various devices, the ordinary shareholders have been deprived of all effective voice in their government, which is in the hands of a small number of too often self-perpetuating directors. (DAE 76)

My view would be that the power should be diffused and democratic, and, while it is necessary technically that certain people should have executive power, they should always be under the control of the democracy and capable of being turned out. It can only be made democratic, I think, by being put under the state. I do not see any other way of making it democratic. (TEP 4)

EDUCATION

If the object were to make pupils think, rather than to make them accept certain conclusions, education would be conducted quite differently: there would be less rapidity of instruction and more discussion, more occasions when pupils were encouraged to express themselves, more attempts to make education concern itself with matters in which the pupils felt some interest. (PSR 176-7)

The scientific educator has two things to think about: in the first place, he must produce emotions in the right proportions; and in the second place, he must attach them to the right objects. The first is probably, in the last analysis, a matter of chemistry; the second is a matter of "conditioning" in the sense of Pavlov and Watson. (SAE 89)

Education, considered as a process of forming our mental habits and our outlook on the world, is to be judged successful in proportion as its outcome approximates to this ideal; in proportion, that is to say, as it gives us a true view of our place in society, of the relation of the whole human society to its non-human environment, and of the nature of the non-human world as it is in itself apart from our desires and interests. (ML 39)

Education should have two objects: first, to give definite knowledge—reading and writing, language and mathematics, and so on; secondly, to create those mental habits which will enable people to acquire knowledge and form sound judgments for themselves. (FT 323)
see DISCIPLINE

EDUCATION ABROAD

If it were customary for young people to receive part of their education abroad, it is to be hoped that this insularity might be diminished on both sides of the ocean. (CAB 58)

EDUCATION, AUTHORITY AND DISCIPLINE IN

Consideration for others does not, with most children, arise spontaneously, but has to be taught, and can hardly be taught except by the exercise of authority. This is perhaps the most important argument against the abdication of the adults. (IPI 242)

EDUCATION, CLASSICAL

One defect, however, does seem inherent in a purely classical education—namely, a too exclusive emphasis on the past. By the study of what is absolutely ended and can never be renewed, a habit of criticism towards the present and the future is engendered. The qualities in which the present excels are qualities to which the study of the past does not direct attention, and to which, therefore, the student of Greek civilization may easily become blind. (ML 35)

EDUCATION, HIGHER

It is one of the defects of modern higher education that it has become too much a training in the acquisition of certain kinds of skill, and too little an enlargement of the mind and heart by an impartial survey of the world. (CH 225)

EDUCATION, INDIVIDUALITY IN

The problem for the educator who is not content with obedience and discipline as sources of social cohesion is difficult, but not insoluble. He has to preserve individuality without producing anarchy. This means that what is necessary in the way of social cooperation must be not very difficult, and must not involve any very severe repression of impulse. This, in turn, means that the child must, from the first, be so handled as to have only slight impulses towards rage and cruelty and destruction; that he must, in the absence of evidence to the contrary, expect his companions to be friendly; and that he must find his environment a help rather than a hindrance so long as his activities are not such as to cause injury to others. (WWP 185-6)

EDUCATION, LIBERAL

This is the task of a liberal education: to give a sense of the value of things other than domination, to help to create wise citizens of a free community, and through the combination of citizenship with liberty in individual creativeness to enable men to give to human life that splendor which some few have shown that it can achieve. (P 305)

EDUCATION, STATE

State education is obviously necessary, but as obviously involves dangers against which there ought to be safeguards. The evils to be feared were seen in their full magnitude in Nazi Germany and are still seen in Russia. (UE 113)

EDUCATION, UNIVERSAL COMPULSORY

There must exist in a modern community a sufficient number

of men who possess the technical skill required to preserve the mechanical apparatus upon which our physical comforts depend. It is, moreover, inconvenient if any large percentage of the population is unable to read and write. For these reasons we are all in favor of universal compulsory education. (UE 115)

EDUCATOR, THE

Love of power is the chief danger of the educator, as of the politician; the man who can be trusted in education must care for his pupils on their own account, not merely as potential soldiers in an army of propagandists for a cause. (P 304)

EFFERENT
see AFFERENT

EGO

Similarly, when we say, "I think first this and then that," we ought not to mean that there is a single entity "I" which "has" two successive thoughts. We ought to mean only that there are two successive thoughts which have causal relations of the kind that makes us call them parts of one biography, in the same sort of way in which successive notes may be parts of one tune; and that these thoughts are connected with the body which is speaking in the way (to be further investigated) in which thoughts and bodies are connected. (OP 163)

Now if there is such a thing as the Ego, it must be a particular or a system of particulars. If the latter, it can be defined, and becomes identical with what I have called a "biography." If the former, we must know of it (if we know of it at all) either by inference or by observation. I agree with Hume that I do not know of it by observation. If it is arrived at by inference, the inference is of just that kind that I seek to invalidate by the principle of substituting constructions for inferences. The basis of this principle is that, where a suitable construction is possible, this very fact invalidates the inference, since it shows that the supposed inferred entity is not necessary for the interpretation of the propositions of the science in question. (RTC 698-9)

EGOISM
see DEMOCRACY

EINSTEIN
see SCIENCE, PROGRESS OF

ELECTIONS, SOVIET

Various methods are adopted in Russia for giving the victory to Government candidates. In the first place, the voting is by show of hands, so that all who vote against the Government are marked men. In the second place, no candidate who is not a Communist can have any printing done, the printing works being all in the hands of the State. In the third place, he cannot address any meetings, because the halls all belong to the State. The whole of the press is, of course, official; no independent daily is permitted. (PTB 74-5)

ELECTRICITY

Some readers may expect me at this stage to tell them what electricity "really is." The fact is that I have already said what it is. It is not a thing, like St. Paul's Cathedral; it is a way in which things behave. When we have told how things behave when they are electrified, and under what circumstances *they* are electrified, we have told all there is to tell. (ABCA 24)

EMOTIONS, CULTIVATION OF

Emotions that have desirable social consequences are not so easily generated as hate and rage and fear. In their creation, much depends upon early childhood; much, also, upon economic circumstances. Something, however, can be done, in the course of ordinary education, to provide the nourishment upon which the better emotions can grow, and to bring about the realization of what may give value to human life. (P 301-2)

EMOTIONS, QUALITY OF

Let us take first the question of the quality of the emotions. One may in a sense divide emotional attitudes into positive and negative; the emotions of hate, rage, and fear are negative, while emotions of affection, pleasure, and experimentation are positive. Speaking broadly, it is a good thing to have much of the positive emotions and little of the negative. There are, of course, exceptions. It is useful to be afraid of snakes, tigers, precipices, and interviewers. (SAE 89)

EMPEDOCLES

The originality of Empedocles, outside science, consists in the doctrine of the four elements and in the use of the two principles of Love and Strife to explain change. He rejected monism, and regarded the course of nature as regulated by chance and necessity rather than by purpose. In these respects his philosophy was more scientific than those of Parmenides, Plato, and Aristotle. In other respects, it is true, he acquiesced in current superstitions; but in this he was no worse than many more recent men of science. (HWP 57-8)

EMPIRICAL KNOWLEDGE
see A PRIORI KNOWLEDGE

EMPIRICISM

Assuming "perceptive premisses" to have been adequately defined, let us return to the definition of "empiricism." My momentary knowledge consists largely of memory, and my individual knowledge consists largely of testimony. But memory, when it is veridical, is related to a previous perceptive premiss, and testimony, when it is veridical, is related to some one else's perceptive premiss. Social empiricism takes these perceptive premisses of other times or other persons as *the* empirical premisses for what is now accepted, and thus evades the problems connected with memory and testimony. (IMT 169)

In this sense, it must be admitted, empiricism as a theory of knowledge has proved inadequate, though less so than any previous theory of knowledge. Indeed, such inadequacies as we have seemed to find in empiricism have been discovered by strict adherence to a doctrine by which empiricist philosophy has been inspired: that all human knowledge is uncertain, inexact, and partial. To this doctrine we have not found any limitation whatever. (HK 507)

I will observe, however, that empiricism, as a theory of knowledge, is self-refuting. For, however it may be formulated, it must involve *some* general proposition about the dependence of knowledge upon experience; and any such proposition, if true, must have as a consequence that itself cannot be known. While, therefore, empiricism may be true, it cannot, if true, be known to be so. This, however, is a large problem. (IMT 207)

To this extent, Hume has proved that pure empiricism is not a sufficient basis for science. But if this one principle is admitted, everything else can proceed in accordance with the theory that all our knowledge is based on experience. It must be granted that this is a serious departure from pure empiricism, and that those who are not empiricists may ask why, if one departure is allowed, others are to be forbidden. These, however, are questions not directly

raised by Hume's arguments. What these arguments prove—and I do not think the proof can be controverted—is that induction is an independent logical principle, incapable of being inferred either from experience or from other logical principles, and that without this principle science is impossible. (HWP 674)
see ALL.; VERIFICATION

EMPIRICISM, MODERN ANALYTIC

Modern analytical empiricism, of which I have been giving an outline, differs from that of Locke, Berkeley, and Hume by its incorporation of mathematics and its development of a powerful logical technique. It is thus able, in regard to certain problems, to achieve definite answers, which have the quality of science rather than of philosophy. It has the advantage, as compared with the philosophies of the system-builders, of being able to tackle its problems one at a time, instead of having to invent at one stroke a block theory of the whole universe. Its methods, in this respect, resemble those of science. I have no doubt that, in so far as philosophical knowledge is possible, it is by such methods, that it must be sought. I have also no doubt that, by these methods, many ancient problems are completely soluble. (HWP 834)

EMPIRICISTS

The empiricists—who are best represented by the British philosophers, Locke, Berkeley, and Hume—maintained that all our knowledge is derived from experience . . . .(PP 114)

ENDOWMENTS

Endowments have a considerable effect in making the religious side of education more conservative than it would otherwise be. The connection of religion with private property arises through the fact that men leave their money to religious bodies, and that this secures, for centuries after their death, the propagation of the particular brand of superstition in which they believed. (ESO 202)

ENDS

The main things which seem to me important on their own account, and not merely as means to other things, are: knowledge, art, instinctive happiness, and relations of friendship or affection. (PC 5)
see MEANS

ENDS, CHOICE OF
see ETHICS, SCIENCE AND

ENERGY, KINETIC

The kinetic energy of a particle is half the mass multiplied by the square of the velocity. The kinetic energy of a number of particles is the sum of the kinetic energies of the separate particles. (ABCR 155)

ENERGY, POTENTIAL

The potential energy is more difficult to define. It represents any state of strain, which can only be preserved by the application of force. To take the easiest case: If a weight is lifted to a height and kept suspended, it has potential energy, because, if left to itself, it will fall. Its potential energy is equal to the kinetic energy which it would acquire in falling through the same distance through which it was lifted. (ABCR 155)

ENVIRONMENT
see TWINS, IDENTICAL

ENVY

Envy, the third of the psychological causes to which we attributed what is bad in the actual world, depends in most natures upon that kind of fundamental discontent which springs from a lack of free development, from thwarted instinct, and from the impossibility of realizing an imagined happiness. Envy cannot be cured by preaching; preaching, at the best, will only alter its manifestations and lead it to adopt more subtle forms of concealment. Except in those rare natures in which generosity dominates in spite of circumstances, the only cure for envy is freedom and the joy of life. (RF 162)

Of all the characteristics of ordinary human nature envy is the most unfortunate; not only does the envious person wish to inflict misfortune and do so whenever he can with impunity, but he is also himself rendered unhappy by envy. Instead of deriving pleasure from what he has, he derives pain from what others have. (CH 85)

EPICURUS

The philosophy of Epicurus, like all those of his age (with the partial exception of Scepticism), was primarily designed to secure tranquillity. He considered pleasure to be the good, and adhered,

with remarkable consistency, to all the consequences of this view.
(HWP 243)

EPISTEMOLOGY

Epistemology involves both logical and psychological elements.
Logically, we have to consider the inferential relation (usually not
that of strict deduction) between basic propositions and those that
we believe because of them; also the logical relations which often
subsist between different basic propositions, causing them, if we
accept certain general principles, to fit into a system which, as a
whole, strengthens the probability of each of its constituents; also
the logical character of basic propositions themselves. Psychologically, we have to examine the relation of basic propositions to experiences, the degree of doubt or certainty that we feel in regard to
any of them, and the methods of diminishing the former and increasing the latter. (IMT 18)

EQUALITY AND DEMOCRACY

All this is connected with what I believe to be a wrong conception of democracy. Democracy demands that no one should have
special privileges, but it does not demand that people should be all
alike. There is a tendency in America to think that any man who
ventures to be different from the majority of his neighbors in any
way is setting himself up and claiming to be better than his neighbors.

This view is fatal to excellence. A community requires many
different kinds of work, and each kind of work requires, if it is to
be well done, its own kind of character and aptitude. (CAB 59)

ERASMUS

The only book by Erasmus that is still read is *The Praise of
Folly*. The conception of this book came to him in 1509, while he
was crossing the Alps on the way from Italy to England. He wrote
it quickly in London, at the house of Sir Thomas More, to whom
it is dedicated, with a playful suggestion of appropriateness since
"moros" means "fool." The book is spoken by Folly in her own
person; she sings her own praises with great gusto, and her text is
enlivened still further with illustrations by Holbein. She covers all
parts of human life, and all classes and professions. But for her,
the human race would die out, for who can marry without folly?
(HWP 514)

ERASTIANISM

Erastianism is the doctrine that the Church should be subject to the State. (HWP 363)

ERROR
see REACTIONS SUSPENDED; TRUTH

ERROR, PROBABLE
see APPROXIMATION

ESSENCE

The divorce of essence from existence, in which I formerly believed as completely as Santayana does, has come to seem to me questionable. I re-read recently his criticism of me in *Winds of Doctrine* (1913), and found myself, broadly speaking, in agreement with him whenever he thought me in the wrong, but not when he thought me in the right. My views have changed so much that I could read what he said with almost as much detachment as if it applied to some one else. (POS 459)

ETERNITY, UNDER THE ASPECT OF

Spinoza, who was one of the wisest of men and who lived consistently in accordance with his own wisdom, advised men to view passing events "under the aspect of eternity." Those who can learn to do this will find a painful present much more bearable than it would otherwise be. (IWS 17)

ETHICAL TEST

I shall therefore assume, without more ado, that actions are to be judged by the results to be expected from actions of that kind, and not by some supposed *a priori* moral code. I do not mean—what would be obviously impracticable—that we should habitually calculate the effects of our actions. What I mean is that in deciding what sort of moral instruction should be given to the young, or what sort of actions should be punished by the criminal law, we should do our best to consider what sort of actions will promote or hinder the general well-being. (PIC 166)

ETHICS

We all think electricity is entirely governed by natural laws, and yet we think it is rational to put up lightning conductors. Well, I should say that an ethic is, as it were, a lightning conductor for human passions, to enable them within a deterministic world to work in a way that produces a minimum of disaster. (SPE 107)

Ethics is in origin the art of recommending to others the sacrifices required for co-operation with oneself. Hence, by reflexion, it comes, through the operation of social justice, to recommend sacrifices by oneself, but all ethics, however refined, remains more or less subjective. Even vegetarians do not hesitate, for example, to save the life of a man in a fever, although in doing so they destroy the lives of many millions of microbes. (ML 108-9)

see ARISTOTLE'S ETHICS; CASUISTRY; DESIRES AND ETHICS; IMPERATIVE. CRITICISM OF THE CATEGORICAL; IMPULSES, REPRESSIVE; MOTIVES; VALUES, SUBJECTIVITY OF

ETHICS, CHRISTIAN

The fundamental defect of Christian ethics consists in the fact that it labels certain classes of acts "sins" and others "virtues" on grounds that have nothing to do with their social consequences. An ethic not derived from superstition must decide first upon the kind of social effects which it desires to achieve and the kind which it desires to avoid. It must then decide, as far as our knowledge permits, what acts will promote the desired consequences; these acts it will praise, while those having a contrary tendency it will condemn. (ESO 110-1)

ETHICS, FUNDAMENTAL PRINCIPLES OF

see UTILITARIANISM

ETHICS, MUNDANE BASIS OF

We have seen a great system of cruel falsehood, the Nazi system, lead a nation to disaster at immense cost to its opponents. It is not by such systems that happiness is to be achieved; even without the help of revelation it is not difficult to see that human welfare requires a less ferocious ethic. More and more people are becoming unable to accept traditional beliefs. If they think that, apart from these beliefs, there is no reason for kindly behaviour the results may be needlessly unfortunate. That is why it is important to show that no supernatural reasons are needed to make men kind and to prove that only through kindness can the human race achieve happiness. (FAR 6)

ETHICS, PERSONAL

I come now to the question of personal ethics, as opposed to the question of social and political institutions. No man is wholly free, and no man is wholly a slave. To the extent to which a man has freedom, he needs a personal morality to guide his conduct.

There are some who would say that a man need only obey the accepted moral code of his community. But I do not think any student of anthropology could be content with this answer. Such practices as cannibalism, human sacrifice, and head hunting have died out as a result of moral protests against conventional moral opinion. If a man seriously desires to live the best life that is open to him, he must learn to be critical of the tribal customs and tribal beliefs that are generally accepted among his neighbours. (AAI 109)

ETHICS, SCIENCE AND

Science can, if rulers so desire, create sentiments which will avert disaster and facilitate cooperation. At present there are powerful rulers who have no such wish. But the possibility exists, and science can be just as potent for good as for evil. It is not science, however, which will determine how science is used. Science, by itself, cannot supply us with an ethic. It can show us how to achieve a given end, and it may show us that some ends cannot be achieved. But among ends that can be achieved our choice must be decided by other than purely scientific considerations. (STS 33)

ETHICS, SPINOZA'S

The basis of his ethic, so far as I accept his ethic is that one can discover by experience that there is a certain kind of way of living which seems to most of those who have tried it to be a good way and which is the way which Spinoza recommends—a way in which you get rid of indignation and fear and irrational hope and a number of the things that produce anxiety and perturbation in life, and acquire a certain kind of calm. The kind of calm which Spinoza recommends is, I think, attainable without adopting his metaphysic. (SPE 112-3)

EUCLID

Euclid, who was still, when I was young, the sole acknowledged text-book of geometry for boys, lived in Alexandria, about 300 B.C., a few years after the death of Alexander and Aristotle. Most of his *Elements* was not original, but the order of propositions, and the logical structure, were largely his. The more one studies geometry, the more admirable these are seen to be. (HWP 211)

EUGENICS

Eugenics is of two sorts, positive and negative. The former is concerned with the encouragement of good stocks, the latter with

the discouragement of bad ones. The latter is at present more practicable. (MM 258)

Unfortunately the concern of biology is with the most intimate
part of human life, where emotions, morals, and religion alike stand
in the way of progress. It may be doubted whether human nature
could bear so great an interference with the life of instinct as would
be involved in a really effective application of eugenics. Whatever
may be thought disagreeable in the machine age would be greatly
intensified by the application of science to parenthood, and men
might well think the price not worth paying. (S 81)

EUTHANASIA

The whole conception of "Sin" is one which I find very puzzling,
doubtless owing to my sinful nature. If "Sin" consisted in causing
needless suffering, I could understand, but on the contrary, sin often
consists in avoiding needless suffering. Some years ago, in the English House of Lords, a bill was introduced to legalize euthanasia in
cases of painful and incurable disease. The patient's consent was
to be necessary, as well as several medical certificates. To me, in
my simplicity, it would seem natural to require the patient's consent,
but the late Archbishop of Canterbury, the English official expert
on Sin, explained the erroneousness of such a view. The patient's
consent turns euthanasia into suicide, and suicide is sin. Their Lord-
ships listened to the voice of authority and rejected the bill. (UE 76)

EVENT

The only way to get clear is to make a fresh start, with *events*
instead of bodies. In physics, an "event" is anything which, according to the old notions, would be said to have both a date and a
place. An explosion, a flash of lightning, the starting of a light-wave
from an atom, the arrival of the light-wave at some other body, any
of these would be an "event". Some strings of events make up what
we regard as the history of one body; some make up the course of
one light-wave; and so on. The unity of a body is a unity of history
—it is like the unity of a tune, which takes time to play, and does
not exist whole in any one moment. What exists at any one moment
is only what we call an "event." (OP 110)
see MATTER

EVENT, CO-ORDINATES OF THE

Four numbers are needed to fix the position of an event in the
world; these correspond to the time and the three dimensions of

space in the old reckoning. These four numbers are called the co-ordinates of the event. They may be assigned on any principle which gives neighbouring co-ordinates to neighbouring events; subject to this condition, they are merely conventional. (OP 111)

EVENT, PHYSICAL AND MENTAL

Let us first define more exactly what we mean by a "physical" event. I should define it as an event which, if known to occur, is inferred, and which is not known to be mental. And I define a "mental" event (to repeat) as one with which someone is acquainted otherwise than by inference. Thus a "physical" event is one which is either totally unknown, or, if known at all, is not known to anyone except by inference—or, perhaps we should say, is not known to be known to anyone except by inference. (HK 229)

EVENTS

We shall find, if I am not mistaken, that the objects which are mathematically primitive in physics, such as electrons, protons, and points in space-time, are all logically complex structures composed of entities which are metaphysically more primitive, which may be conveniently called "events." (AOM 9)

And what we can primarily infer from percepts, assuming the validity of physics, are groups of events, again not substances. It is a mere linguistic convenience to regard a group of events as states of a "thing," or "substance," or "piece of matter." This infer-ence was originally made on the ground of the logic which philoso-phers inherited from common sense. By defining a "thing" as the group of what would formerly have been its "states," we alter nothing in the detail of physics, and avoid an inference as precarious as it is useless. (AOM 284)
see MIND

EVIL

When it is realized that the fundamental evils are due to the blind empire of matter, and are the wholly necessary effects of forces which have no consciousness and are therefore neither good nor bad in themselves, indignation becomes absurd, like Xerxes chastising the Hellespont. Thus the realisation of necessity is the liberation from indignation. This alone, however, will not prevent an undue preoccupation with evil. It is obvious that some things that exist are good, some bad, and we have no means of knowing whether the good or the bad preponderate. (ER 57)

EVILS

When we consider the evils in the lives we know of, we find that they may be roughly divided into three classes. There are, first, those due to physical nature: among these are death, pain and the difficulty of making the soil yield a subsistence. These we will call "physical evils." Second, we may put those that spring from defects in the character or aptitudes of the sufferer: among these are ignorance, lack of will, and violent passions. These we will call "evils of character." Third come those that depend upon the power of one individual or group over another: these comprise not only obvious tyranny, but all interference with free development, whether by force or by excessive mental influence such as may occur in education. These we will call "evils of power." A social system may be judged by its bearing upon these three kinds of evils. (RF 188)

EVILS, CONSCIOUSNESS OF

No one can be a Radical without being profoundly conscious of the things that are amiss in the world, which most people at most times wish to ignore. And consciousness of evils is naturally associated with hatred of those who seem to cause them. Very often, hatred and envy of the successful is the *cause* of Radicalism; but when it is not, it is usually one of its effects. (WRU 14)

EVOLUTIONISM

Evolutionism, in basing itself upon the notion of *progress*, which is change from the worse to the better, allows the notion of time, as it seems to me, to become its tyrant rather than its servant, and thereby loses that impartiality of contemplation which is the source of all that is best in philosophic thought and feeling. (ML 26)

The second type, which may be called evolutionism, derived its predominance from Darwin, and must be reckoned as having had Herbert Spencer for its first philosophical representative; but in recent times it has become, chiefly through William James and M. Bergson, far bolder and far more searching in its innovations than it was in the hands of Herbert Spencer. (KEW 4)
see VITALISM

EXAMINATIONS

As matters stand today, many teachers are unable to do the best of which they are capable. For this there are a number of reasons, some more or less accidental, others very deep-seated. To begin with the former, most teachers are overworked and are compelled to prepare their pupils for examinations rather than to give them a liberalizing mental training. (UE 119)

EXCITEMENT

A person accustomed to too much excitement is like a person with a morbid craving for pepper, who comes at last to be unable even to taste a quantity of pepper which would cause any one else to choke. There is an element of boredom which is inseparable from the avoidance of too much excitement, and too much excitement not only undermines the health, but dulls the palate for every kind of pleasure, substituting titillations for profound organic satisfactions, cleverness for wisdom, and jagged surprises for beauty. I do not wish to push to extremes the objection to excitement. A certain amount of it is wholesome, but, like almost everything else, the matter is quantitative. (CH 61-2)

EXCLUDED MIDDLE, LAW OF
see TRUTH-FUNCTION, THEORY OF

EXECUTIVE, THE POWER OF THE
see MAJORITY, POWER OF THE

EXISTENCE
see ESSENCE

EXORCISM

The formula of exorcism became longer and longer, and more and more filled with obscenities. By such means, the Jesuits of Vienna in 1583, cast out 12,652 devils. When, however, such mild methods failed, the patient was scourged; if the demon still refused to leave him, he was tortured. For centuries, innumerable helpless lunatics were thus given over to the cruelty of barbarous gaolers. Even when the superstitious beliefs by which cruelty had originally been inspired were no longer accepted, the tradition survived that the insane should be treated harshly. (RAS 92-3)

EXPERIENCE

The essence of "experience" is the modification of behaviour produced by what is experienced. We might, in fact, define one chain of experience, or one biography, as a series of occurrences linked by mnemic causation. I think it is this characteristic, more than any other, that distinguishes sciences dealing with living organisms from physics. (AM 83)

EXPRESSES
see SENTENCES, INDICATIVE

F

FACT

I mean by a "fact" something which is there, whether anybody thinks so or not. If I look up a railway timetable and find that there is a train to Edinburgh at 10 A.M., then, if the timetable is correct, there is an actual train, which is a "fact." The statement in the timetable is itself a "fact," whether true or false, but it only *states* a fact if it is true, i.e., if there really is a train. Most facts are independent of our volitions; that is why they are called "hard," "stubborn," or "ineluctable." Physical facts, for the most part, are independent, not only of our volitions but even of our existence. (HK 143)

FACTUAL PREMISS

I shall give the name "factual premiss" to any uninferred proposition which asserts something having a date and which I believe after a critical scrutiny. I do not mean that the date is part of the assertion, but merely that some kind of temporal occurrence is what is involved in the truth of the assertion. (IMT 190)

FALSE

see SENTENCES, INDICATIVE

FALSEHOOD

The ultimate test of falsehood is *never*, I think, the nature of the consequences of a belief, but the association between words and sensible or remembered facts. A belief is "verified" when a situation arises which gives a feeling of expectedness in connection with it; it is falsified when the feeling is one of surprise. But this only applies to beliefs which await some future contingency for verification or refutation. (OP 258)
see TRUTH

FAMILY RELATION

A man and woman who love each other and their children ought to be able to act spontaneously as the heart dictates. They will need much thought and knowledge, but these they will acquire out of parental affection. They must not demand from their children what they get from each other, but if they are happy in each other they will feel no impulse to do so. If the children are properly cared for, they will feel for their parents a natural affection which will be no barriers to independence. What is needed is not ascetic self-denial, but freedom and expansiveness of instinct, adequately informed by intelligence and knowledge. (EEC 198)

FASCISM

Fascism is a complex movement; its German and Italian forms differ widely, and in other countries, if it spreads, it may assume still other shapes. It has, however, certain essentials, without which it would cease to be Fascism. It is anti-democratic, it is nationalistic, it is capitalistic, and it appeals to those sections of the middle class which suffer through modern developments and expect to suffer still more if Socialism or Communism become established. Communism, also, is anti-democratic, but only for a time, at least, so far as its theoretical statements can be accepted as giving its real policy; moreover, it aims at serving the interests of wage-earners, who are a majority in advanced countries, and are intended by Communists to become the whole population. Fascism is anti-democratic in a more fundamental sense. It does not accept the greatest happiness of the greatest number as the right principle in statesmanship, but selects certain individuals, nations, and classes as "the best," and as alone worthy of consideration. The remainder are to be compelled by force to serve the interests of the elect. (IPI 130-1)

FASCISM, ANCESTORS OF

The founders of the school of thought out of which Fascism has grown all have certain common characteristics. They seek the good in *will* rather than in feeling or cognition; they value power more than happiness; they prefer force to argument, war to peace, aristocracy to democracy, propaganda to scientific impartiality. They advocate a Spartan form of austerity, as opposed to the Christian form; that is to say, they view austerity as a means of obtaining mastery over others not as a self-discipline which helps to produce virtue, and happiness only in the next world. The later ones among them are imbued with popular Darwinism, and regard the struggle for existence as the source of a higher species; but it is to be rather a struggle between races than one between individuals, such as the apostles of free competition advocated. Pleasure and knowledge, conceived as ends, appear to them unduly passive. For pleasure they substitute glory, and, for knowledge, the pragmatic assertion that what they desire is true. In Fichte, Carlyle, and Mazzini, these doctrines are still enveloped in a mantle of conventional moralistic cant; in Nietzsche they first step forth naked and unashamed. (IPI 104-5)

FASCISM, DEFEAT OF

What will the world gain by the defeat of the fascist Powers if, in the process, the fascist form of government becomes everywhere triumphant? (CAN 9)

FATE

The notion of fate or destiny is one which has hung over mankind from ancient times. The Greeks thought of it as superior even to the gods and holding sway over Zeus as well as over mortals. It was reinforced when, after Alexander's conquests in the East, astrology became fashionable. It came to be thought that the stars control human affairs and that a man born under such and such a star was bound to have a life in conformity with his horoscope. . . This conception, very rightly, was vigorously opposed by the Church, since it seemed to relieve a man of moral responsibility. (TRF 5)

FATIGUE, NERVOUS

The kind of fatigue that is most serious in the present day in advanced communities is nervous fatigue. This kind, oddly enough, is most pronounced among the well-to-do, and tends to be much less among wage earners than it is among business men and brain workers. (CH 69)

FEAR
see PERFECTION

FEAR AND RELIGION

Religion is based, I think, primarily and mainly upon fear. It is partly the terror of the unknown, and partly, as I have said, the wish to feel that you have a kind of elder brother who will stand

by you in all your troubles and disputes. Fear is the basis of the
whole thing—fear of the mysterious, fear of defeat, fear of death.
Fear is the parent of cruelty, and therefore it is no wonder if cruelty
and religion go hand-in-hand. (WNC 29)

FEAR, DISASTROUS RESULTS OF

Intellectually, also, fear has disastrous results. There is the
fear of any unusual opinion which prevents men from thinking
straight on any subject on which their neighbors have foolish opinions. Then there is the fear of death, which prevents men from
thinking straight on theological subjects; and then there is the
fear of self-direction, which leads men to seek some authority to
which they can submit their judgment. These various forms of
fear are responsible for quite half the stupidity in the world. (EDTF
229-30)

FEAR, EFFECT OF

There are various kinds of fear; of these, physical fear, which
alone is traditionally despised, is by far the least harmful. Moral
and intellectual fears are far worse. All fear inspires a greater or
less degree of rage, which, since it dare not vent itself upon the
dreaded object, finds an outlet in tyranny over whatever is weaker.
Just as in the holders of power cruelty begets fear, so in their slaves
fear begets cruelty. Fear of social disapproval is probably one of
the chief causes of meanness and unkindness in the modern world.
(EDTF 220-1)

FEAR, FREEDOM FROM

I do not wish to suggest that absence of fear is alone enough
to produce a good human being; undoubtedly other things are
necessary. But I do suggest that freedom from fear is *one* of the
most important things to aim at, and is perhaps more easily a-
chieved by a wise education than any other equally desirable quality. (EDTF 228)

FEARS, REAL

There is another class of fears where danger is real but can
be eliminated by sufficient skill. The simplest examples of this are
physical dangers such as are incurred in mountain-climbing. But
there are a large number of others. Take, for example, the danger
of social disapproval. It is quite true that one man may steal a

horse while another man may not look over the hedge; this difference depends mainly upon a certain kind of difference in instinctive attitude toward other people. The man who expects to be
ill-treated will be, while the man who approaches his fellows in
fearless friendliness will find this attitude justified by results. Boys
who are afraid of dogs run away from them, which causes the dogs
to come yapping at their heels, while boys who like dogs find that
dogs like them. (EDTF 225-6)

FEDERALISM

The problem of delimiting the powers of various bodies will,
of course, be one presenting many difficulties. The general principle
should be to leave to smaller bodies all functions which do not prevent the larger bodies from fulfilling their purpose. Confining ourselves, for the moment, to geographical bodies, there should be a
hierarchy from the world government to parish councils. (AAI 99)

In international affairs the same formula of federalism will
apply: self-determination for every group in regard to matters which
concern it much more vitally than they concern others, and government by a neutral authority embracing rival groups in all matters
in which conflicting interest of groups come into play; but always
with the fixed principle that the functions of government are to be
reduced to the bare minimum compatible with justice and the prevention of private violence. (RF 161)

A federal system is desirable whenever the local interests and
sentiments of the constituent units are stronger than the interests
and sentiments connected with the federation. If there were ever
an international government, it would obviously have to be a federation of national governments, with strictly defined powers. (P
280)

FEDERATION, WORLD

If a group of Western Powers are genuinely anxious to create
a supra-national sense of solidarity among the nations composing
the group, there are certain things that they must do. First, they
must rewrite the textbooks of history used in schools, which should
become the same in all countries concerned. The new textbooks
should lay stress on whatever cultural unity exists, and should minimize cultural differences. They should carefully abstain from glorification of any one member nation at the expense of any other.

They should make past wars between member nations appear as foolish civil wars. And they should suggest that the nations composing the group can do great things for mankind in the future, provided they remain friends and not enemies.

Next, they should have a common flag, and a common supranational anthem. The Stars and Stripes and the Union Jack must no longer obtrude themselves on the consciousness of children, and it must not be for "God Save the King" that we all stand up. But these powerful methods of emotional stimulation must not be discarded; they must merely be transferred to new symbols. I am sure the reader will feel a vehement resistance to this suggestion. I feel it myself. But the strength of our unreflecting resistance is the best proof of the necessity of the change that I am advocating. (GAT 35-6)

The Federation will require a Constitution, a Legislature, a Judiciary, and an Executive. I suggest something on the following lines.

The Constitution shall provide (a) that any member of the Federation which is subjected to aggression by another power (whether a member of the Federation or not) shall be defended by the Federation as a whole, and that a member which is pronounced guilty of aggression shall *ipso facto* lose its membership; (b) that the Federation as a whole shall have an Air Force, but no separate State in the Federation shall have an independent Air Force. The ultimate aim should be Federation control of *all* armaments. (AWF 4)

FEELING OF KNOWLEDGE AND OF DOUBT

Whether a sentence gives us a *feeling* of knowledge or of doubt depends upon whether it leaves open alternatives calling for different actions and emotions or not. Every disjunction which is not logically exhaustive (i.e., not such as "A or not-A") gives *some* information about the world, if it is true, but the information may leave us so hesitant as to what to do that it is *felt* as ignorance. (IMT 106)

FIELD

The *field* of a relation consists of its domain and converse domain together. (IMP 32)

FIRST CAUSE ARGUMENT
see GOD

FOLLIES OF MAN
see HISTORY

FORCE
The fact is that the whole conception of "force" is a mistake. The sun does not exert force on the planets; in Einstein's law of gravitation, the planet only pays attention to what it finds in its own neighborhood. The way in which this works will be explained in a later chapter; for the present we are only concerned with the necessity of abandoning the notion of "force," which was due to misleading conceptions derived from the sense of touch. (ABCR 11-2)

A government must possess force, but cannot be a satisfactory government unless force is seldom necessary. All the kinds of freedom advocated by liberals disappear when security disappears, and security depends upon a wide diffusion of contentment. This in turn is impossible when the general level of prosperity is falling. Liberalism flourished in the nineteenth century because of economic progress; it is in eclipse now because of economic retrogression. (FAG 256)

FOREIGN NATIONS, ATTITUDE TOWARD
Broadly speaking, there are four possible attitudes toward foreign nations, and the internal economy will depend largely upon which of these is adopted. The four attitudes I have in mind are: (1) isolationism, (2) imperialism, (3) membership in a bloc combined with balance-of-power politics, and (4) membership in a new and more vigorous League of Nations, intended to become worldwide as soon as possible. To decide among these four a certain awareness of the outer world and the psychology of other nations is an indispensable requisite. (CGS 168)

FOREIGNERS, EDUCATION ABOUT
To this day, it is hardly possible to imagine anything more civilized than a cultivated Chinese. All this should be more widely known, and a similar work should be done in diffusing appreciation of what has been achieved in India, in Persia, and by the Arabs in their great days. By this means the somewhat condescending attitude of white men towards Asiatics might be transformed into the respect which is felt towards those whom we acknowledge as equals. (EIU 21)

FRASER, A.C.

Amberley, while in Edinburgh, lived at the house of Professor Alexander Campbell Fraser, the editor of Locke and Berkeley. The Professor taught him philosophy, and Mrs. Fraser mothered him, with the result that he was always happy in their society. I well remember the Professor as a kindly old gentleman with a long beard and a Scotch accent. He held the chair of Logic and Metaphysics until 1891, and in 1896 he published his Gifford Lectures on "The Philosophy of Theism." He succeeded Sir William Hamilton (whom Mill "examined"), but did not carry on his predecessor's Kantian tendencies; British (and especially Scottish) common sense was more to his liking. (API 216-7)

FREE MAN

Man is yet free, during his brief years, to examine, to criticise, to know, and in imagination to create. To him alone, in the world with which he is acquainted, this freedom belongs; and in this lies his superiority to the resistless forces that control his outward life. (ML 48)

FREE MAN'S WORSHIP

To abandon the struggle for private happiness, to expel all eagerness of temporary desire, to burn with passion for eternal things— this is emancipation, and this is the free man's worship. And this liberation is effected by a contemplation of Fate; for Fate itself is subdued by the mind which leaves nothing to be purged by the purifying fire of Time. (ML 55-6)

FREE SPEECH

There is of course one obvious limitation upon the principle of free speech; if an act is illegal, it is logical to make it illegal to advocate it. This principle justifies the authorities in prohibiting incitement to assassination or violent revolution. But in practice this principle does not by any means cover the ground. If there is to be any personal liberty, men must be free to urge a change in the laws. (FAG 254)

FREE THOUGHT

We may say that thought is free when it is exposed to free competition among beliefs—i.e., when all beliefs are able to state their case, and no legal or pecuniary advantages or disadvantages attach to beliefs. (FT 8)

FREE WILL

The first dogma which I came to disbelieve was that of free will. It seemed to me that all motions of matter were determined by the laws of dynamics and could not therefore be influenced by the human will, even in the instance of matter forming part of a human body. I had never heard of Cartesianism, or, indeed, of any of the great philosophies, but my thoughts ran spontaneously on Cartesian lines. (WIBII 10)

Freedom, in short, in any valuable sense, demands only that our volitions shall be, as they are, the result of our own desires, not of an outside force compelling us to will what we would rather not will. Everything else is confusion of thought, due to the feeling that knowledge *compels* the happening of what it knows when this is future, though it is at once obvious that knowledge has no such power in regard to the past. Free will, therefore, is true in the only form, which is important; and the desire for other forms is a mere effect of insufficient analysis. (KEW 255-256)

From this dilemma some men seek to escape by assuming freedom in human beings and determinism everywhere else, others by ingeniously sophistical attempts at a logical reconciliation of freedom with determinism. In fact, we have no reason to adopt either alternative, but we also have no reason to suppose that the truth, whatever it may be, is such as to combine the agreeable features of both, or is in any degree determinable by relation to our desires. (RAS 177)

FREEDOM

From the submission of our desires springs the virtue of resignation; from the freedom of our thoughts springs the whole world of art and philosophy, and the vision of beauty by which, at last, we half reconquer the reluctant world. But the vision of beauty is possible only to unfettered contemplation, to thoughts not weighted by the load of eager wishes; and thus Freedom comes only to those who no longer ask life that it shall yield them any of those personal goods that are subject to the mutations of Time. (ML 51)
see JUSTICE AND FREEDOM

FREEDOM, LOSS OF
see 'NINETIES, THE

FREEDOM, MENTAL

In everything that lies outside the provision of the necessaries of life, there must be individualism, personal initiative, variety. The fight for freedom is not to be won by any mere change in our economic system. It is to be won only by a constant resistance to the tyranny of officials, and a constant realization that mental freedom is the most precious of all goods. (FIE 163-4)

FREEDOM OF OPINION

Freedom of opinion is closely connected with free speech, but has a wider scope. The Inquisition made a point of investigating, by means of torture, the secret opinions that men endeavored to keep to themselves. When men confessed to unorthodox opinions, they were punished even if it could not be proved that they had ever before given utterance to them. This practice has been revived in the dictatorial countries, Germany, Italy, and Russia. The reason, in each case, is that the government feels itself unstable. One of the most important conditions of freedom, in the matter of opinion as in other matters, is governmental security. (FAG 255)

FUNCTION, NEGATIVE

The simplest of such functions is the negative, "not-p." This is that function of p which is true when p is false, and false when p is true. (IMP 146)

FUNCTION, PROPOSITIONAL

A "propositional function," in fact, is an expression containing one or more undetermined constituents, such that, when values are assigned to these constituents, the expression becomes a proposition. In other words, it is a function whose values are propositions. (IMP 155-6)

FUNCTIONS, DESCRIPTIVE AND PROPOSITIONAL

The notion of *function* need not be confined to numbers, or to the uses to which mathematicians have accustomed us; it can be extended to all cases of one-many relations, and "the father of x" is just as legitimately a function of which x is the argument as is "the logarithm of x." Functions in this sense are *descriptive* functions. As we shall see later, there are functions of a still more general and more fundamental sort, namely, *propositional* functions . . . (IMP 46)

G

GALILEO

Galileo was the first to establish the law of falling bodies. This law, given the concept of "acceleration," is of the utmost simplicity. It says that, when a body is falling freely, its acceleration is constant, except in so far as the resistance of the air may interfere; further, the acceleration is the same for all bodies, heavy or light, great or small. The complete proof of this law was not possible until the air pump had been invented, which was about 1654. After this, it was possible to observe bodies falling in what was practically a vacuum, and it was found that feathers fall as fast as lead. (HWP 532)

see INTELLIGENCE, IMPORTANCE OF

GENERA

see AVICENNA

GENERALIZATION

The process of substituting either some value or all values of a variable is called "generalization." It is not convenient to confine this term to the case of all values. (IMT 333)

GEODESIC

An adventurous pedestrian in the Alps may wish to go from a place in one valley to a place in another by the shortest route—*i.e.* the shortest compatible with remaining all the time on the earth's surface. He cannot determine the shortest route by looking at a large-scale map and drawing a straight line between the two places, for if this line involves a greater average of gradient than another it may be longer, in distance as well as in time, than another route which slopes gradually to the head of a pass and then down again. What the traveller is seeking is a "geodesic"—*i.e.* the shortest line that can be drawn on the earth's surface between two points. (AOM 72)

GEODESICS

But when we speak of a "triangle," we must explain what we mean, because on most surfaces there are no straight lines. On a sphere, we shall replace straight lines by great circles, which are the nearest possible approach to straight lines. In general, we shall take, instead of straight lines, the lines that give the shortest route on the surface from place to place. Such lines are called "geodesics." On the earth, the geodesics are great circles. In general, they are the shortest way of traveling from point to point if you are unable to leave the surface. (ABCR 104-5)

GEOGRAPHY

I should teach geography partly by pictures and tales about travellers, but mainly by the cinema, showing what the traveller sees on his journey. The knowledge of geographical facts is useful, but without intrinsic intellectual value; when, however, geography is made vivid by pictures, it has the merit of giving food for imagination. It is good to know that there are hot countries and cold countries, flat countries and mountainous countries, black men, yellow men, brown men, and red men, as well as white men. This kind of knowledge diminishes the tyranny of familiar surroundings over the imagination, and makes it possible in later life to *feel* that distant countries really exist, which otherwise is very difficult except by travelling. (EEC 265)

GEOMETRY
see ARITHMETIC

GEOMETRY, EUCLIDEAN AND NON-EUCLIDEAN

Geometry throws no more light upon the nature of space than Arithmetic throws upon the population of the United States. Geometry is a whole collection of deductive sciences based on a corresponding collection of sets of axioms. One set of axioms is Euclid's; other equally good sets of axioms lead to other results. Whether Euclid's axioms are true, is a question as to which the pure mathematician is indifferent; and, what is more, it is a question which it is theoretically impossible to answer with certainty in the affirmative. (ML 92)

GEOMETRY, NON-EUCLIDEAN

Lobatchevski, by inventing non-Euclidean geometry, undermined the mathematical argument of Kant's transcendental aesthetic. Weier-

strass proved that continuity does not involve infinitesimals; George
Cantor invented a theory of continuity and a theory of infinity which
did away with all the old paradoxes upon which philosophers had
battened. Frege showed that arithmetic follows from logic, which
Kant had denied. All these results were obtained by ordinary mathe-
matical methods, and were as indubitable as the multiplication table.
Philosophers met the situation by not reading the authors concerned.
(SE 73)

GOD

If everything must have a cause, then God must have a cause.
If there can be anything without a cause, it may just as well be
the world as God, so that there cannot be any validity in that argument. It is exactly of the same nature as the Indian's view, that
the world rested upon an elephant and the elephant rested upon
a tortoise; and when they said, "How about the tortoise?" the Indian said, "Suppose we change the subject." The argument is really
no better than that. (WNC 11)

There are, roughly speaking, two functions which a Christian
God has to fulfil. He has to be a Providence and a Creator. Leibniz
merged the first of these functions in the second, though he often
denied that he had done so. (PL 183)

Why did God issue just those natural laws and no others? If
you say that he did it simply from his own good pleasure, and without any reason, you then find that there is something which is not
subject to law, and so your train of natural law is interrupted. If
you say, as more orthodox theologians do, that in all the laws which
God issued he had a reason for giving those laws rather than others—
the reason, of course, being to create the best universe, although
you would never think it to look at it—if there was a reason for the
laws which God gave, then God himself was subject to law, and
therefore you do not get any advantage by introducing God as intermediary. (WNC 13-14)

When you come to look into this argument from design, it is
a most astonishing thing that people can believe that this world, with
all the things that are in it, with all its defects, should be the best
that omnipotence and omniscience has been able to produce in millions of years. I really cannot believe it. (WNC 15)

GOOD, DOING

Our motives in doing good are seldom as pure as we imagine

them to be. Love of power is insidious; it has many disguises, and is often the source of the pleasure we derive from doing what we believe to be good to other people. Not infrequently, yet another element enters in. "Doing good" to people generally consists in depriving them of some pleasure: drink, or gambling, or idleness, or what not. In this case there is an element which is typical of much social morality, namely, envy of those who are in a position to commit sins from which we have to abstain if we are to retain the respect of our friends. (CH 117)

GOOD LIFE, THE

To live a good life in the fullest sense a man must have a good education, friends, love, children (if he desires them), a sufficient income to keep him from want and grave anxiety, good health, and work which is not uninteresting. All these things, in varying degrees, depend upon the community, and are helped or hindered by political events. The good life must be lived in a good society and is not fully possible otherwise. (WIB 60-1)

The good life is one inspired by love and guided by knowledge. (WIB 20)

GOVERNMENT, REPRESENTATIVE

There is one thing of great importance that we owe to the Middle Ages, and that is representative government. (IPI 189)

GOVERNMENT, SCIENTIFIC

When I speak of scientific government I ought, perhaps, to explain what I mean by the term. I do not mean simply a government composed of men of science. There were many men of science in the government of Napoleon, including Laplace, who, however, proved so incompetent that he had to be dismissed in a very short time. I should not consider Napoleon's government scientific while it contained Laplace, or unscientific when it lost him. I should define a government as in a greater or less degree scientific in proportion as it can produce intended results: the greater the number of results that it can both intend and produce, the more scientific it is. (SO 227)

GOVERNMENT, THE PRIMARY AIMS OF

The *primary* aims of government, I suggest, should be three: security, justice, and conservation. These are things of the utmost importance to human happiness, and they are things which only government can bring about. At the same time, no one of them is absolute; each may, in some circumstances, have to be sacrificed in some degree for the sake of a greater degree of some other good. (AAI 89)

GRAVITATION, UNIVERSAL
see NEWTON

GREAT MEN
The great are not solitary; out of the night come the voices of those who have gone before, clear and courageous; and so through the ages they march, a mighty procession, proud, undaunted, unconquerable. To join in this glorious company, to swell the immortal paeon of those whom fate could not subdue—this may not be happiness; but what is happiness to those whose souls are filled with that celestial music? (OH 213-4)

GREEK CIVILIZATION
The distinctive Western character begins with the Greeks, who invented the habit of deductive reasoning and the science of geometry. Their other merits were either not distinctive or lost in the Dark Ages. In literature and art they may have been supreme, but they did not differ very profoundly from various other ancient nations. In experimental science they produced a few men, notably Archimedes, who anticipated modern methods, but these men did not succeed in establishing a school or a tradition. (IPI 185-6)

GUILD SOCIALISM
The view of the Guild Socialists is that State Socialism takes account of men only as consumers, while Syndicalism takes account of them only as producers. "The problem," say the Guild Socialists, "is to reconcile the two points of view. That is what advocates of National Guilds set out to do." (RF 83)

H

HABIT
All kinds of matter to some extent, but some kinds of matter (viz. nervous tissue) more particularly, are liable to form "habits," i.e. to alter their structure in a given environment in such a way that, when they are subsequently in a similar environment, they react in a new way, but if similar environments recur often, the reaction in the end becomes nearly uniform, while remaining different from the reaction on the first occasion. (LA 381)
see INSTINCT

HABIT FORMATION IN INFANCY
Two considerations come in when we are considering habit-formation in infancy. The first and paramount consideration is health; the second is character. We want the child to become the sort of person that will be liked and will be able to cope with life successfully. Fortunately, health and character point in the same direction: what is good for one is good also for the other. (EEC 89-90)

HABITS, ACQUIRED
Our habitual knowledge is not always in our minds, but is called up by the appropriate stimuli. If we are asked "What is the capital of France?" we answer "Paris," because of past experience; the past experience is as essential as the present question in the causation of our response. Thus all our habitual knowledge consists of acquired habits, and comes under the head of mnemic phenomena. (AM 79-80)

HAPPINESS
Happiness, if it is to have any depth and solidity, demands a life built round some central purpose of a kind demanding continuous activity and permitting of progressively increasing success.

The purpose must be one which has its root in instinct, such as love of power or love of honour, or parental affection. (WIH 59)

Fundamental happiness depends more than anything else upon what may be called a friendly interest in persons and things. (CH 155)

The secret of happiness is this: let your interests be as wide as possible, and let your reactions to the things and persons that interest you be as far as possible friendly rather than hostile. (CH 157)

see BENTHAM; CREATIVITY

HAPPINESS AND VIEWING LIFE AS A WHOLE
see WORK

HAPPINESS, DIVERSITY IN
see MORE'S UTOPIA

HAPPINESS, GREATEST

The "greatest happiness principle" was the most famous formula of the Benthamite school. According to this principle, actions are good when they promote the greatest happiness of the greatest number, and bad when they do not. (FO 91)

HAPPY LIFE, CONDITIONS OF A

The conditions of a happy life, it seems to me, are: first, health and a fair degree of economic security; second, work which is satisfying both because it is felt to be worth doing and because it utilizes whatever skill a man possesses without making impossible demands; third, personal relations that are satisfying, and especially a happy family life; fourth, a width of interests which makes many things enjoyable. (WIH 63-4)

HARMONY IN LIFE

If a man's life is to be satisfactory, whether from his own point of view or from that of the world at large, it requires two kinds of harmony: an internal harmony of intelligence, emotion, and will, and an external harmony with the wills of others. In both these respects, existing education is defective. (ESO 237)

HATRED
see SOCIALISM

HATRED, PSYCHOLOGY OF

We must therefore find some other non-human object of hatred, if men are to be prevented from hating their neighbours in other countries. One might hate matter, like the Manicheans, or ignorance, or disease. To hate these things would do good; and by a little symbolism it could be made to satisfy our instinctive craving for hatred. But to hate other groups of human beings can only do harm, and it is monstrous that education should aim at instilling such hatred by means of lies and suppressions. (FIE 157)

HEGEL

Hegel asserts that the real is rational, and the rational is real. But when he says this he does not mean by "the real" what an empiricist would mean. He admits, and even urges, that what to the empiricist appear to be facts are, and must be, irrational; it is only after their apparent character has been transformed by viewing them as aspects of the whole that they are seen to be rational. Nevertheless, the identification of the real and the rational leads unavoidably to some of the complacency inseparable from the belief that "whatever is, is right." (HWP 731)

HEISENBERG
see UNCERTAINTY, HEISENBERG'S PRINCIPLE OF

HERACLITUS

Heraclitus himself, for all his belief in change, allowed *something* everlasting. The conception of eternity (as opposed to endless duration), which comes from Parmenides, is not to be found in Heraclitus, but in his philosophy the central. fire never dies: the world "was ever, is now, and ever shall be, an ever-living Fire." But fire is something continually changing, and its permanence is rather that of a process than that of a substance—though this view should not be attributed to Heraclitus. (HWP 46)

HERD PRESSURE

Too much herd pressure interferes with individuality, and with the development of all such interests as are not common among average healthy boys, e.g., science and art, literature and history, and everything else that makes civilization. It cannot be denied, however, that emulation within the herd has its good points. It encourages physical prowess, and it discourages all kinds of sneaking underhand meanness. Within limits, therefore, it has its uses. (ESO 92-3)

HERD, TYRANNY OF THE

There is one aspect of American life which I have not yet touched on, and which I think wholly undesirable—I mean, the tyranny of the herd. Eccentricity is frowned upon, and unusual opinions bring social penalties upon those who hold them. (PCI 17)
see AMERICA AND TYRANNY OF THE HERD

HERE

It is to be observed that "here" and "now" depend upon perception; in a purely material universe there would be no "here" and "now." Perception is not impartial, but proceeds from a center; our perceptual world is (so to speak) a perspective view of the common world. (HK 92)

We may define "here" as the place, in perspective space, which is occupied by our private world. Thus we can now understand what is meant by speaking of a thing as near to or far from "here." (KEW 97)

HEREDITARY

A property is said to be "hereditary" in the natural-number series if, whenever it belongs to a number n, it also belongs to $n +$ 1, the successor of n. Similarly a class is said to be "hereditary" if, whenever n is a member of the class, so is $n + 1$. (IMP 21)

HEREDITY
see TWINS, IDENTICAL

HEROISM

Heroism is a valuable quality, but admiration of it cannot be made the basis of a theory of politics. (WWP 170)

HISTORY

History has always interested me more than anything else except philosophy and mathematics. I have never been able to accept any general scheme of historical development, such as that of Hegel or that of Marx. Nevertheless, general trends can be studied, and the study is profitable in relation to the present. (MMD 18-9)

I have seen cruelty, persecution, and superstition increasing by leaps and bounds, until we have almost reached the point where praise of rationality is held to mark a man as an old fogey regrettably surviving from a bygone age. All this is depressing, but gloom is a useless emotion. In order to escape from it, I have been driven to study the past with more attention than I had formerly given to it, and have found, as Erasmus found, that folly is perennial and yet the human race has survived. That follies of our times are easier to bear when they are seen against the background of past follies. (UE 71)

Whether history is a science or not, it certainly can be an art, and I, for my part, value it quite as much for its intrinsic interest as for what it can establish in the way of causal laws. I value it also for the knowledge it gives of human beings in circumstances very different from our own—not mainly analytic scientific knowledge, but the sort of knowledge that a dog-lover has of his dog. History has perhaps its greatest value in enlarging the world of our imagination, making us, in thought and feeling, citizens of a larger universe than that of our daily preoccupations. In this way it contributes not only to knowledge, but to wisdom. (RTC 741)

I think the course of history is subject to laws and is probably for a sufficiently wise person deterministic; but nobody is wise enough. It is far too complicated and nobody can work it out; and the person who says he has done so is a charlatan. (HPH 414)

HISTORY, FUNCTION OF

Nevertheless, history has a function in regard to current affairs, but a function less direct, less exact, and less decisive. It may, in the first place, suggest minor maxims, whose truth, when they are once propounded, can be seen without the help of the events that suggested them. This is largely the case in economics, where most of the motives concerned are simple. It is the case also, for a similar reason in regard to strategy. Wherever, out of the facts, a simple deductive argument from indubitable premises can be elicited, history may yield useful precepts. But these will only apply where the end is given, and are therefore of a technical nature. They can never tell the statesman what end to pursue, but only, within certain limits, how some of the more definite ends, such as wealth, or victory in war, are to be attained. (OH 211)

HISTORY, MATERIALISTIC CONCEPTION OF

Marx holds that in the main all the phenomena of human society have their origin in material conditions, and these he takes to be embodied in economic systems. Political constitutions, laws, religions, philosophies—all these he regards as, in their broad outlines, expressions of the economic *regime* in the society that gives rise to them. (RF 7)

It (the materialistic conception of history) means that all the mass-phenomena of history are determined by economic motives. This view has no essential connection with materialism in the philosophic sense. Materialism in the philosophic sense may be defined as the theory that all apparently mental occurrences either are really physical, or at any rate have purely physical causes. Materialism in this sense also was preached by Marx, and is accepted by all orthodox Marxians. (PTB 123)

HISTORY, ORDINARY PEOPLE IN

In all these views there are elements of truth: the Middle Ages were rude, they were knightly, they were pious. But if we wish to see a period truly, we must not see it contrasted with our own, whether to its advantage or disadvantage: we must try to see it as it was to those who lived in it. Above all, we must remember that, in every epoch, most people are ordinary people, concerned with their daily bread rather than with the great themes of which historians treat. (LMA 295)

HISTORY, PHILOSOPHY OF

I should regard men like Hegel, Marx, and Spengler as having a philosophy of history, in the sense that they believe in sweeping laws of historical development, either progressive or cyclic. For such vast laws, I should say, there is not, and never can be, any adequate evidence; they are reflections of our own moods upon the cosmos. (RTC 734)

HISTORY, TEACHING OF

History ought to be taught in exactly the same way in all countries of the world, and history textbooks ought to be drawn up by and another from Soviet Russia. History should be world history the League of Nations, with an assistant from the United States, rather than national history, and should emphasise matters of cultural importance rather than wars. (ESO 135)

HISTORY, THE SCIENCE OF

History, considered as a body of truth, seems destined long to remain almost purely descriptive. Such generalisations as have been suggested—omitting the sphere of economics—are, for the most part, so plainly unwarranted as to be not even worthy of refutation. Burke argued that all revolutions end in military tyrannies, and predicted Napoleon. In so far as his argument was based on the analogy of Cromwell, it was a very lucky hit; but certainly not a scientific law. It is true that numerous instances are not always necessary to establish a law, provided the essential and relevant cir- cumstances can be easily disentangled. But, in history, so many circumstances of a small and accidental nature are relevant, that no broad and simple uniformities are possible. (OH 209)

HOBBES

Hobbes prefers monarchy, but all his abstract arguments are equally applicable to all forms of government in which there is one supreme authority not limited by the legal rights of other bodies. He could tolerate Parliament alone, but not a system in which governmental power is shared between king and Parliament. This is the exact antithesis to the views of Locke and Montesquieu. The English Civil War occurred, says Hobbes, because power was divided between King, Lord, and Commons. (HWP 551)

HOLISTIC

see ANALYTIC

HOLMES, OLIVER WENDELL

I will only say, to begin with, that Europeans with pretensions to culture are too apt to remember Hollywood with a sniff, and forget the respect due to such men as Holmes, who was, after all, equally a product of America. (PCI 3)

HOMER

The first notable product of the Hellenic civilization was Homer. Everything about Homer is conjectural, but the best opinion seems to be that he was a series of poets rather than an individual. Prob- ably the Iliad and the Odyssey between them took about two hundred years to complete, some say from 750 to 550 B. C., while others hold that "Homer" was nearly complete at the end of the eighth century. (HWP 10)

HONESTY

A rather more serious matter, to which similar considerations apply, is honesty. I do not mean this term in any fancy sense; I mean merely respect for the property of others. This is not a natural characteristic of human beings. The undisciplined human being ap- propriates the property of others whenever he considers it safe to do so. Perhaps even the disciplined human being does this not infrequently, but discipline has taught him that theft is often not safe when at first sight it seems so. (ESO 36)

HOPE

And so, to the man tempted by despair, I say: Remind yourself that the world is what we make it, and that to the making of it each one of us can contribute something. This thought makes hope possible: and in this hope, though life will still be painful, it will be no longer purposeless. (APFY 7)

HUMAN EXCELLENCE

At the same time, when I examine my own conception of human excellence, I find that, doubtless owing to early environment, it contains many elements which have hitherto been associated with aristocracy, such as fearlessness, independence of judgment, emancipation from the herd, and leisurely culture. Is it possible to preserve these qualities, and even make them widespread, in an industrial community? And is it possible to dissociate them from the typical aristocratic vices: limitation of sympathy, haughtiness, and cruelty to those outside a charmed circle? These bad qualities could not exist in a community in which the aristocratic virtues were universal. But that could only be achieved through economic security and leisure, which are the two sources of what is good in aristocracies. It has at last become technically possible through the progress of machinery and the consequent increased productivity of labor, to create a society in which every man and woman has economic security and sufficient leisure—for complete leisure is neither necessary nor desirable. But although the technical possibility exists, there are formidable political and psychological obstacles. It would be necessary to the creation of such a society to secure three conditions: first, a more even distribution of the produce of labor; second, security against large-scale wars; and third, a population which is stationary or very nearly so. (ISP xv-xvi)

HUMAN NATURE, TRANSFORMATION OF

The ultimate source of the whole train of evils lies in the Bolshevik outlook on life: in its dogmatism of hatred and its belief that human nature can be completely transformed by force. (PTB 180)

If human nature were unchangeable, as ignorant people still suppose it to be, the situation would indeed be hopeless. But we now know, thanks to psychologists and physiologists, that what passes as "human nature" is at most one-tenth nature, the other nine-tenths being nurture. What is called human nature can be almost completely changed by changes in early education. And these changes could be such as to preserve sufficient seriousness in life without the spice of danger, if thought and energy were devoted to that end. Two things are necessary for this purpose: the development of constructive impulses in the young, and opportunities for their existence in adult life. (SE 254-5)

HUMAN RACE, THE

Unfortunately, there is no impartial arbiter to decide on the merits of the human race; but for my part, when I consider their poison gases, their researches into bacteriological warfare, their meannesses, cruelties and oppressions, I find them, considered as the crowning gem of creation, somewhat lacking in lustre. (SO 122)

HUMAN WELFARE
see DESIRES AND ETHICS

HUMAN WELFARE, INDIVIDUAL CONTRIBUTION TO

It may seem to you conceited to suppose that you can do anything important toward improving the lot of mankind. But this is a fallacy. You must believe that *you* can help bring about a better world. A good society is produced only by good individuals, just as truly as a majority in a presidential election is produced by the votes of single electors. Everybody can do something toward creating in his own environment kindly feelings rather than anger, reasonableness rather than hysteria, happiness rather than misery. (APFY 5)

HUMANISM

Those who attempt to make a religion of humanism, which recognizes nothing greater than man, do not satisfy my emotions. And yet I am unable to believe that, in the world as known, there is anything that I can value outside human beings, and, to a much lesser extent, animals. Not the starry heavens, but their effects on human percipients, have excellence; to admire the universe for its size is slavish and absurd; impersonal non-human truth appears to be a delusion. And so my intellect goes with the humanists, though my emotions violently rebel. In this respect the "consolations of philosophy" are not for me. (MMD 19-20)

HUMANITY

The conception is that of the human race as a whole, fighting against chaos without and darkness within, the little tiny lamp of reason growing gradually into a great light by which the night is dispelled. The divisions between races, nations and creeds should be treated as follies, distracting us in the battle against Chaos and Old Night, which is our one truly human activity. (EEC 267)

Beyond all these partial reconciliations there lies an ultimate goal, still distant, but never to be despaired of as unattainable. This goal is the recognition of the human race as all one family, whose common interests far outweigh any causes of conflict not dependent upon mutual ill will. (EIU 21)

As soon as we begin to view mankind as a whole, we see there is a certain common fund of achievement and that there are certain common hopes of improvement, which afford a rational basis for cooperation. It is these that should be emphasized by the world university in its teaching of history, as also of economics and the social sciences generally. (EAW 199)

HUME

David Hume (1711-1776) is one of the most important among philosophers, because he developed to its logical conclusion the empirical philosophy of Locke and Berkeley, and by making it self-consistent made it incredible. He represents, in a certain sense, a dead end; in his direction, it is impossible to go further. To refute him has been, ever since he wrote, a favourite pastime among metaphysicians. For my part, I find none of their refutations convincing; nevertheless I cannot but hope that something less sceptical than Hume's system may be discoverable. (HWP 659)
see EMPIRICISM

HUNGER

The characteristic mark by which we recognize a series of actions which display hunger is not the animal's mental state, which we cannot observe, but something in its bodily behaviour; it is this observable trait in the bodily behaviour that I am proposing to call "hunger," not some possibly mythical and certainly unknowable ingredient of the animal's mind. (AM 63)

HU SHIH

Men with the requisite gifts exist in China; I might mention, as an example personally known to me, Dr. Hu Shih. He has great learning, wide culture, remarkable energy, and a fearless passion for reform; his writings in the vernacular inspire enthusiasm among progressive Chinese. He is in favor of assimilating all that is good in Western culture, but by no means a slavish admirer of our ways. (PC 264)

HYDROGEN ATOM

The hydrogen atom which is the simplest, consists of one proton with one electron going round it as a planet goes round the sun. The electron may be lost, and the proton left alone; the atom is then positively electrified. But when it has its electron, it is, as a whole, electrically neutral, since the positive electricity of the proton is exactly balanced by the negative electricity of the electron. (OP 100)

HYPOTHESIS, ACTING ON

For it is not enough to recognize that all our knowledge is, in a greater or less degree, uncertain and vague; it is necessary, at the same time, to learn to act upon the best hypothesis without dogmatically believing it. (UE 28)

HYSTERIA, MASS

Mass hysteria is a phenomenon not confined to human beings; it may be seen in any gregarious species. I once saw a photograph of a large herd of wild elephants in Central Africa seeing an airplane for the first time, and all in a state of wild collective terror. The elephant, at most times, is a calm and sagacious beast, but this unprecedented phenomenon of a noisy, unknown animal in the sky had thrown the whole herd completely off its balance. Each separate animal was terrified, and its terror communicated itself to the others, causing a vast multiplication of panic. As, however, there were no journalists among them, the terror died down when the airplane was out of sight. (TFD 7)

I

. . ."I" is the biography to which "this" belongs. But although we have explained the use of the word "this," we have done so by depriving the word itself of all significance in isolation. We cannot therefore be sure that the above definition of "I" can be maintained. (IMT 141)

IDEA

He (Berkeley) gives the name "idea" to anything which is *immediately* known, as, for example, sense-data are known. (PP 61)

IDEA, GENERAL

Thus we may say that a word embodies a vague idea when its effects are appropriate to an individual, but are the same for various similar individuals, while a word embodies a general idea when its effects are different from those appropriate to individuals. In what this difference consists it is, however, not easy to say. I am inclined to think that it consists merely in the knowledge that no one individual is represented, so that what distinguishes a general idea from a vague idea is merely the presence of a certain accompanying belief. (AM 221-2)

IDEA, VAGUE

see IDEA, GENERAL

IDEAL, RUSSIAN

The Russian Government has a different conception of the ends of life. The individual is thought of no importance; he is expendable. What is important is the state, which is regarded as something almost divine and having a welfare of its own not consisting in the welfare of citizens. This view, which Marx took over from Hegel, is fundamentally opposed to the Christian ethic, which in the West is accepted by free thinkers as much as by Christians. In the Soviet world human dignity counts for nothing. (IWS 17)

IDEAL, WESTERN

In the West, we see man's greatness in the individual life. A great society for us is one which is composed of individuals who, as far as is humanly possible, are happy, free and creative. We do not think that individuals should be alike. We conceive society as like an orchestra, in which the different performers have different parts to play and different instruments upon which to perform, and in which cooperation results from a conscious common purpose. (IWS 5)

IDEALISM

We can begin to state the difference between realism and idealism in terms of this opposition of contents and objects. Speaking quite roughly and approximately, we may say that idealism tends to suppress the object, while realism tends to suppress the content. Idealism, accordingly, says that nothing can be known except thoughts, and all the reality that we know is mental; while realism maintains that we know objects directly, in sensation certainly, and perhaps in memory and thought. (AM 19-20)
see PHYSICS; REALISM

IDEALISTS

Those who maintain that mind is the reality and matter an evil dream are called "idealists"—a word which has a different meaning in philosophy from that which it bears in ordinary life. (AM 10)

As explained above, very many philosophers, perhaps most, have held that whatever is real must be in some sense mental, or at any rate that whatever we can know anything about must be in some sense mental. Such philosophers are called "idealists." (PP 56)

Such philosophers are called "idealists." When they come to explaining matter, they either say, like Berkeley, that matter is really nothing but a collection of ideas, or they say, like Leibniz (1646-1716), that what appears as matter is really a collection of more or less rudimentary minds. (PP 21-2)

IDEAS

From memory it is an easy step to what are called "ideas"—not in the Platonic sense, but in that of Locke, Berkeley and Hume, in which they are opposed to "impressions." You may be conscious of a friend either by seeing him or by "thinking" of him; and by "thought" you can be conscious of objects which cannot be seen, such as the human race, or physiology. "Thought" in the narrower sense is that form of consciousness which consists in "ideas" as opposed to impressions or mere memories. (AM 13)

ILLUSIONS
see REAL OBJECTS

IMAGES

Images, as opposed to sensations, can only be defined by their different causation: they are caused by association with a sensation, not by a stimulus external to the nervous system—or perhaps one should say external to the brain, where the higher animals are concerned. The occurrence of a sensation or image does not in itself constitute knowledge but any sensation or image may come to be known if the conditions are suitable. (AM 109-110)

Images come in various ways, and play various parts. There are those that come as accretions to a case of sensation, which are not recognised as images except by the psychologist; these form, for example, the tactual quality of things we only see, and the visual quality of things we only touch. I think dreams belong, in part, to this class of images: some dreams result from misinterpreting some ordinary stimulus, and in these cases the images are those suggested by a sensation, but suggested more uncritically than if we were awake. Then there are images which are not attached to a present reality, but to one which we locate in the past; these are present in memory, not necessarily always, but sometimes. Then there are images not attached to reality at all so far as our feeling about them goes: images which merely float into our heads in reverie or in passionate desire. And finally there are images which are called up voluntarily, for example, in considering how to decorate a room. (OP 186)

We might attempt to distinguish images from sensations by our absence of belief in the "physical reality" of images. When we are aware that what we are experiencing is an image, we do not give it the kind of belief that we should give to a sensation: we do not think that it has the same power of producing knowledge of the "external world." Images are "imaginary"; in *some* sense they are "unreal." But this difference is hard to analyse or state correctly. What we call the "unreality" of images requires interpretation: it cannot mean what would be expressed by saying "there's no such thing." Images are just as truly part of the actual world as sensations are. All that we really mean by calling an image "unreal" is that it does not have the concomitants which it would have if it were a sensation. (AM 148)

When you hear New York spoken of, some image probably comes into your mind, either of the place itself (if you have been there), or of some picture of it (if you have not). The image is due to your past experience, as well as to the present stimulus of the words "New York." Similarly, the images you have in dreams are all dependent upon your past experience, as well as upon the present stimulus to dreaming. It is generally believed that all images, in their simpler parts, are copies of sensations; if so, their mnemic character is evident. (AM 80)

IMAGINATION
see PERCEPTION

IMMORTALITY

What science has to say on the subject of immortality is not very definite. There is, indeed, one line of argument in favour of survival after death, which is, at least in intention, completely scientific—I mean the line of argument associated with psychical research. I have not myself sufficient knowledge on this subject to judge of the evidence already available, but it is clear that there could be evidence which would convince reasonable men. To this, however, certain provisos must be added. In the first place, the evidence, at the best, would prove only that we survive death, not that we survive forever. (RAS 141-2)

Believers in immortality will object to physiological arguments, such as I have been using, on the ground that soul and body are totally disparate, and that the soul is something quite other than its empirical manifestations through our bodily organs. I believe this to be a metaphysical superstition. Mind and matter alike are for certain purposes convenient terms, but are not ultimate realities. Electrons and protons, like the soul, are logical fictions; each is really a history, a series of events, not a single persistent entity. (WIB 9)

Immortality, if we could believe in it, would enable us to shake off this gloom about the physical world. We should hold that although our souls, during their sojourn here on earth are in bondage to matter and physical laws, they pass from earth into an eternal world beyond the empire of decay which science seems to reveal in the sensible world. But it is impossible to believe this unless we think that a human being consists of two parts—soul and body—which are separable and can continue independently of each other. Unfortunately all the evidence is against this. (FAR 5)

If there is a future life, and if heaven is the reward for misery here below, we do right to obstruct all amelioration of terrestrial conditions, and we must admire the unselfishness of those captains of industry who allow others to monopolise the profitable brief sorrow on earth. But if the belief in a hereafter is mistaken, we shall have thrown away the substance for the shadow, and shall be as unfortunate as those who invest a life-time's savings in enterprises that go bankrupt. (ESO 108-9)
see ARISTOTLE'S VIEW OF IMMORTALITY

IMMORTALITY, PERSONAL

The question of personal immortality stands on a somewhat different footing. Here evidence either way is possible. Persons are part of the everyday world with which science is concerned, and the conditions which determine their existence are discoverable. A drop of water is not immortal; it can be resolved into oxygen and hydrogen. If, therefore, a drop of water were to maintain that it had a quality of aqueousness which would survive its dissolution, we should be inclined to be sceptical. In like manner we know that the brain is not immortal, and that the organized energy of a living body becomes as it were, demobilized at death, and therefore not available for collective action. (WIB 6-7)

IMPARTIALITY

There is another intellectual virtue, which is that of generality or impartiality. I recommend the following exercise: When, in a sentence expressing political opinion, there are words that arouse powerful but different emotions in different readers, try replacing them by symbols, A,B,C, and so on, and forgetting the particular significance of the symbols. Suppose A is England, B is Germany and C is Russia. So long as you remember what the letters mean, most of the things you will believe will depend upon whether you are English, German, or Russian, which is logically irrelevant. (UE 31)

IMPERATIVE, CRITICISM OF THE CATEGORICAL

But there are some acts which Kant would certainly think wrong but which cannot be shown to be wrong by his principles, for instance suicide; it would be quite possible for a melancholic to wish that everybody should commit suicide. His maxim seems, in fact, to give a necessary but not a sufficient criterion of virtue. To get a *sufficient* criterion, we should have to abandon Kant's purely formal point of view, and take some account of the effects of actions. Kant, however, states emphatically that virtue does not depend upon the intended results of an action, but only on the principle of which it is itself a result; and if this is conceded, nothing more concrete than his maxim is possible. (HWP 711)

IMPERATIVES, HYPOTHETICAL AND CATEGORICAL

There are two sorts of imperatives: the *hypothetical* imperative which says "You must do so-and-so if you wish to achieve such-and-such an end"; and the *categorical* imperative, which says that a certain kind of action is objectively necessary, without regard to any end. The categorical imperative is synthetic and *a priori*. Its character is deduced by Kant from the concept of Law. (HWP 710)

IMPERIALISM

The imperialism of single nations, such as the British, the French, and the Dutch, has become an anachronism, and an invitation to war, because it is no longer backed by irresistible military force. But in certain parts of the world, if there is not to be dangerous chaos, national imperialism will have to be succeeded by an international control. The principle of national independence, if treated as absolute, is anarchic, and makes the prevention of war impossible. (ISIP 232)
see AMERICA AND IMPERIALISM; FOREIGN NATIONS, ATTITUDE TOWARD

IMPLICATION

Last take *implication*, i.e., "p implies q" or "if p, then q." This is to be understood in the widest sense that will allow us to infer the truth of q if we know the truth of p. Thus we interpret it as meaning: "Unless p is false, q is true," or "either p is false or q is true." (The fact that "implies" is capable of other meanings does not concern us; this is the meaning which is convenient for us.) That is to say, "p implies q" is to mean "not-p or q": its truth-value is to be truth if p is false, likewise if q is true, and is to be falsehood if p is true and q is false. (IMP 147)

IMPLIED BY
see CONTAIN

IMPULSE, HAPPINESS AND NATURAL

Healthy, outward-looking men and women are not to be produced by the thwarting of natural impulse, but by the equal and balanced development of all the impulses essential to a happy life. (MM 293)

IMPULSES

There are two kinds of impulses, corresponding to the two kinds of goods. There are *possessive* impulses, which aim at acquiring or retaining private goods that cannot be shared; these center in the impulse of property. And there are *creative* or constructive impulses, which aim at bringing into the world or making available for use the kind of goods in which there is no privacy and no possession. (PI 8)

Life should not be too closely regulated or too methodical; our impulses, when not positively destructive or injurious to others, ought if possible to have free play; there should be room for adventure. (WIB 84)

IMPULSES, CURBING

We have all kinds of shocking impulses and also creative impulses which society forbids us to indulge, and the alternatives that it supplies in the shape of football matches and all-in wrestling are hardly adequate. Anyone who hopes that in time it may be possible to abolish war should give serious thought to the problem of satisfying harmlessly the instincts that we inherit from long generations of savages. For my part I find a sufficient outlet in detective stories where I alternatively identify myself with the murderer and the huntsman-detective, but I know there are those to whom this vicarious outlet is too mild, and for them something stronger should be provided. (SC 1010)

IMPULSES, EXPANSIVE
see IMPULSES, REPRESSIVE

IMPULSES, MAJOR

I think we want our lives to be expansive and creative, we want to live to a very great extent upon impulse; and when I say impulse I don't mean every transitory impulse of every passing moment—I mean those major impulses that really govern our lives. There are in some people great artistic impulses, in others scientific, and in others this or that form of affection or creativeness. And if you deny those impulses, provided that they do not infringe upon the liberty of another, you stunt your growth. (FAH 29-30)

IMPULSES, PREDATORY

It is obvious that predatory impulses inspired Napoleon and Hitler and still inspire Stalin. I am not sure whether the attitude of both Britain and America toward Iranian oil and Malayan rubber is free from a similar taint. . It is the existence of predatory impulses on one side that justifies fear on the other, and unless predatory impulses can be restrained, even the most desirable forms of international cooperation will remain impossible. (KF 54)

IMPULSES, REPRESSIVE

I think that if we are going to have a true morality, if we are going to have an outlook upon life which is going to make life richer and freer and happier, it must not be a repressive outlook, it must not be an outlook based upon any kind of restrictions or prohibitions; it must be an outlook based upon the things that we love rather than those that we hate. There are a number of emotions which guide our lives, and roughly you can divide them into those that are repressive and those that are expansive. Repressive emotions are cruelty, fear, jealousy; expansive emotions are such as hope, love of art, impulse of constructiveness, love, affection, intellectual curiosity, and kindliness; and they make more of life instead of less. I think that the essence of true morality consists in living by the expansive impulses and not by the repressive ones. (FAH 23-4)

INCARNATION, DOCTRINE OF THE

At last Pope Leo—the same Pope who turned Attila from attacking Rome—in the year of the battle of Chalons secured the summoning of an oecumenical Council at Chalcedon in 451, which condemned the Monophysites and finally decided the orthodox doctrine of the Incarnation. The Council of Ephesus had decided that there is only one *Person* of Christ, but the Council of Chalcedon decided that He exists in two *natures*, one human and one divine. The influence of the Pope was paramount in securing this decision. (HWP 369)

INCOMPATIBILITY

Take next *incompatibility*, i.e. "p and q are not both true." This is negation of conjunction; it is also the disjunction of the negations of p and q, i.e. it is "not-p or not-q." Its truth-value is truth when p is false and likewise when q is false; its truth-value is falsehood when p and q are both true. (IMP 147)

INDETERMINACY, PRINCIPLE OF

The Principle of Indeterminacy states that it is impossible to determine with precision both the position and the momentum of a particle; there will be a margin of error in each, and the product of the two errors is constant. That is to say, the more accurately we determine the one, the less accurately we shall be determining the other, and *vice versa*. The margin of error involved is, of course, very small. (SO 104)

INDICATES
see SENTENCES, INDICATIVE

INDIVIDUALISM, LOSS OF

There is one regrettable feature of scientific civilization as hitherto developed: I mean, the diminution in the value and independence of the individual. Great enterprises tend more and more to be collective, and in an industrialized world the interference of the community with the individual must be more intense than it need be in a commercial or agricultural regime. Although machinery makes man collectively more lordly in his attitude towards nature, it tends to make the individual man more submissive to his group. (S 77-8)

INDIVIDUALITY
see EDUCATION, INDIVIDUALITY IN

INDIVIDUALITY, REVERENCE FOR HUMAN

I have selected this chapter because reverence for human individuality and mental initiative are, in my opinion, of the utmost importance, and are increasingly threatened in our highly organized and centralized societies. (LIWB 447)

INDIVIDUALS

We shall further define "individuals" or "particulars" as the objects that can be named by proper names. (IMP 142)

INDIVIDUATION

Among the properties of individual things, some are essential, others accidental; the accidental properties of a thing are those it can lose without losing its identity—such as wearing a hat, if you are a man. The question now arises: given two individual things belonging to the same species, do they always differ in essence, or is it

possible for the essence to be exactly the same in both? Saint Thomas holds the latter view as regards material substances, the former as regards those that are immaterial. Duns Scotus holds that there are *always* differences of essence between two different individual things. (HWP 467)
see DUNS SCOTUS

INDUCTION

In practice, inference is of two kinds, one typified by induction, the other by mathematical reasoning. The former is by far the more important, since, as we have seen, it covers all use of signs and all empirical generalisations as well as the habits of which they are the verbal expression. (OP 83)

I propose to assume the validity of induction, not because I know of any conclusive grounds in its favour, but because it seems, in some form, essential to science and not deductible from anything very different from itself. (AOM 167)

As a practice, induction is nothing but our old friend, the law of conditioned reflexes or of association. A child touches a knob that gives him an electric shock; after that, he avoids touching the knob. If he is old enough to speak he may state that the knob hurts when it is touched; he has made an induction based on a single instance. But the induction will exist as a bodily habit even if he is too young to speak, and it occurs equally among animals, provided they are not too low in the scale. The theories of induction in logic are what Freudians call a "rationalisation"; that is to say, they consist of reasons invented afterwards to prove that what we have been doing is sensible. (OP 80-1)

Induction is a matter about which nobody has clear ideas. None of the arguments set forth to try to prove the validity of induction is convincing. In accepting induction we are performing an act of faith. Faith is a "grand" word. What I really mean is that we are acting from habit. (TWW 19)
see DEDUCTION; EMPIRICISM; PROBABILITY

INDUCTION AND SACRED BOOKS

The conflict between Galileo and the Inquisition is not merely the conflict between free thought and bigotry or between science and religion; it is a conflict between the spirit of induction and the spirit of deduction. Those who believe in deduction as the method of arriving at knowledge are compelled to find their premises somewhere, usually in a sacred book. Deduction from inspired books is the method of arriving at truth employed by jurists, Christians, Mohammedans, and Communists. Since deduction as a means of obtaining knowledge collapses when doubt is thrown upon its premises, those who believe in deduction must necessarily be bitter against men who question the authority of the sacred books. (SO 33)

INDUCTION, ANIMAL AND SCIENTIFIC

Animal induction differs from scientific induction in various ways: one of these is that the former, but not the latter, involves expectation. When, in the experience of an animal, an event of kind A has been quickly followed by an event of kind B, if B is emotionally interesting the animal comes to expect B whenever A occurs. How many experiences are necessary depends upon the degree of emotion aroused by B; if B is very pleasurable or very painful, one experience may suffice. As soon as the animal has acquired the habit of expecting B when it sees A, it behaves, *in the presence of* A, as a man would who believed the general proposition "A is always followed by B." But the animal is at no time believing anything that can only be expressed in words by mentioning both A and B. (IMT 314)

INDUCTION BY SIMPLE ENUMERATION

The problem of induction by simple enumeration remains unsolved to this day. Bacon was quite right in rejecting simple enumeration where the details of scientific investigation are concerned, for in dealing with details we may assume general laws on the basis of which so long as they are taken as valid, more or less cogent methods can be built up. John Stuart Mill framed four canons of inductive method, which can be usefully employed so long as the law of causality is assumed; but this law itself, he had to confess, is to be accepted solely on the basis of induction by simple enumeration. The thing that is achieved by the theoretical organization of science is the collection of all subordinate inductions into a few that are very comprehensive—perhaps only one. Such comprehensive inductions are confirmed by so many instances that it is thought legitimate to accept, as regards them, an induction by simple enumeration. This situation is profoundly unsatisfactory, but neither Bacon nor any of his successors have a way out of it. (HWP 545)

INDUCTION, HYPOTHETICAL

Third: what is called "hypothetical induction," in which some general theory is regarded as probable because all its hitherto observed consequences have been verified, does not differ in any essential respect from induction by simple enumeration. For, if p is the theory in question, A the class of relevant phenomena, and B the class of consequences of p, then p is equivalent to "All A is B," and the evidence for p is obtained by a simple enumeration. (HK 417)

INDUCTIVE PROPERTY

A property is said to be "inductive" when it is a hereditary property which belongs to O. Similarly a class is "inductive" when it is a hereditary class of which O is a member. (IMP 21-2)

INDUSTRIALISM

Industrialism is essentially production (including distribution) by methods requiring much fixed capital, i.e., much expenditure of labor in producing implements for the production of commodities which satisfy our needs and desires. It is an extension of the habit of using tools. (PIC 8-9)

Industrialism does not consist merely in large undertakings requiring a great number of workmen. The building of the pyramids was a vast undertaking, but was not industrial. The essence of industrialism is the employment of elaborate machinery and other means, such as railways, of diminishing the total labor of production. All the characteristics of industrialism are exemplified by the substitution of a bridge for a ferry, in spite of the fact that bridges existed before the industrial era. (WIG 141)

INFERENCE

Inference from a group of events to other events can only be justified if the world has certain characteristics which are not logically necessary. So far as deductive logic can show, any collection of events might be the whole universe; if, then, I am ever to be able to infer events, I must accept principles of inference which lie outside deductive logic. All inference from events to events demands some kind of interconnection between different occurrences. Such interconnection is traditionally asserted in the principle of causality or natural law. It is implied, as we shall find, in whatever limited validity may be assigned to induction by simple enumeration: But the traditional ways of formulating the kind of interconnection that must be postulated are in many ways defective, some being too stringent and some not sufficiently so. (HK xii-xiii)

INFERENCE, ANIMAL

I give the name "animal inference" to the process of spontaneous interpretation of sensations. When a dog hears himself called in tones to which he is accustomed, he looks round and runs in the direction of the sound. He may be deceived, like the dog looking into the gramophone in the advertisement of "His Master's Voice." But since inferences of this sort are generated by the repeated experiences that give rise to habit, his inference must be one which has usually been right in his past life, since otherwise the habit would not have been generated. (HK 167-8)

INFERENCE, PRINCIPLE OF
see PROBABILITY

INFINITE

A collection of terms is infinite when it contains as parts other collections which have just as many terms as it has. (ML 86)

INFINITY

What is infinity? If any philosopher had been asked for a definition of infinity, he might have produced some unintelligible rigmarole, but he would certainly not have been able to give a definition that had any meaning at all. Twenty years ago, roughly speaking, Dedekind and Cantor asked this question, and what is more remarkable, they answered it. They found, that is to say, a perfectly precise definition of an infinite number or an infinite collection of things. This was the first and perhaps the greatest step. (ML 85)

INFINITY, AXIOM OF

The axiom of infinity is an assumption which may be enunciated as follows: —"If n be any inductive cardinal number, there is at least one class of individuals having n terms." (IMP 131)

INQUIRY AND LOGIC
see LOGIC

INQUISITION

The ferreting out of heresy had been the business of the bishops, but it became too onerous to be performed by men who had other duties, and in 1233 Gregory IX founded the Inquisition, to take over this part of the work of the episcopate. After 1254, those accused by the Inquisition were not allowed counsel. If condemned, their property was confiscated—in France, to the crown. When an accused person

was found guilty, he was handed over to the secular arm with a prayer
that his life might be spared; but if the secular authorities failed to
burn him, they were liable to be themselves brought before the Inquisition. It dealt not only with heresy in the ordinary sense, but
with sorcery and witchcraft. In Spain, it was mainly directed against
crypto-Jews. Its work was performed mainly by Dominicans and
Franciscans. It never penetrated to Scandinavia or England, but the
English were quite ready to make use of it against Joan of Arc. On
the whole, it was very successful; at the outset, it completely stamped
out the Albigensian heresy. (HWP 448-9)
see DICTATORSHIP

INSECTS, MEN AND

Amid wars and rumors of wars, while "disarmament" proposals
and non-aggression pacts threaten the human race with unprecedented
disaster, another conflict, perhaps even more important, is receiving
much less notice than it deserves—I mean the conflict between men
and insects. (IPI 231)

INSIGHT
see REASON

INSTINCT

In spite of these qualifications, the broad distinction between
instinct and habit is undeniable. To take extreme cases, every animal
at birth can take food by instinct, before it has had opportunity to
learn; on the other hand, no one can ride a bicycle by instinct, though,
after learning, the necessary movements become just as automatic as
if they were instinctive. (AM 51)

The popular conception of instinct errs by imagining it to be
infallible and preternaturally wise, as well as incapable of modification. This is a complete delusion. Instinct, as a rule, is very rough
and ready, able to achieve its result under ordinary circumstances,
but easily misled by anything unusual. (AM 55)

The essence of instinct, one might say, is that it provides a mechanism for acting without foresight in a manner which is usually
advantageous biologically. It is partly for this reason that it is so
important to understand the fundamental position of instinct in prompt-
ing both animal and human behaviour. (AM 57)

INSTINCT, LIFE OF

The life of instinct includes all that man shares with the lower animals, all that is concerned with self-preservation and reproduction and the desires and impulses derivative from these. It includes vanity and love of possessions, love of family, and even much of what makes love of country. It includes all the impulses that are essentially concerned with the biological success of oneself or one's group. . . . (PSR 224)

INSTRUMENTALISM

But contempt for philosophy, if developed to the point at which it becomes systematic is itself a philosophy; it is a philosophy which, in America, is called "instrumentalism." (UE 1)

More and more, science becomes the art of manipulating nature, not a theoretical understanding of nature. The hope of understanding the world is itself one of those day-dreams that science tends to dissipate. This was not formerly the case; it is an outcome of the physics of the last twenty-five years. Undoubtedly it tends to strengthen the instrumentalist philosophy. (S 77)

INSULARITY
see EDUCATION ABROAD

INTELLECTUAL, FUNCTION OF THE

If the intellectual has any function in society, it is to preserve a cool and unbiased judgment in the face of all solicitations to passion. I found, however, that most intellectuals have no belief in the utility of the intellect except in quiet times. (WIBII 13)

INTELLECTUAL INTEGRITY

Intellectual integrity is a personal virtue, not always easy to combine with co-operation in a collective enterprise. But on a long view its social utility is very great, and Amberley deserves to be honoured for having practised it fearlessly in spite of all the specious arguments of ambition and Party. (API 262)

INTELLIGENCE

Education, the press, politics, religion—in a word, all the great forces in the world—are at present on the side of irrationality; they are in the hands of men who flatter King Demos in order to lead him astray. The remedy does not lie in anything heroically cataclysmic, but in the efforts of individuals towards a more sane and balanced view of our relations to our neighbors and to the world. It is to intelligence, increasingly widespread, that we must look for the solution of the ills from which our world is suffering. (SE 54)

INTELLIGENCE, IMPORTANCE OF

It is customary amongst a certain school of sociologists to minimize the importance of intelligence, and to attribute all great events to large impersonal causes. I believe this to be an entire delusion. I believe that if a hundred of the men of the seventeenth century had been killed in infancy, the modern world would not exist. And of these hundred, Galileo is the chief. (SO 34)

INTERACTION

The conclusion to which the above somewhat discursive discussion has seemed to lead is that the fundamental postulate is that of "causal lines." This postulate enables us to infer, from any given event, *something* (though not much) as to what is probable at all neighboring times and some neighboring places. So long as a causal line is not entangled with another, a good deal can be inferred, but where there is entanglement (i.e., interaction) the postulate alone allows a much more restricted inference. However, when quantitative measurement is possible, the measurably different possibilities after an interaction are finite in number, and therefore observation plus induction can make a general law highly probable. In this kind of way, step by step, it would seem that scientific generalizations can be justified. (HK 481-2)

INTERNATIONAL GOVERNMENT

A complete international government, with legislative, executive, and judiciary, and a monopoly of armed force, is the most essential condition of individual liberty in a technically scientific world. Not, of course, that it will secure *complete* liberty; that, I repeat, is only possible for omnipotence, and there cannot be two omnipotent individuals in the world. The man whose desire for liberty is wholly self-centered is therefore driven, if he feels strong enough, to seek world dictatorship; but the man whose desire for liberty is social, or who feels too weak to secure more than his fair share, will seek to maximize liberty by means of law and government, and will oppose anarchic power in all its various forms. (FAG 258-9)

INTERNATIONAL LAW

There is hope that law, rather than private force, may come to govern the relations of nations within the present century. If this hope is not realized we face utter disaster; if it is realized, the world will be far better than at any previous period in the history of man. (UE 44)

Until the relations of nations are as much governed by law as the relations of citizens within a nation, it will be impossible to feel that civilization is secure. (STGS 62)

INTERNATIONAL MILITARY FORCE
see COLLECTIVE SECURITY; WARS OF PRINCIPLE

INTERNATIONAL POLICE

The international authority ought to possess an army and navy, and these ought to be the only army and navy in existence. The only legitimate use of force is to diminish the total amount of force exercised in the world. So long as men are free to indulge their predatory instincts, some men or groups of men will take advantage of this freedom for oppression and robbery. Just as the police are necessary to prevent the use of force by private citizens, so an international police will be necessary to prevent the lawless use of force by separate states. (PI 156-7)

INTERNATIONAL PRODUCTION
see PRODUCTION

INTERNATIONALISM

The international spirit which we should wish to see produced will be something added to love of country, not something taken away. Just as patriotism does not prevent a man from feeling family affection, so the international spirit ought not to prevent a man from feeling affection for his own country. But it will somewhat alter the character of that affection. (PI 170)

Take, first, international government. The necessity for this is patent to every person capable of political thought, but nationalistic passions stand in the way. Each nation is proud of its independence; each nation is willing to fight till the last gasp to preserve its freedom. This, of course, is mere anarchy, and it leads to conditions exactly analogous to those in the feudal ages before the bold, bad barons were forced in the end to submit to the authority of the king. (WIBII 17-8)
see LIBERTY

— 113 —

INTERNATIONALISM, EDUCATION FOR

The feeling that mankind are all one family, and that the division into nations is a trivial folly, could very easily be produced in the average boy or girl if education were directed to that end. (FIE 157)

INTERVAL

An observer in the sun will think the motion of the train quite trivial, and will judge that you have traveled the distance traveled by the earth in its orbit and its diurnal rotation. On the other hand, a flea in the railway carriage will judge that you have not moved at all in space, but have afforded him a period of pleasure which he will measure by his "proper" time, not by Greenwich Observatory. It cannot be said that you or the sun dweller or the flea are mistaken: each is equally justified, and is only wrong if he ascribes an objective validity to his subjective measures. The distance in space between two events is, therefore, not in itself a physical fact. But, as we shall see, there is a physical fact which can be inferred from the distance in time together with the distance in space. This is what is called the "interval" in space time. (ABCR 53)

INTROSPECTION

I contend that the ultimate constituents of matter are not atoms or electrons, but sensations, and other things similar to sensations as regards extent and duration. As against the view that introspection reveals a mental world radically different from sensations, I propose to argue that thoughts, beliefs, desires, pleasures, pains and emotions are all built up out of sensations and images alone, and that there is reason to think that images do not differ from sensations in their intrinsic character. We thus effect a mutual *rapprochement* of mind and matter, and reduce the ultimate data of introspection (in our second sense) to images alone. (AM 121-2)

A sensation *seems* to give us knowledge of a present physical object, while an image does not, except when it amounts to a hallucination, and in this case the seeming is deceptive. Thus the whole context of the two occurrences is different. But in themselves they do not differ profoundly, and there is no reason to invoke two different ways of knowing for the one and for the other. Consequently introspection as a separate kind of knowledge disappears. (AM 110)

INTUITION

Intuition, in fact, is an aspect and development of instinct, and, like all instinct, is admirable in those customary surroundings which have moulded the habits of the animal in question, but totally incompetent as soon as the surroundings are changed in a way which demands some non-habitual mode of action. (ML 17)

IRRATIONALISM
see RATIONALISM

IRRATIONALISM, MODERN
The irrationalists of our time aim, not at salvation, but at power. They thus develop an ethic which is opposed to that of Christianity and of Buddhism; and through their lust of dominion they are of necessity involved in politics. Their genealogy among writers is Fichte, Carlyle, Mazzini, Nietzsche—with supporters such as Treitschke, Rudyard Kipling, Houston Chamberlain and Bergson. (IPI 102-103)*

IRRATIONALIZING
see RATIONALIZING

ISLAM
Islam, on the contrary, was from its very beginning a political religion. Mahomet made himself a ruler of men, and the caliphs who succeeded him remained so until the conclusion of the Great War. It is typical of the difference between Islam and Christianity that the caliph combined within himself both temporal and spiritual authority, which to a Mahometan are not distinct, whereas Christianity, by its non-political character, was led to create two rival politicians, namely, the Pope and the Emperor, of whom the former based his claims to temporal power upon the unimportance of secular rule. (ESO 16-7)

ISOLATIONISM
see FOREIGN NATIONS, ATTITUDE TOWARD

ISOLATIONISM AND IMPERIALISM
Isolationism combined with imperialism is ignorant and stupid; divorced from imperialism, it is much more defensible. (WWP 57)

ISOTOPES
When two elements have the same atomic number, they are called "isotopes." Apart from radio-activity, the only discoverable property in which isotopes differ is atomic weight. They have the same net charge in the nucleus, and therefore the same number of planetary electrons, and the same possible orbits of the electrons. Consequently

their chemical properties are the same, their optical spectra are the same, and even their x-ray spectra are the same. (ABCA 118-9)

The discovery of radio-activity necessitated new views as to "atoms". It was found that an atom of one radio-active element can break up into an atom of another element and an atom of helium, and that there is also another way in which it can change. It was found also that there can be different elements having the same place in the series; these are called "isotopes". (OP 99)

J

JAMES, WILLIAM

I think it may be wagered that no one except William James has ever lived who would have thought of comparing Hegelianism to a seaside boarding-house. In 1884 this article had no effect, because Hegelianism was still on the up-grade, and philosophers had not learnt to admit that their temperaments had anything to do with their opinions. In 1912 (the date of the reprint) the atmosphere had changed through many causes—among others the influence of William James upon his pupils. I cannot claim to have known him more than superficially except from his writings, but it seems to me that one may distinguish three strands in his nature, all of which contributed to form his outlook. Last in time but first in its philosophical manifestations was the influence of his training in physiology and medicine, which gave him a scientific and slightly materialistic bias as compared to purely literary philosophers who derived their inspiration from Plato, Aristotle, and Hegel. This strand dominated his *Psychology* except in a few crucial passages, such as his discussion of free will. The second element of his philosophic make-up was a mystical and religious bias inherited from his father and shared with his brother. This inspired the *Will to Believe* and his interest in psychical research. Thirdly, there was an attempt, made with all the earnestness of a New England conscience, to exterminate the natural fastidiousness which he also shared with his brother, and replace it by democratic sentiment a la Walt Whitman. (SE 59-60)

Among eminent philosophers, excluding men still alive, the most personally impressive to me, was William James. This was in spite of a complete naturalness and absence of all apparent consciousness of being a great man. No degree of democratic feeling and of desire to identify himself with the common herd could make him anything but a natural aristocrat, a man whose personal distinction commanded respect. (UE 167)

Between James and Dr. Dewey there is a difference of emphasis. Dr. Dewey's outlook is scientific, and his arguments are largely derived from an examination of scientific method, but James is concerned primarily with religion and morals. Roughly speaking, he is prepared to advocate any doctrine which tends to make people virtuous and happy; if it does so, it is "true" in the sense in which he uses that word. (HWP 816)

JEALOUSY

Jealousy is, of course, a special form of envy: envy of love. The old often envy the young; when they do, they are apt to treat them cruelly. (WIB 76)

JEFFERSON

see DEMOCRACY, JEFFERSONIAN

JOHN SCOTUS

John supported free will, and this might have passed uncensored; but what roused indignation was the purely philosophic character of his argument. Not that he professed to controvert anything accepted in theology, but that he maintained the equal, or even superior, authority of a philosophy independent of revelation. He contended that reason and revelation are both sources of truth, and therefore cannot conflict; but if they ever *seem* to conflict, reason is to be preferred. (HWP 403)

JUDGMENT, ANALYTIC

The notion that all *a priori* truths are analytic is essentially connected with the doctrine of subject and predicate. An analytic judgment is one in which the predicate is contained in the subject. The subject is supposed defined by a number of predicates, one or more of which are singled out for predication in an analytic judgment. (PL 17)

JUSTICE

But in seeking justice by means of elaborate systems we have been in danger of forgetting that justice alone is not enough. Daily joys, times of liberation from care, adventure, and opportunity for creative activities, are at least as important as justice in bringing about a life that men can feel to be worth living. (AAI 121)

Only justice can give security; and by "justice" I mean the recognition of the equal claims of all human beings. (WIB 72)
see LIBERTY

JUSTICE AND FREEDOM

The greatest possible amount of free development of individuals is, to my mind, the goal at which a social system ought to aim. To secure this end, we need a compromise between justice and freedom: justice, to secure opportunity and the necessaries of life for all; freedom as to the use made of opportunity, so long as that use does not infringe justice . . . Justice and freedom have different spheres: the sphere of justice is the external conditions of a good life; the sphere of freedom is the personal pursuit of happiness or whatever constitutes the individual's conception of well-being. (PIC 279)

JUSTICE, GREEK CONCEPTION OF

This conception of justice—of not overstepping eternally fixed bounds—was one of the most profound of Greek beliefs. The gods were subject to justice just as much as men were, but this supreme power was not itself personal, and was not a supreme God. (HWP 27)

K

KANT

Although he had been brought up as a pietist, he was a Liberal both in politics and in theology; he sympathized with the French Revolution until the Reign of Terror, and was a believer in democracy. His philosophy, as we shall see, allowed an appeal to the heart against the cold dictates of theoretical reason, which might, with a little exaggeration, be regarded as a pedantic version.of the Savoyard Vicar. His principle that every man is to be regarded as an end in himself is a form of the doctrine of the Rights of Man; and his love of freedom is shown in his saying (about children as well as adults) that "there can be nothing more dreadful than that the actions of a man should be subject to the will of another." (HWP 705)

see IMPERATIVES, HYPOTHETICAL AND CATEGORICAL

KEPLER

Kepler's great achievement was the discovery of his three laws of planetary motion. Two of these he published in 1609, and the third in 1619. His first law states: The planets describe elliptic orbits, of which the sun occupies one focus. His second law states: The line joining a planet to the sun sweeps out equal areas in equal times. His third law states: The square of the period of revolution of a planet is proportioned to the cube of its average distance from the sun. (HWP 530)

KEYNES

see PROBABILITY

KINDLY FEELING

From the point of view of worldly wisdom, hostile feeling and limitation of sympathy are folly. Their fruits are war, death, oppression, and torture, not only for their original victims but, in the long run, also for the perpetrators or their descendants. Whereas if we could all learn to love our neighbours the world would quickly become a paradise for us all. (FAR 2)

KLEPTOMANIA

Kleptomania consists of stealing things, which often the thief does not really want, in circumstances where he is pretty sure to be caught. It has as a rule some psychological source: the kleptomaniac, unconsciously to himself, is stealing love, or objects having some sexual significance. Kleptomania cannot be dealt with by punishment, but only by psychological understanding. (ESO 36)

KNOW

On the whole, I prefer to use the word "know" in a sense which implies that the knowing is different from what is known, and to accept the consequence that, as a rule, we do not know our present experiences. (IMT 59)

KNOWING

This objective way of viewing knowledge is, to my mind, much more fruitful than the way which has been customary in philosophy. I mean that, if we wish to give a definition of "knowing", we ought to define it as a manner of reacting to the environment, not as involving something (a "state of mind") which only the person who has the knowledge can observe. (OP 17)

KNOWLEDGE

"Knowledge," in my opinion, is a much less precise concept than is generally thought, and has its roots more deeply embedded in unverbalized animal behavior than most philosophers have been willing to admit. The logically basic assumptions to which our analysis leads us are psychologically the end of a long series of refinements which starts from habits of expectations in animals, such as that what has a certain kind of smell will be good to eat. To ask, therefore, whether we "know" the postulates of scientific inference is not so definite a question as it seems. The answer must be: in one sense, yes, in another sense, no; but in the sense in which "no" is the right answer we know nothing whatever, and "knowledge" in this sense is a delusive vision. The perplexities of philosophers are due, in a large measure, to their unwillingness to awaken from this blissful dream. (HK xv-xvi)

"Knowledge" is a vague concept for two reasons. First because the meaning of a word is always more or less vague except in logic and pure mathematics; and second, because all that we count as knowledge is in a greater or less degree uncertain, and there is no way of deciding how much uncertainty makes a belief unworthy to be called "knowledge," any more than how much loss of hair makes a man bald. (HK 98)

The distinction of the empirical and the *a priori* seems to depend upon confounding sources of knowledge with grounds of truth. There is no doubt a great difference between *knowledge* gained by perception, and *knowledge* gained by reasoning; but that does not show a corresponding difference as to what is known. (PL 24)
see REACTIONS, SUSPENDED

KNOWLEDGE BY ACQUAINTANCE

We shall say that we have *acquaintance* with anything of which we are directly aware, without the intermediary of any process of inference or any knowledge of truths. (PP 73)

KNOWLEDGE BY DESCRIPTION

My knowledge of the table as a physical object, on the contrary, is not direct knowledge. Such as it is, it is obtained through acquaintance with the sense-data that make up the appearance of the table. We have seen that it is possible, without absurdity, to doubt whether there is a table at all, whereas it is not possible to doubt the sense-data. My knowledge of the table is of the kind which we shall call "knowledge by description." (PP 74)

KNOWLEDGE BY DESCRIPTION AND BY ACQUAINTANCE

We have acquaintance with sense-data, with many universals, and possibly with ourselves, but not with physical objects or other minds. We have *descriptive* knowledge of an object when we know that it is *the* object having some property or properties with which we are acquainted; that is to say, when we know that the property or properties in question belong to one object and no more, we are said to have knowledge of that one object by description, whether or not we are acquainted with the object. Our knowledge of physical objects and of other minds is only knowledge by description, the descriptions involved being usually such as involve sense-data. All propositions intelligible to us, whether or not they primarily concern things only known to us by description, are composed wholly of constituents with which we are acquainted, for a constituent with which we are not acquainted is unintelligible to us. (ML 231)

KNOWLEDGE BY INTROSPECTION

The next extension to be considered is acquaintance by *introspection*. We are not only aware of things, but we are often aware of being aware of them. When I see the sun, I am often aware of my seeing the sun; thus "my seeing the sun" is an object with which I have acquaintance. (PP 76-7)

KNOWLEDGE, GENERAL

By "general knowledge" I mean knowledge of the truth or falsehood of sentences containing the word "all" or the word "some" or logical equivalents of these words. The word "some" might be thought to involve less generality than the word "all," but this would be a mistake. This appears from the fact that the negation of a some-sentence is an all-sentence, and vice versa. (HK 129)

KNOWLEDGE-REACTIONS
see MIND

KNOWLEDGE, "USELESS"

Perhaps the most important advantage of "useless" knowledge is that it promotes a contemplative habit of mind. There is in the world much too much readiness, not only for action without adequate previous reflection, but also for some sort of action on occasions on which wisdom would counsel inaction. (IPI 48)

L

LABOR
see HUMAN EXCELLENCE

LANGUAGE

We have arrived, in this chapter, at a result which has been, in a sense, the goal of all our discussions. The result I have in mind is this: that complete metaphysical agnosticism is not compatible with the maintenance of linguistic propositions. Some modern philosophers hold that we know much about language, but nothing about anything else. This view forgets that language is an empirical phenomenon like another, and that a man who is metaphysically agnostic must deny that he knows when he uses a word. For my part, I believe that, partly by means of the study of syntax, we can arrive at considerable knowledge concerning the structure of the world. (IMT 437-8)

Language has two interconnected merits: first, that it is social, and second, that it supplies public expression for "thoughts" which would otherwise remain private. Without language, or some prelinguistic analogue, our knowledge of the environment is confined to what our own senses have shown us, together with such inferences as our congenital constitution may prompt; but by the help of speech we are able to know what others can relate, and to relate what is no longer sensibly present but only remembered. (HK 59)

The essence of language lies, not in the use of this or that special means of communication, but in the employment of fixed associations (however these may have originated) in order that something now sensible—a spoken word, a picture, a gesture, or what not—may call up the "idea" of something else. Whenever this is done, what is now sensible may be called a "sign" or "symbol," and that of which it is intended to call up the "idea" may be called its "meaning." (AM 191)

LANGUAGE, PRIMARY OR OBJECT

We can now partially define the primary or object-language as a language consisting wholly of "object-words," where "object-words" are defined, logically, as words having meaning in isolation, and, psychologically, as words which have been learnt without it being necessary to have previously learnt any other words. (IMT 79-80)

LAO-TZE

The oldest known Chinese sage is Lao-Tze, the founder of Taoism. "Lao-Tze" is not really a proper name, but means merely "the old philosopher." He was (according to tradition) an older contemporary of Confucius, and his philosophy is to my mind far more interesting. He held that every person, every animal, and every thing has a certain way or manner of behaving which is natural to him, or her, or it, and that we ought to conform to this way ourselves and encourage others to conform to it. (PC 198)

LAW

The second argument of principle against the method of minority violence is that abandonment of law, when it becomes widespread, lets loose the wild beast, and gives a free rein to the primitive lusts and egoisms which civilization in some degree curbs. Every student of medieval thought must have been struck by the extraordinarily high value placed upon law in that period. The reason was, that, in countries infested by robber barons, law was the first requisite for progress. We, in the modern world, take it for granted that most people will be law-abiding, and we hardly realize what centuries of effort have gone to making such an assumption possible. (PTB 147-8)
see LIBERTY

LAW, AUTHORITY OF

But in regard to departures on conscientious grounds from what is thought right by the society to which a man belongs, we must distinguish between the authority of custom and the authority of law. Very much stronger grounds are needed to justify an action which is illegal than to justify one which contravenes conventional morality. The reason is that respect for law is an indispensable condition for the existence of any tolerable social order. When a man considers a certain law to be bad, he has a right, and may have a duty, to try to get it changed, but it is only in rare cases that he does right to break it. (AAI 109)

LAW, INTERNATIONAL

In the interrelations of States nothing of the same sort exists. There is, it is true, a body of conventions called "international law," and there are innumerable treaties between High Contracting Powers. But the conventions and the treaties differ from anything that could properly be called law by the absence of sanction: there is no police force able or willing to enforce their observance. (JWT 21)

LAW, PERIODIC

The elements can be arranged in a series by means of what is called their "atomic weight." By chemical methods, we can remove one element from a compound and replace it by an equal number of atoms of another element; we can observe how much this alters the weight of the compound, and thus we can compare the weight of one kind of atom with the weight of another. (ABCA 14)

LAW, RESPECT FOR

If the method of sanctions is to be used effectively, the sentiment behind it must be respect for law, not love of peace. It is true that, if respect for international law were sufficiently strong, peace would result in the long run; but it would result in consequence of a series of wars from which pacifists would shrink. Respect for law may inspire a wish to punish the criminal, and may thus afford an incentive to war; but love of peace, if used as an incentive to war, produces an inner conflict which is likely to prevent effective action. (WWP 75)

LAW, RULE OF

Means must be found of subjecting the relations of nations to the rule of law, so that a single nation will no longer be, as at present, the judge of its own cause. If this is not done, the world will quickly return to barbarism. (ISOS 40)

The only escape is to have the greatest possible number of disputes settled by legal process and not by a trial of strength. Thus, here again the preservation of internal liberty and external control go hand in hand, and both equally depend upon what is *prima facie* a restraint upon liberty, namely an extension of the domain of law and of the public force necessary for its enforcement. (ISOS 42)

LAWS, DIFFERENTIAL

The principle I mean is that of "differential laws," as it may be called. This means that any connection which may exist between distant events is the result of integration from a law giving a 'rate of change at every point of some route from the one to the other. One may give a simple illustration of a differential law from the "curve of pursuit": a man is walking along a straight road, and his dog is in a field beside the road; the man whistles to the dog, and the dog runs towards him. We suppose that at each moment the dog runs exactly towards where his master is at that moment. (AOM 101)

LAWS, PHYSICAL

Laws embodied in differential equations may possibly be exact, but cannot be known to be so. All that we can know empirically is approximate and liable to exceptions; the exact laws that are assumed in physics are known to be somewhere near the truth, but are not known to be true just as they stand. The laws that we actually know empirically have the form of the traditional causal laws, except that they are not to be regarded as universal or necessary. (AM 95)

LAZINESS

But I have hopes of laziness as a gospel. I think that if our education were strenuously directed to that end, by men with all the fierce energy produced by our present creed and way of life, it might be possible to induce people to be lazy. I do not mean that no one should work at all, but that few people should work more than is necessary for getting a living. (LAM 117)

LEAGUE OF NATIONS, DEFECTS OF

All the defects of the League may be summed up in the one fact that it is not a government. A government has legislative, executive, and judicial functions; it does not require unanimity, but can act by a majority. The League of Nations has no legislative body: neither the Council nor the Assembly can coerce dissentient members, nor can treaties be revised without the consent of the signatories. The League has no executive: the only force at its disposal is that of member States, which is used or withheld as national governments decide, not as the League may demand. (WWP 69-70)

LEARN, THE WISH TO

The spontaneous wish to learn, which every normal child possesses, as shown in its efforts to walk and talk, should be the driving-force in education. The substitution of this driving-force for the rod is one of the great advances of our time. (EEC 42)

LEARNED REACTION

What I am saying is that, genetically and causally, there is no important difference between the most elaborate induction and the most elementary "learned reaction." The one is merely a developed form of the other, not something radically different. And our determination to believe in the results of induction, even if, as logicians, we see no reason to do so, is really due to the potency of the principle of association; it is an example—perhaps the most important example of what Dr. Santayana calls "animal faith." (OP 84)

LEGITIMACY, THE PRINCIPLE OF

The principle of legitimacy asserts, speaking broadly, that territories ought to belong to their hereditary sovereigns, unless voluntarily parted with in exchange for some compensation. (FO 17)

LEIBNIZ

But being the champion of orthodoxy against the decried atheist, Leibniz shrank from the consequences of his views, and took refuge in the perpetual iteration of edifying phrases. The whole tendency of his temperament, as of his philosophy, was to exalt enlightenment, education, and learning, at the expense of ignorant good intentions. This tendency might have found a logical expression in his Ethics. But he preferred to support Sin and Hell, and to remain, in what concerned the Church, the champion of ignorance and obscurantism. This is the reason why the best parts of his philosophy are the most abstract, and the worst those which most nearly concern human life. (PL 202)

LEISURE

Coming now to that great majority who will not choose idleness, I think we may assume that, with the help of science, and by the elimination of the vast amount of unproductive work involved in internal and international competition, the whole community could be kept in comfort by means of four hours' work a day. (RF 193)

Modern technique has made it possible for leisure, within limits, to be not the prerogative of small privileged classes, but a right evenly distributed throughout the community. (IPI 17)

But it would be possible to reduce compulsory work to a rather small amount. Probably with our present technique it could be reduced to four hours a day, and with every technical advance the amount could be diminished. (PIC 281)

see HUMAN EXCELLENCE

LEISURE, USE OF

It will be said that, while a little leisure is pleasant, men would not know how to fill their days if they had only four hours of work out of the twenty-four. In so far as this is true in the modern world, it is a condemnation of our civilization; it would not have been true at any earlier period. There was formerly a capacity for light-heartedness and play which has been to some extent inhibited by the cult of efficiency. The modern man thinks that everything ought to be done for the sake of something else, and never for its own sake. (IPI 28)

LENIN

see DICTATORSHIP; POWER, UNRESTRICTED

LIBERAL ATTITUDE

Unfortunately the atomic bomb is a swifter exterminator than the stake, and cannot safely be allowed so long a run. We must hope that a more rational outlook can be made to prevail, for only through a revival of Liberal tentativeness and tolerance can our world survive. (UE 17)

LIBERAL CREED

The Liberal creed, in practice, is one of live-and-let-live, of toleration and freedom so far as public order permits, of moderation and absence of fanaticism in political programs. Even democracy, when it becomes fanatical, as it did among Rousseau's disciples in the French Revolution, ceases to be Liberal; indeed, a fanatical belief in democracy makes democratic institutions impossible, as appeared in England under Cromwell and in France under Robespierre. The genuine liberal does not say "this is true"; he says, "I am inclined to think that under present circumstances this opinion is probably the best." (UE 15)

LIBERALISM

Political change throughout the century was inspired by two systems of thought, Liberalism and Radicalism. Of these, Liberalism was eighteenth-century in origin, and had inspired the American and French Revolutions. It stood for liberty, both individual and national, with as little government as possible; indeed, the functions of government were reduced by many Liberals to the prevention of crime. In agricultural communities it was successful in producing stable conditions and a fairly contented population; but it had little to offer to industrial wage-earners, since its philosophy suggested no way of curbing economic power in the hands of individuals. It succeeded in establishing Parliaments, with a greater or less degree of power, in every country of Europe and America, as well as in Japan and China; but the resultant benefits were, in many parts of the world, not very noticeable. (FO 447-8)

This is the essential difference between the Liberal outlook and that of the totalitarian State, that the former regards the welfare of the State as residing ultimately in the welfare of the individual, while the latter regards the State as the end and individuals merely as indispensable ingredients, whose welfare must be subordinated to a mystical totality which is a cloak for the interests of the rulers. (P 302-3)

The essence of the Liberal outlook lies not in *what* opinions are held, but in *how* they are held: instead of being held dogmatically, they are held tentatively, and with a consciousness that new evidence may at any moment lead to their abandonment. This is the way in which opinions are held in science, as opposed to the way in which they are held in theology. The decisions of the Council of Nicaea are still authoritative, but in science fourth-century opinions no longer carry any weight. In the U. S. S. R. the dicta of Marx on dialectical materialism are so unquestioned that they help to determine the view of geneticists on how to obtain the best breed of wheat, though elsewhere it is thought that experiment is the right way to study such problems. Science is empirical, tentative, and undogmatic; all immutable dogma is unscientific. The scientific outlook, accordingly, is the intellectual counterpart of what is, in the practical sphere, the outlook of Liberalism. (UE 15-6)
see DEMOCRACY; FORCE

LIBERALISM, EMPIRICIST

I conclude that, in our day as in the time of Locke, empiricist Liberalism (which is not incompatible with *democratic* socialism) is the only philosophy that can be adopted by a man who, on the one hand, demands some scientific evidence for his beliefs, and, on the other hand, desires human happiness more than the prevalence of this or that party or creed. (UE 20)

LIBERALISM, ESSENCE OF

In general, important civilizations start with a rigid and super-stitious system, gradually relaxed, and leading, at a certain stage, to a period of brilliant genius, while the good of the old tradition remains and the evil inherent in its dissolution has not yet developed. But as the evil unfolds, it leads to anarchy, thence, inevitably, to a new tyranny, producing a new synthesis secured by a new system of dogma. The doctrine of liberalism is an attempt to escape from this endless oscillation. The essence of liberalism is an attempt to secure a social order not based on irrational dogma, and insuring stability without involving more restraints than are necessary for the preservation of the community. Whether this attempt can succeed only the future can determine. (HWP xxiii)

LIBERTY

The liberty of the individual should be respected where his actions do not directly, obviously, and indubitably do harm to other people. Otherwise our persecuting instincts will produce a stereotyped society as in sixteenth-century Spain. The danger is real and press-ing. (SE 186)

"Liberty" is a good watchword, but it is not sufficient as an international principle. There should be liberty to do certain kinds of things, but not certain other kinds. Primarily, there should be no liberty to make aggressive war. It is obvious that this requires some supernational authority with a preponderance of armed forces and with a judicial body entrusted with the duty of pronouncing quickly whether, in a given case, aggression has taken place. (PPW 88)

The whole realm of the possessive impulses, and of the use of force to which they give rise, stands in need of control by a public neutral authority, in the interests of liberty no less than of justice. Within a nation, this public authority will naturally be the state; in relations between nations, if the present anarchy is to cease, it will have to be some international parliament. (PI 135-6)

There can be no widespread liberty except under the reign of law, for when men are lawless only the strongest are free, and they only until they are overcome by someone still stronger. The tyrant in a lawless community is like the King of the Wood, "who slays the slayer and must himself be slain." Whoever, in the name of liberty, impairs respect for the law, incurs a grave responsibility;

yet, since the law is often oppressive and incapable of being amended legally, revolution must be allowed to be sometimes necessary. (FAG 256)

The question of the degree of liberty that is compatible with order is one that cannot be settled in the abstract. The only thing that can be said in the abstract is that, where there is no technical reason for a collective decision, there should be some strong reason connected with public order if freedom is to be interfered with. (P 277)
see COMMUNISM AND LIBERTY

LIFE, ATTITUDES TOWARD

The three attitudes most prevalent in people's philosophy are the practical, the mystical, and the scientific. Each is insufficient as covering the whole of life; each becomes fallacious when it tries to extend beyond its proper sphere. The practical attitude asks: "What shall I do?" The mystical attitude asks: "What shall I feel?" The scientific attitude asks: "What shall I believe, or what can I know?" (TWW 11)

LIFE, MAN'S TRUE

Man's true life does not consist in the business of filling his belly and clothing his body, but in art and thought and love, in the creation and contemplation of beauty and in the scientific understanding of the world. If the world is to be regenerated, it is in these things not only in material goods, that all must be enabled to participate. (PIC 40-1)

LIFE, THE AMERICAN WAY OF
see LOYALTIES, CURRENT

LIFE, THE FULL

Instinct, mind, and spirit are all essential to a full life; each has its own excellence and its own corruptions. Each can attain a spurious excellence at the expense of the others; each has a tendency to encroach upon the others; but in the life which is to be sought all three will be developed in coordination, and intimately blended in a single harmonious whole. (PSR 227)

LIFE, WAY OF

The Chinese have discovered, and have practised for many

centuries, a way of life which, if it could be adopted by all the world, would make all the world happy. We Europeans have not. Our way of life demands strife, exploitation, restless change, discontent, and destruction. Efficiency directed to destruction can only end in annihilation, and it is to this consummation that our civilization is tending, if it cannot learn some of that wisdom for which it despises the East. (PC 12)

LIST
see PROTECTION

LITERATURE, TEACHING OF
The teaching of Literature is a matter as to which it is easy to make mistakes. There is not the slightest use, either for young or old, in being well-informed *about* literature, knowing the dates of the poets, the names of their works, and so on. Everything that can be put into a handbook is worthless. What is valuable is great familiarity with certain examples of good literature—such familiarity as will influence the style, not only of writing, but of thought. (EEC 269)

LOCKE
A characteristic of Locke, which descended from him to the whole Liberal movement, is lack of dogmatism. Some few certainties he takes over from his predecessors: our own existence, the existence of God, and the truth of mathematics. But wherever his doctrines differ from those of his forerunners, they are to the effect that truth is hard to ascertain, and that a rational man will hold his opinions with some measure of doubt. This temper of mind is obviously connected with religious toleration, with the success of parliamentary democracy, with *laissez-faire*, and with the whole system of liberal maxims. Although he is a deeply religious man, a devout believer in Christianity who accepts revelation as a source of knowledge, he nevertheless hedges round professed revelations with rational safeguards. (HWP 606-7)

LOGIC
Activity can supply only one half of wisdom; the other half depends upon receptive passivity. Ultimately, the controversy between those who base logic upon "truth" and those who base it upon "in-

quiry" arises from a difference of values, and cannot be argued without, at some point, begging the question. (DNL 156)

In logic, it is a waste of time to deal with inferences concerning particular cases: we deal throughout with completely general and purely formal implications, leaving it to other sciences to discover when the hypotheses are verified and when they are not. (KEW 47)

Although we can no longer be satisfied to define logical propositions as those that follow from the law of contradiction, we can and must still admit that they are a wholly different class of propositions from those that we come to know empirically. They all have the characteristic which, a moment ago, we agreed to call "tautology." This, combined with the fact that they can be expressed wholly in terms of variables and logical constants (a logical constant being something which remains constant in a proposition even when *all* its constituents are changed)—will give the definition of logic or pure mathematics. (IMP 204-5)
see ARISTOTLE'S LOGIC

LOGIC, GREEK

It has only been very slowly that scientific method, which seeks to reach principles inductively from observation of particular facts, has replaced the Hellenic belief in deduction for luminous axioms derived from the mind of the philosopher. For this reason, apart from others, it is a mistake to treat the Greeks with superstitious reverence. (HWP 39)

LOGICAL ATOMISM

I hold that logic is what is fundamental in philosophy, and that schools should be characterized rather by their logic than by their metaphysic. My own logic is atomic, and it is this aspect upon which I should wish to lay stress. Therefore I prefer to describe my philosophy as "logical atomism," rather than as "realism," whether with or without some prefixed adjective. (LA 359)

The third type, which may be called "logical atomism" for want of a better name, has gradually crept into philosophy through the critical scrutiny of mathematics. This type of philosophy, which is the one that I wish to advocate, has not as yet many whole-hearted adherents, but the "new realism" which owes its inception to Harvard is very largely impregnated with its spirit. It represents, I believe, the same kind of advance as was introduced into physics by Galileo: the substitution of piecemeal, detailed, and verifiable results for large untested generalities recommended only by a certain appeal to imagination. (KEW 4)

The philosophy which I wish to advocate may be called logical atomism or absolute pluralism, because, while maintaining that there are many things, it denies that there is a whole composed of those things. We shall see, therefore, that philosophical propositions, instead of being concerned with the whole of things collectively, are concerned with all things distributively; and not only must they be concerned with all things, but they must be concerned with such properties of all things as do not depend upon the accidental nature of the things that there happen to be, but are true of any possible world, independently of such facts as can only be discovered by our senses. (ML 111)

LOGICAL TYPE

The definition of a logical type is as follows: A and B are of the same logical type if, and only if, given any fact of which A is a constituent, there is a corresponding fact which has B as a constituent, which either results by substituting B for A, or is the negation of what so results. (LA 369-70)

LOVE

Love is a word which covers a variety of feelings; I have used it purposely, as I wish to include them all. Love as an emotion—which is what I am speaking about, for love "on principle" does not seem to me genuine—moves between two poles: on the one side, pure delight in contemplation; on the other, pure benevolence. (WIB 22)

My attitude, however, is not really one of hostility to moral rules; it is essentially that expressed by Saint Paul in the famous passage on charity. I do not always find myself in agreement with that apostle, but on this point my feeling is exactly the same as his—namely, that no obedience to moral rules can take the place of love, and that where love is genuine, it will, if combined with intelligence, suffice to generate whatever moral rules are necessary. (WIBII 15)

LOVE, INCULCATION OF

Love cannot exist as a duty: to tell a child that it *ought* to love its parents and its brothers and sisters is utterly useless, if not worse. Parents who wish to be loved must behave so as to elicit love, and must try to give to their children those physical and mental characteristics which produce expansive affections. (EEC 188)

LOYALTIES, CURRENT

In our own day two widespread creeds embrace the loyalty of a very large part of mankind. One of these, the creed of communism, has the advantage of intense fanaticism and embodiment in a sacred book. The other, less definite, is nevertheless potent—it may be called 'the American way of life.' (SC 992)

LUNATICS, CERTIFIED AND UNCERTIFIED

Certified lunatics are shut up because of their proneness to violence when their pretensions are questioned; the *uncertified* variety are given the control of powerful armies, and can inflict death and disaster upon all sane men within their reach. The success of insanity, in literature, in philosophy, and in politics, is one of the peculiarities of our age. And the successful form of insanity proceeds almost entirely from impulses towards power. (P 259)

LYING

Indeed, no man who thinks truthfully can believe that it is *always* wrong to speak untruthfully. Those who hold that a lie is always wrong have to supplement this view by a great deal of casuistry and considerable practice in misleading ambiguities, by means of which they deceive without admitting to themselves that they are lying. (EEC 157)

M

MACHIAVELLI

His most famous work, *The Prince*, was written in 1513, and dedicated to Lorenzo the Magnificent, since he hoped (vainly, as it proved) to win the favour of the Medici. Its tone is perhaps partly due to this practical purpose; his longer work, the *Discourses*, which he was writing at the same time, is markedly more republican and more liberal. He says at the beginning of *The Prince* that he will not speak of republics in this book, since he has dealt with them elsewhere. Those who do not read also the *Discourses* are likely to get a very one-sided view of his doctrine. (HWP 505)

MACHINERY, EFFECT OF

Meanwhile machines deprive us of two things which are certainly important ingredients of human happiness, namely, spontaneity and variety. Machines have their own pace, and their own insistent demands: a man who has an expensive plant must keep it working. The great trouble with the machine, from the point of view of the emotions, is its *regularity*. And, of course, conversely, the great objection to the emotions, from the point of view of the machine, is their *irregularity*. (SE 87)

MAJORITY, POWER OF THE

I think it must be admitted that, if any important economic change is to be successfully carried out, a government will need some years of free initiative. This, however, is not incompatible with democracy, which consists in the occasional exercise of popular control, but does not demand the constant hampering of the executive. The ultimate power of the majority is very important to minimize the harshness inevitably involved in great changes, and to prevent a rapidity of transformation which causes a revulsion of feeling. I do not believe, therefore, that an authoritarian government is better than a democracy, though I believe that, in times of crisis, a strong and temporarily unhampered executive is necessary. (FOD 381)

MAN, EVANESCENCE OF

Even within the life of our planet man is only a brief interlude. Non-human life existed countless ages before man was evolved. Man, even if he does not commit scientific suicide, will perish ultimately through failure of water or air or warmth. It is difficult to believe that Omnipotence needed so vast a setting for so small and transitory a result. (FAR 4)

MAN, GOAL OF

Mankind has become so much one family that we cannot insure our own prosperity except by insuring that of everyone else. If you wish to be happy yourself, you must resign yourself to seeing others also happy. Whether science can continue, and whether, while it continues, it can do more good than harm, depends upon the capacity of mankind to learn this simple lesson. Perhaps it is necessary that all should learn it, but it must be learned by all who have great power, and among those some still have a long way to go. (STS 33)

MAN, THE HAPPY

The happy man is the man who lives objectively, who has free affections and wide interests, who secures his happiness through these interests and affections and through the fact that they, in turn, make him an object of interest and affection to many others. (CH 244)

In fact the whole antithesis between self and the rest of the world, which is implied in the doctrine of self-denial, disappears as soon as we have any genuine interest in persons or things outside ourselves. Through such interests a man comes to feel himself part of the stream of life, not a hard separate entity like a billiard ball, which can have no relation with other such entities except that of collision. (CH 248)

MAN, THE LOT OF

The universe is vast and men are but tiny specks on an insignificant planet. But the more we realize our minuteness and our impotence in the face of cosmic forces, the more astonishing becomes what human beings have achieved. It is to the possible achievements of man that our ultimate loyalty is due, and in that thought the brief troubles of our unquiet epoch become endurable. (IWS 18)

MAN, THE PURPOSE OF

We, too, in all our deeds, bear our part in a process of which we cannot guess the development: even the obscurest are actors in a drama of which we know that it is great. Whether any purpose that we value will be achieved, we cannot tell; but the drama itself, in any case, is full of Titanic grandeur. This quality it is the business of the historian to extract from the bewildering multitude of irrelevant details. (OH 214)

MANICHAEISM

Manichaeism combined Christian and Zoroastrian elements, teaching that evil is a positive principle, embodied in matter, while the good principle is embodied in spirit. It condemned meat-eating, and all sex, even in marriage. (HWP 325)

MANKIND

The whole world of art and literature and learning is international; what is done in one country is not done for that country, but for mankind. If we ask ourselves what are the things that raise mankind above the brutes, what are the things that make us think the human race more valuable than any species of animals, we shall find that none of them are things in which any one nation can have exclusive property, but all are things in which the whole world can share. Those who have any care for these things, those who wish to see mankind fruitful in the work which men alone can do, will take little account of national boundaries, and have little care to what state a man happens to owe allegiance. (PI 166-7)

MANKIND, FAMILY OF

There will have to be a realization at once intellectual and moral that we are all one family, and that the happiness of no one branch of this family can be built securely upon the ruin of another. At the present time, moral defects stand in the way of clear thinking, and muddled thinking encourages moral defects. Perhaps, though I scarcely dare to hope it, the hydrogen bomb will terrify mankind into sanity and tolerance. If this should happen we shall have reason to bless its inventors. (UE 165)

MANKIND, HOPES FOR

If we had the buoyancy and the hope that are justified by the facts, we should find it a thousand times easier than we do now to conquer our difficulties and to bring the rest of the world, or at any rate the greater part of it, into a mood of eager cooperation. But we can only do this if our hopes are generous. We cannot keep to ourselves the goods that we now enjoy. If we are to continue to enjoy them, we must see to it that the whole world shares with us. It is chiefly fear that now prevents this generosity of feeling, and if we are to end our troubles, we must learn, even in our inmost thoughts, to replace our fears by hopes. (TRF 25)

MANKIND, THE FUTURE OF

Before the end of the present century, unless something quite unforeseeable occurs, one of three possibilities will have been realized. These three are: I. The end of human life, perhaps of all life on our planet. II. A reversion to barbarism after a catastrophic diminution of the population of the globe. III. A unification of the world under a single government, possessing a monopoly of all the major weapons of war. I do not pretend to know which of these will happen, or even which is the most likely. What I do contend, without any hesitation, is that the kind of system to which we have been accustomed cannot possibly continue. (UE 34)

MAN'S POWER

Brief and powerless is Man's life; on him and all his race the slow, sure doom falls pitiless and dark. Blind to good and evil, reckless of destruction,omnipotent matter rolls on its relentless way; for Man, condemned to-day to lose his dearest, to-morrow himself to pass through the gate of darkness, it remains only to cherish, ere yet the blow falls, the lofty thoughts that ennoble his little day; disdaining the coward terrors of the slave of Fate, to worship at the shrine that his own hands have built; undismayed by the empire of chance, to preserve a mind free from the wanton tyranny that rules his outward life; proudly defiant of the irresistible forces that tolerate, for a moment, his knowledge and his condemnation, to sustain alone, a weary but unyielding Atlas, the world that his own ideals have fashioned despite the trampling march of unconscious power. (ML 56-7)

MAN'S TRUE LIFE

I wish to warn the advocates of economic reconstruction against the danger of adopting the vices of their opponents by regarding man as a tool for producing goods rather than goods as a subordinate necessity for liberating the non-material side of human life. Man's true life does not consist in the business of filling his belly and clothing his body, but in art and thought and love, in the creation and contemplation of beauty, and in the scientific understanding of the world. If the world is to be regenerated, it is in these things, not only in material goods, that all must be enabled to participate. (WIG 147)

MARRIAGE

It is therefore possible for a civilized man and woman to be happy in marriage, although if this is to be the case a number of conditions must be fulfilled. There must be a feeling of complete equality on both sides; there must be no interference with mutual freedom; there must be the most complete physical and mental intimacy; and there must be a certain similarity in regards to standards of values. (It is fatal, for example, if one values only money while the other values only good work.) Given all these conditions, I believe marriage to be the best and most important relation that can exist between two human beings. (MM 143)

MARRIAGE, DISSOLUTION OF

To the eye of the sane maker of laws it would seem that the special contract of partnership known as marriage should be dissolved altogether when it has failed in its object and when the partners are no longer carrying on business together, but living separate (subject always to the one special difficulty of the partnership assets which have been created in the shape of children) . . . . (WMD 134)

MARRIAGE, ESSENCE OF A GOOD

The essence of a good marriage is respect for each other's personality combined with that deep intimacy, physical, mental, and spiritual, which makes a serious love between man and woman the most fructifying of all human experiences. (MM 320)

MARRIAGE, THE NEW IDEAL OF

I doubt if there is any radical core except in some form of religion, so firmly and sincerely believed in as to dominate even the life of instinct. The individual is not the end and aim of his own being: outside the individual, there is the community, the future of mankind, the immensity of the universe in which all our hopes and

fears are a mere pin-point. A man and woman with reverence for
the spirit of life in each other, with an equal sense of their own unimportance beside the whole life of man, may become comrades
without interference with liberty, and may achieve the union of
instinct without doing violence to the life of mind and spirit. As
religion dominated the old form of marriage, so religion must dominate the new. But it must be a new religion, based upon liberty,
justice and love, not upon authority and law and hell-fire. (MPQ 461)

MARSIGLIO

Marsiglio of Padua (1270-1342), on the contrary, inaugurated
the new form of opposition to the Pope, in which the Emperor has
mainly a role of decorative dignity. He was a close friend of William
of Occam, whose political opinions he influenced. Politically, he is
more important than Occam. He holds that the legislator is the
majority of the people, and that the majority has the right to punish
princes. He applies popular sovereignty also to the Church, and he
includes the laity. (HWP 470)

MARX

Considered purely as a philosopher, Marx has grave shortcom-
ings. He is too practical, too much wrapped up in the problems of
his time. His purview is confined to this planet, and, within this
planet, to Man. Since Copernicus, it has been evident that Man has
not the cosmic importance which he formerly arrogated to himself.
No man who has failed to assimilate this fact has a right to call
his philosophy scientific. (HWP 788)
see SOCIALISM

MASS

When we substitute space-time for time, we find that the measured mass (as opposed to the proper mass) is a quantity of the same
kind as the momentum in a given direction; it might be called the
momentum in the time direction. The measured mass is obtained by
multiplying the invariant mass by the *time* traversed in traveling
through unit interval; the momentum is obtained by multiplying the
same invariant mass by the *distance* traversed (in the given direction) in traveling through unit interval. (ABCR 152)

MATERIALISM

see AMERICA AND MATERIALISM; HISTORY,
MATERIALISTIC CONCEPTION OF; PHYSICS

MATERIALISM, AMERICAN

I do not think Americans are in any degree more "materialistic," in the popular sense of that word, than people of other nations. We think they worship the "almighty dollar" because they succeeded in getting it. But a needy aristocrat or a French peasant will do things for the sake of money that shock every decent American. (PCI 16)

MATERIALISTS

Those who argue that matter is the reality and mind a mere property of protoplasm are called "materialists." They have been rare among philosophers, but common, at certain periods, among men of science. (AM 10)

MATHEMATICAL LOGIC

The new philosophy is not merely critical. It is constructive, but as science is constructive, bit by bit and tentatively. It has a special technical method of construction, namely, mathematical logic, a new branch of mathematics, much more akin to philosophy than any of the traditional branches. Mathematical logic makes it possible, as it never was before, to see what is the outcome, for philosophy, of a given body of scientific doctrine, what entities must be assumed, and what relations between them. (SE 74)

Mathematics, rightly viewed, possesses not only truth, but supreme beauty—a beauty cold and austere, like that of sculpture, without appeal to any part of our weaker nature, without the gorgeous trappings of painting or music, yet sublimely pure, and capable of a stern perfection such as only the greatest art can show. (ML 60)

MATHEMATICS

Well, I think mathematics has the advantage of teaching you the habit of thinking without passion. That seems to me the great merit of mathematics. You learn to use your mind primarily upon material where passion doesn't come in, and having trained it in that way you can then use it passionlessly upon matters about which you feel passionately. Then you're much more likely to come to true conclusions. (SPE 113-4)

MATHEMATICS AND NATURE

We are certainly stimulated by our experience to the creation of the concept of number—the connection of the decimal system with our ten fingers is enough to prove this. If one could imagine intelligent beings living on the sun, where everything is gaseous, they would presumably have no concept of number, any more than of "things." They might have mathematics, but the most elementary branch would be topology. Some solar Einstein might invent arithmetic, and imagine a world to which it would be applicable, but the subject would be considered too difficult for schoolboys. Perhaps, conversely, Heraclitus would not have invented his philosophy if he had lived in a northern country where rivers are frozen in winter. The influence of temperature on metaphysics would be a pleasant subject for some new Gulliver. I think the general tendency of such reflections is to throw doubt on the view that concepts arise independently of sensible experience. (RTC 697)

MATHEMATICS AND PHILOSOPHY

The principles of mathematics have always had an important relation to philosophy. Mathematics apparently contains *a priori* knowledge of a high degree of certainty, and most philosophy aspires to *a priori* knowledge. Ever since Zeno the Eleatic, philosophers of an idealistic caste have sought to throw discredit on mathematics by manufacturing contradictions which were designed to show that mathematicians had not arrived at real metaphysical truth, and that the philosophers were able to supply a better brand. There is a great deal of this in Kant, and still more in Hegel. (SE 73)

MATHEMATICS, PURE
see LOGIC

MATTER

A piece of matter, as it is known empirically, is not a single existing thing, but a system of existing things. When several people simultaneously see the same table, they all see something different; therefore "the" table, which they are supposed all to see, must be either a hypothesis or a construction. "The" table is to be neutral as between different observers: it does not favour the aspect seen by one man at the expense of that seen by another. (AM 97)

The main point for the philosophers in the modern theory is the disappearance of matter as a "thing". It has been replaced by emanations from a locality—the sort of influences that characterise haunted rooms in ghost stories. As we shall see in the next chapter, the theory of relativity leads to a similar destruction of the solidity of matter, by a different line of argument. All sorts of events happen in the physical world, but tables and chairs, the sun and moon, and even our daily bread, have become pale abstractions, mere laws exhibited in the successions of events which radiate from certain regions. (OP 106)

The word matter is, in philosophy, the name of a problem. Assuming that, in perception, we are assured of the existence of something other than ourselves—an assumption which, as we saw in the last chapter, Leibniz made on very inadequate grounds—the question inevitably arises: of what nature is this something external to ourselves? In so far as it appears to be in space, we name it matter. (PL 75)

Instead of supposing, as we naturally do when we start from an uncritical acceptance of the apparent dicta of physics, that *matter* is what is "really real" in the physical world, and that the immediate objects of sense are mere phantasms, we must regard matter as a logical construction, of which the constituents will be just such evanescent particulars as may, when an observer happens to be present, become data of sense to that observer. What physics regards as the sun of eight minutes ago will be a whole assemblage of particulars, existing at different times, spreading out from a centre with the velocity of light, and containing among their number all those visual data which are seen by people who are now looking at the sun. Thus the sun of eight minutes ago is a class of particulars, and what I see when I now look at the sun is one member of this class. (ML 137)

The physicists have now all but succeeded in reducing matter to two different kinds of units, one (the proton or hydrogen nucleus) bearing positive electricity, and the other (the electron) bearing negative electricity. (ABCA 13)

Briefly, omitting niceties and qualifications, my view is this: A piece of matter is a system of events; if the piece of matter is to be as small as possible, these events must all overlap, or be "compresent." Every event occupies a finite amount of space-time, i. e., over-laps with events which do not overlap with each other. Certain collections of events are "points" or perhaps minimum volumes, since the existence of collections generating points is uncertain. Causal laws enable us to arrange points (or minimum volumes) in a four-dimensional order. Therefore when the causal relations of an event are known, its position in space-time follows tautologically. (RTC 705)

In the old view, a piece of matter was something which survived all through time, while never being at more than one place at a given time. This way of looking at things is obviously connected with the complete separation of space and time in which people formerly believed. When we substitute space-time for space and time, we shall naturally expect to derive the physical world from constituents which are as limited in time as in space. Such constituents are what we call "events." An event does not persist and move, like the traditional piece of matter; it merely exists for its little moment and then ceases. A piece of matter will thus be resolved into a series of events. (ABCR 208-9)

The collection of all physical objects is called "matter." (PP 18)
see ASCETIC; EVENTS

MATTER, CHEMICAL IMPERIALISM OF LIVING

Every living thing is a sort of imperialist, seeking to transform as much as possible of its environment into itself and its seed. The distinction between self and posterity is one which does not exist in a developed form in asexual unicellular organisms; many things, even in human life, can only be completely understood by forgetting it. We may regard the whole of evolution as flowing from this "chemical imperialism" of living matter. (OP 27)

MEAN, TO

To mean is to intend, and in the use of words there is generally an intention, which is more or less social. When you say "I am hot," you give information, and as a rule you intend to do so. When you give information, you enable your hearer to act with reference to a fact of which he is not directly aware; that is to say, the sounds that he hears stimulate an action, on his part, which is appropriate to an experience that you are having but he is not. (IMT 63)

MEANING

It is common to distinguish two aspects, *meaning* and *denotation*, in such phrases as "the author of Waverley." The meaning will be a certain complex, consisting (at least) of authorship and Waverley with some relation; the denotation will be Scott. (ML 223-4)

When through the law of conditioned reflexes, A has come to

be a cause of C, we will call A an "associative" cause of C, and C an "associative" effect of A. We shall say that, to a given person, the word A, when he hears it, "means" C, if the associative effects of A are closely similar to those of C; and we shall say that the word A, when he utters it, "means" C, if the utterance of A is an associative effect of C, or of something previously associated with C. To put the matter more concretely, the word "Peter" means a certain person if the associated effects of hearing the word "Peter" are closely similar to those of seeing Peter, and the associative causes of uttering the word "Peter" are occurrences previously associated with Peter. Of course as our experience increases in complexity this simple schema becomes obscured and overlaid, but I think it remains fundamentally true. (OP 52)

see LANGUAGE

MEANS

Men who boast of being what is called "practical" are for the most part exclusively preoccupied with means. But theirs is only one-half of wisdom. When we take account of the other half, which is concerned with ends, the economic process and the whole of human life take on an entirely new aspect. (AAI 115)

MEASURE

An instrument is a "measure" of a set of stimuli which are serially ordered when its responses, in all cases where they are relevantly different, are arranged in a series in the same order. (AM 183)

MECHANISTIC OUTLOOK

Perhaps it is not clear what I mean by "the mechanistic outlook." I mean something which exists equally in imperialism, Bolshevism, and the Y.M.C.A.; something which distinguishes all these from the Chinese outlook, and which I, for my part, consider very evil. What I mean is the habit of regarding mankind as raw material, to be molded by our scientific manipulation into whatever form may happen to suit our fancy. (PC 80-1)

MEDIEVAL WORLD

The medieval world, as contrasted with the world of antiquity, is characterized by various forms of dualism. There is the dualism of clergy and laity, the dualism of Latin· and Teuton, the dualism

of the kingdom of God and the kingdoms of this world, the dualism
of the spirit and the flesh. All these are exemplified in the dualism
of Pope and Emperor. (HWP 302)

MEMORY

True memory, which we must now endeavour to understand,
consists of knowledge of past events, but not of all such knowledge.
Some knowledge of past events, for example what we learn through
reading history, is on a par with knowledge we can acquire concerning the future; it is obtained by inference, not (so to speak) spontaneously. (AM 172-3)

The first extension beyond sense-data to be considered is acquaintance by *memory*. It is obvious that we often remember what
we have seen or heard or had otherwise present to our senses, and
that in such cases we are still immediately aware of what we remember, in spite of the fact that it appears as past and not as present.
(PP 76)

MEMORY AS KNOWLEDGE

The kind of memory of which I am now speaking is definite
knowledge of some past event in one's own experience. From time
to time we remember things that have happened to us, because something in the present reminds us of them. Exactly the same present
fact would not call up the same memory if our past experience had
been different. Thus our remembering is caused by—

(1) The present stimulus,

(2) The past occurrence. (AM 82)

MENTAL

My own belief is that the "mental" and the "physical" are not
so disparate as is generally thought. I should define a "mental" occurrence as one which someone knows otherwise than by inference;
the distinction between "mental" and "physical" therefore belongs
to theory of knowledge, not to metaphysics. (HK 209)

The definition of the term "mental" is more difficult, and can
only be satisfactorily given after many difficult controversies have
been discussed and decided. For present purposes therefore I must
content myself with assuming a dogmatic answer to these controversies. I shall call a particular "mental" when it is aware of something,
and I shall call a fact "mental" when it contains a mental particular
as a constituent. (ML 150)
see MIND

MENTAL STUFF

I believe that the stuff of our mental life, as opposed to its relations and structure, consists wholly of sensations and images. (AM 109)

METAPHYSICS
see DISCONTINUITY; LANGUAGE

MICHELSON-MORLEY EXPERIMENT

On the face of it, and apart from hypotheses *ad hoc*, the Michelson-Morley experiment (in conjunction with others) showed that, relatively to the earth, the velocity of light is the same in all directions, and that this is equally true at all times of the year, although the direction of the earth's motion is always changing as it goes round the sun. (ABCR ·33) ·

MILL, JAMES

Mill had become a Radical before he met Bentham; in psychology he was a disciple of Hartley, in economics he accepted Malthus and was a close friend of Ricardo, in politics he was an extreme democrat and a doctrinaire believer in *laissez faire*. He was not an original thinker, but he was clear and vigorous, and had the unquestioning faith of the born disciple, with the disciple's utter contempt for doctrines at variance with the Master's. "I see clearly enough what poor Kant is about," he wrote, after a brief attempt to read that philosopher. Like all his kind, he greatly admired Helvetius, from whom he accepted the current doctrine of the omnipotence of education. (FO 94)

MILL, JOHN STUART
see INDUCTION BY SIMPLE ENUMERATION

MIND

Out of habit, the peculiarities of what we call "mind" can be constructed; a mind is a track of sets of compresent events in a region of space-time where there is matter which is peculiarly liable to form habits. The greater the liability, the more complex and organized the mind becomes. Thus a mind and a brain are not really distinct, but when we speak of a mind we are thinking chiefly of the set of compresent events in the region concerned, and of their several relations to other events forming parts of other periods in the history of the spatio-temporal tube which we are considering, whereas when we speak of the brain we are taking the set of compresent events as a whole, and considering its external relations to other sets of compresent events, also taken as wholes; in a word, we are considering the shape of the tube, not the events of which each cross-section of it is composed. (LA 382)

Thus "mind" and "mental" are merely approximate concepts, giving a convenient shorthand for certain approximate laws. In a completed science, the word "mind" and the word "matter" would both disappear, and would be replaced by causal laws concerning "events", the only events known to us otherwise than in their mathematical and causal properties being percepts, which are events situated in the same region as a brain and having effects of a peculiar sort called "knowledge-reactions." (OP 281)

What is a mind? It is obvious, to begin with, that a mind must be a group of mental events, since we have rejected the view that it is a single simple entity such as the ego was formerly supposed to be. (OP 285)

MIND, ADVOCACY OF THE OPEN

But mankind is so prone to prejudice, party bias, collective hysteria and unthinking acceptance of propaganda, that there is almost always and almost everywhere too little of the open mind, not too much. While, therefore, truth compels me to acknowledge the theoretical limitations of the open mind, in practice I should find it almost always wise to advocate it, since the utmost advocacy is not likely to produce enough of it, and since its absence is one of the chief reasons for the appalling dangers by which, in our age, the human race is beset. (CWA 39)

MIND, CHANGE OF
see MIND, USE OF OPEN

MIND, CLOSED
see MIND, OPEN

MIND, LIFE OF THE

The life of the mind is the life of pursuit of knowledge, from mere childish curiosity up to the greatest efforts of thought. Curiosity exists in animals, and serves an obvious biological purpose; but it is only in men that it passes beyond the investigation of particular objects which may be edible or poisonous, friendly or hostile. Curiosity is the primary impulse out of which the whole edifice of scientific knowledge has grown. (PSR 225)

MIND, LIMITATIONS OF THE OPEN
see MIND, ADVOCACY OF THE OPEN

MIND, OPEN
A completely open mind is either a disease or a pretense; a completely closed mind is a useless assemblage of indefensible prejudices. (CWA 37)

MIND, USE OF OPEN
The right course, whether for an individual or for a nation, is first to think carefully, with a completely open mind, and then having come to a decision, not to reconsider it, unless some very important new fact changes the situation. (CWA 38)

MINORITIES
Where race questions are not involved, a sufficiently determined minority will generally be able to hold its own against the state so far as its own affairs are concerned. It is in the highest degree desirable that this should be possible, and a state which treats minorities ruthlessly is *pro tanto* a bad state. (PIC 200)

MINORITY, GEOGRAPHICAL
There remains, however, a difficult problem, with which any international government will have to deal; I mean, the problem of minorities. This has two forms, according as the minority in question is, or is not, geographically concentrated. When it is, the problem is comparatively simple; it can be met by allowing local autonomy, or virtual independence if necessary, to the minority group. (FOP 11)

MINORITY, NON-GEOGRAPHICAL
The question of minorities that are not geographically concentrated is more difficult. The most prominent example, of course, is that of the Jews. I think the international authority ought to forbid any legal discrimination against any minority group, with the exception of political groups aiming at treason against their national government or against the world federation. (FOP 11)

MISTAKES
By "mistakes" I mean, to begin with, beliefs which are proved

wrong by leading to surprise, as, for instance, that the things one sees in a mirror are "real." If I do not know about radio, I shall think there is a strange man in the house when it is only the news. If you give a savage a box containing a gyrostat, he will think it is bewitched because he cannot turn it round. (RTC 703)

MNEMIC PHENOMENA

Following a suggestion derived from Semon *(Die Mneme*, Leipzig, 1904; 2nd edition, 1908, English translation, Allen & Unwin, 1921; *Die mnemischen Empfindungen,* Leipzig, 1909), we will give the name of "mnemic phenomena" to those responses of an organism which, so far as hitherto observed facts are concerned, can only be brought under causal laws by including past occurrences in the history of the organism as part of the causes of the present response. (AM 78)

MODERATION

The ancients, however, were clearly in the right. In the good life there must be a balance between different activities, and no one of them must be carried so far as to make the others impossible. The gormandizer sacrifices all other pleasures to that of eating, and by so doing diminishes the total happiness of his life. (CH 166)

MODESTY

Modesty is considered a virtue, but for my part I am very doubtful whether, in its more extreme forms, it deserves to be so regarded. Modest people need a great deal of reassuring, and often do not dare to attempt tasks which they are quite capable of performing. Modest people believe themselves to be outshone by those with whom they habitually associate. They are therefore particularly prone to envy, and, through envy, to unhappiness and ill will. For my part, I think there is much to be said for bringing up a boy to think himself a fine fellow. (CH 89)

MONISM
see PLURALISM

MONOPHYSITE HERESY

In 449, after the death of Saint Cyril, a synod at Ephesus tried to carry the triumph further, and thereby fell into the heresy opposite to that of Nestorius; this is called the Monophysite heresy, and maintains that Christ has only one nature. (HWP 369)

MORAL ENDS
see DESIRES

MORAL PRECEPTS, VARIETY OF

When we study in the works of anthropologists the moral precepts which men have considered binding in different times and places we find the most bewildering variety. (SIE 5)

MORAL RULE, SUPREME

The supreme moral rule should, therefore, be: *Act so as to produce harmonious rather than discordant desires.* This rule will apply wherever a man's influence extends: within himself, in his family, his city, his country, even the world as a whole, if he is able to influence it. (OP 234)

MORALITY

On the whole, I think that, speaking philosophically, all acts ought to be judged by their effects; but as this is difficult and uncertain and takes time, it is desirable, in practice, that some kinds of acts should be condemned and others praised without waiting to investigate consequences. I should say, therefore, with the utilitarians, that the right act, in any given circumstances, is that which, on the data, will probably produce the greatest balance of good over evil of all the acts that are possible; but that the performance of such acts may be promoted by the existence of a moral code. (P 246)

MORALITY, CIVIC AND PERSONAL

Throughout recorded history, ethical beliefs have had two very different sources, one political, the other concerned with personal religious and moral convictions. In the Old Testament the two appear quite separately, one as the Law, the other as the Prophets. In the Middle Ages there was the same kind of distinction between the official morality inculcated by the hierarchy and the personal holiness that was taught and practised by the great mystics. This duality of personal and civic morality, which still persists, is one of which any adequate ethical theory must take account. Without civic morality communities perish; without personal morality their survival has no value. Therefore civic and personal morality are equally necessary to a good world. (AAI 110-1)

MORALITY, EFFECTIVENESS OF RULES OF

In seeking a new ethic of sexual behavior, therefore, we must not ourselves be dominated by the ancient irrational passions which gave rise to the old ethic, though we should recognize that they may, by accident, have led to some sound maxims, and that, since they still exist, though perhaps in a weakened form, they are still among the data of our problem. What we have to do positively is to ask ourselves what moral rules are most likely to promote human happiness, remembering always that, whatever the rules may be, they are not likely to be universally observed. That is to say, we have to consider the effect which the rules will in fact have, not that which they would have if they were completely effective. (OSE 39-40)

MORALITY, NEEDED VIRTUES IN
see CHARITY

MORALITY, POSITIVE

In all ages and nations positive morality has consisted almost wholly of prohibitions of various classes of actions, with the addition of a small number of commands to perform certain other actions. (SIE 3)

MORALS, RELATIVITY IN

There is also, in all conventional moralists, a gross ignorance of psychology, making them unable to realize that certain virtues imply certain correlated vices, so that in recommending a virtue the consideration which ought to weigh is: does this virtue, with its correlative vice, outweigh the opposite virtue with its correlative vice? The fact that a virtue is good in itself is not enough; it is necessary to take account of the vices that it entails and the virtues that it excludes. (PIC 161)

MORE'S UTOPIA

More's *Utopia* was in many ways astonishingly liberal. I am not thinking so much of the preaching of communism, which was in the tradition of many religious movements. I am thinking of what is said about war, about religion, and religious toleration, against the wanton killing of animals (there is a most eloquent passage against hunting) and in favour of a mild criminal law. (The book opens with an argument against the death penalty for death.) It must be admitted, however, that life in More's Utopia, as in most others, would be intolerably dull. Diversity is essential to happiness, and in Utopia there is hardly any. This is a defect of all planned social systems, actual as well as imaginary. (HWP 521-2)

MOTION

All motion is relative, and it is a mere convention to take one body as at rest. All such conventions are equally legitimate, though not all are equally convenient. (ABCR 10)

MOTIVES

Nevertheless, it is obvious that there are cases where lying and stealing are justifiable, and the same must be said of murder by those who hold that some wars are righteous. Tolstoy does not judge conduct by its consequences: he considers actions inherently right or wrong. This makes it possible for him to say that no use of force is ever right. But if we judge conduct, as I think we ought, by its power of promoting what we consider a good life or a good society, we cannot expect such simplicity in our moral precepts, and we must expect all of them to be subject to exceptions. (JWT 41)

MOVEMENT, MECHANICAL

see MOVEMENT, VITAL

MOVEMENT, VITAL

The movements of the human body may, none the less, be divided into two classes, which we may call respectively "mechanical" and "vital." As an example of the former, I should give the movement of a man falling from a cliff into the sea. To explain this, in its broad features, it is not necessary to take account of the fact that the man is alive; his centre of gravity moves exactly as that of a stone would move. But when a man climbs up a cliff, he does something that dead matter of the same shape and weight would never do; this is a "vital" movement. (OP 25-6)

MOVEMENTS, MECHANICAL

We may define a movement of an animal's body as "mechanical" when it proceeds as if only dead matter were involved. For example, if you fall over a cliff, you move under the influence of gravitation and your centre of gravity describes just as correct a parabola as if you were already dead. Mechanical movements have not the characteristics of appropriateness, unless by accident, as when a drunken man falls into a waterbutt and is sobered. (AM 46)

MOVEMENTS, VITAL

We may then distinguish "vital" from mechanical movements by the fact that vital movements depend for their causation upon the special properties of the nervous system, while mechanical movements depend only upon the properties which animal bodies share with matter in general. (AM 47)

MYSTICAL ATTITUDE TOWARD LIFE

The mystical attitude is best expressed in the religions of India, although it is also found in Christian mysticism, and in Greek philosophy even before the time of Socrates. It is based almost always on a certain definite experience, the mystical experience. The distinctive feature of the whole thing is emotion. The beliefs it inspires are often bad ones, but the feelings are good ones. (TWW 13)

MYSTICISM

I believe that, when the mystics contrast "reality" with "appearance," the word "reality" has not a logical, but an emotional significance: it means what is, in some sense, important. When it is said that time is "unreal," what should be said is that, in some sense and on some occasions, it is important to conceive the universe as a whole, as the Creator, if He existed, must have conceived it in deciding to create it. When so conceived, all process is within one completed whole: past, present, and future all exist, in some sense, together, and the present does not have that pre-eminent reality which it has to our usual ways of apprehending the world. If this interpretation is accepted, mysticism expresses an emotion, not a fact; it does not assert anything, and therefore can be neither confirmed nor contradicted by science. The fact that mystics do make assertions is owing to their inability to separate emotional importance from scientific validity. It is, of course, not to be expected that they will accept this view, but it is the only one, so far as I can see, which, while admitting something of their claim, is not repugnant to the scientific intelligence. (RAS 194-5)

After Socrates has explained that there is an idea of the good, but not of such things as hair and mud and dirt, Parmenides advises him "not to despise even the meanest things," and this advice shows the genuine scientific temper. It is with this impartial temper that the mystic's apparent insight into a higher reality and a hidden good has to be combined if philosophy is to realize its greatest possibilities. And it is failure in this respect that has made so much of idealistic philosophy thin, lifeless, and insubstantial. It is only in marriage with the world that our ideals can bear fruit: divorced from it, they remain barren. But marriage with the world is not to be achieved by an ideal which shrinks from fact, or demands in advance that the world shall conform to its desires. (ML 7)

Of the reality or unreality of the mystic's world I know nothing.

I have no wish to deny it, nor even to declare that the insight which reveals it is not a genuine insight. What I do wish to maintain and it is here that the scientific attitude becomes imperative—is that insight, untested and unsupported, is an insufficient guarantee of truth, in spite of the fact that much of the most important truth is first suggested by its means. (KEW 21)

MYSTICISM AND SCIENCE

I yet believe that, by sufficient restraint, there is an element of wisdom to be learned from the mystical way of feeling, which does not seem to be attainable in any other manner. If this is the truth, mysticism is to be commended as an attitude towards life, not as a creed about the world. The metaphysical creed, I shall maintain, is a mistaken outcome of the emotion, although this emotion, as colouring and informing all other thoughts and feelings, is the inspirer of whatever is best in Man. Even the cautious and patient investigation of truth by science, which seems the very antithesis of the mystic's swift certainty, may be fostered and nourished by that very spirit of reverence in which mysticism lives and moves. (ML 11-2)

MYSTICISM, GREEK

There was however, in ancient Greece, much that we can feel to have been religion as we understand the term. This was connected, not with the Olympians, but with Dionysus, or Bacchus, whom we think of most naturally as the somewhat disreputable god of wine and drunkenness. The way in which, out of his worship, there arose a profound mysticism, which greatly influenced many of the philosophers, and even had a part in shaping Christian theology, is very remarkable, and must be understood by anyone who wishes to study the development of Greek thought. (HWP 14)

N

NAME

. . . a *name*, which is a simple symbol, directly designating an individual which is its meaning, and having this meaning in its own right, independently of the meaning of all other words. (IMP 174)

NAME, PROPER

To speak for the moment in terms of physics, we give proper names to certain continuous stretches of space-time, such as Socrates, France, or the moon. In former days, it would have been said that we give a proper name to a substance or collection of substances, but now we have to find a different phrase to express the object of a proper name. (IMT 38)

NAMES, GENERAL

Passing on from proper names, we come next to general names, such as "man," "cat," "triangle." A word such as "man" means a whole class of such collections of particulars as have proper names. The several members of the class are assembled together in virtue of some similarity or common property. (AM 194)

NAMES, PROPER

We are thus led to the conception of terms which, when they occur in propositions, can *only* occur as subjects, and never in any other way. This is part of the old scholastic definition of *substance*; but persistence through time, which belonged to that notion, forms no part of the notion with which we are concerned. We shall define "proper names" as those terms which can only occur as *subjects* in propositions (using "subject" in the extended sense just explained). (IMP 142)

NAMES, THEORY OF

The theory of names has been neglected, because its importance is only evident to the logician, and to him names can remain purely hypothetical, since no proposition of logic can contain any actual name. For theory of knowledge, however, it is important to know what sort of objects can have names, assuming that there are names. (IMT 119-120)

NAPOLEON

In Germany, feeling about Napoleon was more divided. There were those who, like Heine, saw him as the mighty missionary of liberalism, the destroyer of serfdom, the enemy of legitimacy; the man who made hereditary princelings tremble; there were others who saw him as Antichrist, the would-be destroyer of the noble German nation, the immoralist who had proved once for all that Teutonic virtue can only be preserved by unquenchable hatred of France. Bismarck effected a synthesis: Napoleon remained Antichrist, but an Antichrist to be imitated, not merely to be abhorred. Nietzsche, who accepted the compromise, remarked with ghoulish joy that the classical age of war is coming, and that we owe this boon, not to the French Revolution, but to Napoleon. And in this way nationalism, Satanism, and hero-worship, the legacy of Byron, became part of the complex soul of Germany. (HWP 751-2)
see DICTATORSHIP

NATION

What constitutes a nation is a sentiment and an instinct, a sentiment of similarity and an instinct of belonging to the same group or herd. (PI 148)

NATION, A

see NATIONALISM

NATIONALISM

The inevitable outcome of the doctrine that each nation should have unrestricted sovereignty is to compel the citizens of each nation to engage in irksome activities and to incur sacrifices, often of life itself, in order to thwart the designs of other nations. (FAG 258)

Nationalism is a development of herd-instinct; it is the habit of taking as one's herd the nation to which one belongs. As to what constitutes a nation, the only thing that can be said definitely is that a nation is a group which is defined geographically. (PIC 16)

Nationalism, in theory, is the doctrine that men, by their sympathies and traditions, form natural groups, called "nations," each of which ought to be united under one central Government. (PSR 27) *see* PATRIOTISM, TRUE

NATURAL LAW ARGUMENT
see GOD

NEEDS, OUR AGE'S
There are certain things that our age needs, and certain things that it should avoid. It needs compassion and a wish that mankind should be happy; it needs the desire for knowledge and the determination to eschew pleasant myths; it needs, above all, courageous hope and the impulse to creativeness. The things that it must avoid and that have brought it to the brink of catastrophe are cruelty, envy, greed, competitiveness, search for irrational subjective certainty, and what Freudians call the death wish. (ISOS 59)

NESTORIANISM
Saint Cyril was pained to learn that Constantinople was being led astray by the teaching of its patriarch Nestorius, who maintained that there were two persons in Christ, one human and one divine. On this ground Nestorius objected to the new practice of calling the Virgin "Mother of God"; she was, he said, only the mother of the human Person, while the divine Person, who was God, had no mother. (HWP 368)

NEUTRAL-MONISM
I shall try to persuade you in the course of these lectures that matter is not so material and mind not so mental as is generally supposed. When we are speaking of matter, it will seem as if we were inclining to idealism; when we are speaking of mind, it will seem as if we were inclining to materialism. Neither is the truth. Our world is to be constructed out of what the American realists call "neutral" entities which have neither the hardness and indestructibility of matter, nor the reference to objects which is supposed to characterize mind. (AM 36)

NEUTRAL STUFF
To show that the traditional separation between physics and psychology, mind and matter, is not metaphysically defensible, will be one of the purposes of this work; but the two will be brought

together, not by subordinating either to the other, but by displaying each as a logical structure composed of what, following Dr. H. M. Sheffer, we shall call "neutral stuff." We shall not contend that there are demonstrative grounds in favour of this construction, but only that it is recommended by the usual scientific ground of economy and comprehensiveness of theoretical explanation. (AOM 10)

NEWTON

Newton (1642-1727) achieved the final and complete triumph for which Copernicus, Kepler, and Galileo had prepared the way. Starting from his three laws of motion—of which the first two are due to Galileo—he proved that Kepler's three laws are equivalent to the proposition that every planet, at every moment, has an acceleration towards the sun which varies inversely as the square of the distance from the sun. He showed that accelerations towards the earth and the sun, following the same formula, explain the moon's motion, and that the acceleration of falling bodies on the earth's surface is again related to that of the moon according to the inverse square law. He defined "force" as the change of motion, i.e., of acceleration. He was thus able to enunciate his law of universal gravitation: "Every body attracts every other with a force directly proportional to the product of their masses, and inversely proportional to the square of the distance between them." From this formula he was able to deduce everything in planetary theory: the motions of the planets and their satellites, the orbits of comets, the tides. It appeared later that even the minute departures from elliptical orbits on the part of the planets were deducible from Newton's law. The triumph was so complete that Newton was in danger of becoming another Aristotle, and imposing an insuperable barrier to progress. In England, it was not till a century after his death that men freed themselves from his authority sufficiently to do important original work in the subjects of which he had treated. (HWP 535)
see SCIENCE, PROGRESS OF

NIETZSCHE

Nietzsche (1844-1900) regarded himself, rightly, as the successor of Schopenhauer, to whom, however, he is superior in many ways, particularly in the consistency and coherence of his doctrine. Schopenhauer's oriental ethic of renunciation seems out of harmony with his metaphysic of the omnipotence of will; in Nietzsche, the will has ethical as well as metaphysical primacy. Nietzsche, though a professor, was a literary rather than an academic philosopher. He invented no new technical theories in ontology or epistemology; his importance is primarily in ethics, and secondarily as an acute historical critic. (HWP 760)

'NINETIES, THE

But in the 'nineties young men desired something more sweeping and passionate, more bold and less bland. The impulse towards destruction and violence which has swept over the world began in the sphere of literature. Ibsen, Strindberg, and Nietzsche were angry men—not primarily angry about this or that, but just angry. And so they each found an outlook on life that justified anger. The young admired their passion, and found in it an outlet for their own feelings of revolt against parental authority. The assertion of freedom seemed sufficiently noble to justify violence; the violence duly ensued, but freedom was lost in the process. (MRR 8)

NOMINALISM
see REALISM

NONE
see ALL

NON-VIOLENCE

The doctrine of non-violence, which has been practised on a large scale in India, can be defended on other than religious grounds. In certain circumstances, it is the best practical policy. These circumstances arise when one party is unarmed but resolute, while the opposing party is armed but irresolute. Killing people who do not resist is a disgusting business, and decent men will yield much, rather than persist in it. But when the enemy is resolute and brutal the method has no success. The Church persecuted heretics and Jews relentlessly, even when they made no attempt at armed resistance. The Japanese, if they conquered India, would make short work of any movement of non-cooperation on the part of Gandhi's followers. Absolute pacifism, therefore, as a method of gaining your ends, is subject to very severe limitations. (FOB 7-8)

NOW
see HERE

NULL-CLASS

The number 0 is the number of terms in a class which has no members, i.e. in the class which is called the "null-class." (IMP 23)

NUMBER

A number is anything which is the number of some class. Such a definition has a verbal appearance of being circular, but in fact it is not. We define "the number of a given class" without using the notion of number in general; therefore we may define number in general in terms of "the number of a given class" without committing any logical error. (IMP 19)

NUMBER, ATOMIC

By means of the periodic law, the elements are placed in a series, beginning with hydrogen and ending with uranium. Counting the four gaps, there are ninety-two places in the series. What is called the "atomic number" of an element is simply its place in this series. (ABCA 18)

NUMBER, ORDINAL

An "ordinal" number means the relation-number of a well-ordered series. It is thus a species of serial number. (IMP 93)

NUMBERS, INDUCTIVE

We may *define* the "inductive" numbers as *all those that possess all inductive properties;* they will be the same as what are called the "natural" numbers, i.e. the ordinary finite whole numbers. To all such numbers, proofs by mathematical induction can be validly applied. They are those numbers, we may loosely say, which can be reached from 0 by successive additions of 1; in other words, they are all the numbers that can be reached by counting. (KEW 214)

NUMBERS, NATURAL

The "natural numbers" are the posterity of 0 with respect to the relation "immediate predecessor" (which is the converse of "successor"). (IMP 22-3)
see NUMBERS, INDUCTIVE

NUMBERS, NON-INDUCTIVE (INFINITE)

But beyond all these numbers (inductive), there are the infinite numbers, and infinite numbers do not have all inductive properties. Such numbers, therefore, may be called non-inductive. All those properties of numbers which are proved by an imaginary step-by-step process from one number to the next are liable to fail when we come to infinite numbers. The first of the infinite numbers has no immediate predecessor, because there is no greatest finite number. (KEW 214)

NUMBERS, SERIES OF NATURAL

Probably only a person with some mathematical knowledge would think of beginning with 0 instead of with 1, but we will presume this degree of knowledge; we will take as our starting point the series:

$$0, 1, 2, 3, \ldots .n, n + 1, \ldots .$$

and it is this series that we shall mean when we speak of the "series of natural numbers." (IMP 3)

O

OATHS

American legislation has always had a surprising belief in the efficiency of oaths. For many decades it has been impossible for an alien to obtain a United States visa until he had sworn that his purpose in visiting America was not the assassination of the President. It was, apparently, assumed that any man who had this purpose would, of course, avow it honestly. (TDF 44)

OBJECT, PHYSICAL

The real table, if it exists, we will call a "physical object." (PP 18)

OBJECT-WORD

An *object-word* is a class of similar noises or utterances such that, from habit, they have become associated with a class of mutually similar occurrences frequently experienced at the same time as one of the noises or utterances in question. (IMT 92)

OBJECT-WORDS

see LANGUAGE, PRIMARY OR OBJECT

OBJECTIVITY

When two people simultaneously have percepts which they regard as belonging to one group, if the inferences of the one differ from those of the other, one of them at least must be drawing false inferences, and must therefore have an element of subjectivity in his perception. It is only where the inferences of the two observers agree that both perceptions may be objective. It will be seen that, according to this view, the objectivity of a perception does not depend only upon what it is in itself, but also upon the experience of the percipient. (AOM 223)

see SUBJECTIVITY

OCCAM'S RAZOR

. . . . . the maxim which inspires all scientific philosophizing, namely "Occam's razor": *Entities are not to be multiplied without necessity.* In other words, in dealing with any subject-matter, find out what entities are undeniably involved, and state everything in terms of these entities. (KEW 113)

Occam is best known for a maxim which is not to be found in his works, but has acquired the name of "Occam's razor." This maxim says: "Entities are not to be multiplied without necessity." Although he did not say this, he said something which has much the same effect, namely: "It is vain to do with more what can be done with fewer." That is to say, if everything in some science can be interpreted without assuming this or that hypothetical entity, there is no ground for assuming it. I have myself found this a most fruitful principle in logical analysis. (HWP 472)

OCCURRENCE, REPRESENTATIONAL
see REFERENCE, EXTERNAL

OEDIPUS COMPLEX

I do not believe that there is, except in rare morbid cases, an "Oedipus Complex", in the sense of a special attraction of sons to mothers and daughters to fathers. The excessive influence of the parent, where it exists, will belong to the parent who has had most to do with the child—generally the mother—without regard to the difference of sex. Of course, it may happen that a daughter who dislikes her mother and sees little of her father will idealize the latter; but in that case the influence is exerted by dreams, not by the actual father. Idealization consists of hanging hopes to a peg; the peg is merely convenient, and has nothing to do with the nature of the hopes. Undue parental influence is quite a different thing from this, since it is connected with the actual person, not with an imaginary portrait. (EEC 190-1)

OLIGARCHY

The natural successor to absolute monarchy is oligarchy. But oligarchy may be of many sorts; it may be the rule of a hereditary aristocracy, of the rich, or of a church or political party. These produce very different results. A hereditary landed aristocracy is apt to be conservative, proud, stupid, and rather brutal; for these reasons among others, it is always worsted in a struggle with the higher bourgeoisie. A government of the rich prevailed in all the free cities of the Middle Ages, and survived in Venice until Napoleon extinguished it. Such governments have been, on the whole, more enlightened and astute than any others known to history. Venice, in particular, steered a prudent course through centuries of complicated intrigue, and had a diplomatic service far more efficient than that of any other State. (P 186-7)

OMNISCIENCE, FIRST-ORDER AND LIMITED FIRST-ORDER

Let us give the name "first-order omniscience" to knowledge of the truth or falsehood of every sentence not containing general words. "Limited first-order omniscience" will mean similar complete knowledge concerning all sentences of a certain form, say the form "x is human." (HK 133)

ONTOLOGICAL ARGUMENT

The ontological argument will be unsound, and God's existence itself, being contingent, must have a sufficient reason which inclines without necessitating. But if this be required, we might just as well admit the preestablished harmony as an ultimate fact, since the assumption of God's existence is insufficient for its explanation. (PL 188-9)

see ANSELM

ONTOLOGICAL ARGUMENT, LATER HISTORY OF THE

This argument has never been accepted by theologians. It was adversely criticized at the time; then it was forgotten till the latter half of the thirteenth century. Thomas Aquinas rejected it, and among theologians his authority has prevailed ever since. But among philosophers it has had a better fate. Descartes revived it in a somewhat amended form; Leibniz thought that it could be made valid by the addition of a supplement to prove that God is *possible*. Kant considered that he had demolished it once for all. Nevertheless, in some sense, it underlies the system of Hegel, and his followers, and reappears in Bradley's principle: "What may be and must be, is." (HWP 417)

OPEN-MINDEDNESS

But since our intellectual life is only a part of our activity, and since curiosity is perpetually coming into conflict with other passions, there is need of certain intellectual virtues, such as open-mindedness. We become impervious to new truth both from habit and from desire: we find it hard to disbelieve what we have emphatically believed for a number of years, and also what ministers to self-esteem or any other fundamental passion. Open-mindedness should therefore be one of the qualities that education aims at producing. (EEC 77)

OPINION, FEAR OF PUBLIC

As a matter of fact, any man who can obviously afford a car but genuinely prefers travel or a good library will in the end be much more respected than if he behaved exactly like every one else. There is of course no point in deliberately flouting public opinion; this is still to be under its domination, though in a topsy-turvy way. But to be genuinely indifferent to it is both a strength and a source of happiness. (CH 136-7)

OPINION, FREEDOM OF

I admit, the issue of academic freedom is not in itself of the first magnitude. But it is part and parcel of the same battle. Let it be remembered that what is at stake, in the greatest issues as well as in those that seem smaller, is the freedom of the individual human spirit to express its beliefs and hopes for mankind, whether they be shared by many or by few or none. New hopes, new beliefs, and new thoughts are at all times necessary to mankind, and it is not out of a dead uniformity that they can be expected to arise. (FAC 33)

If I had considered only my own interests and inclinations I should have retired at once. But however wise such action might have been from a personal point of view, it would also, in my judgment, have been cowardly and selfish. A great many people who realized that their own interests and the principles of toleration and free speech were at stake were anxious from the first to continue the controversy. If I had retired I should have robbed them of their *casus belli* and tacitly assented to the proposition that substantial groups shall be allowed to drive out of public office individuals whose opinions, race, or nationality they find repugnant. This to me would appear immoral. (LBRC April 26, 1940)

OPINION, PROBABLE
see TRUTH

OPINION, SCIENTIFIC AND UNSCIENTIFIC

A scientific opinion is one which there is some reason to believe true; an unscientific opinion is one which is held for some reason other than its probable truth. (SO 15)

OPINION, UNIFORMITY OF

Uniformity in the opinions expressed by teachers is not only not to be sought, but is, if possible, to be avoided, since diversity of opinion among preceptors is essential to any sound education. No man can pass as educated who has heard only one side on questions as to which the public is divided. (FAC 27)

OPPRESSED, VIRTUE OF THE

As appears from the various instances that we have considered, the stage in which superior virtue is attributed to the oppressed is transient and unstable. It begins only when the oppressors come to have a bad conscience, and this only happens when their power is no longer secure. The idealizing of the victim is useful for a time: if virtue is the greatest of goods, and if subjection makes people virtuous, it is kind to refuse them power, since it would destroy their virtue. If it is difficult for a rich man to enter the kingdom of heaven, it is a noble act on his part to keep his wealth and so imperil his eternal bliss for the benefit of his poorer brethren. It was a fine self-sacrifice on the part of men to relieve women of the dirty work of politics. And so on. But sooner or later the oppressed class will argue that its superior virtue is a reason in favor of its having power, and the oppressors will find their own weapons turned against them. (UE 63)

OPTIMISM
see PESSIMISM

OR

But how about "or?" You cannot show a child examples of it in the sensible world. You can say: "Will you have pudding or pie?" but if the child says yes, you cannot find a nutriment which is "pudding-or-pie." And yet "or" has a relation to experience; it is related to the experience of choice. But in choice we have before us two possible courses of action, that is to say, two actual thoughts as to courses of action. These thoughts may not involve explicit sentences, but no change is made in what is essential if we suppose them to be explicit. Thus "or", as an element of experience, presupposes sentences, or something mental related in a similar manner to some other fact. (IMT 89)

ORDER, CYCLIC

Cyclic order, such as that of the points on a circle, cannot be generated by means of three-term relations of "between." We need a relation of four terms, which may be called "separation of couples." The point may be illustrated by considering a journey round the world. One may go from England to New Zealand by way of Suez or by way of San Francisco; we cannot say definitely that either of these two places is "between" England and New Zealand. But if a man chooses that route to go round the world, whichever way round he goes, his times in England and New Zealand are separated from each other by his times in Suez and San Francisco, and conversely. (IMP 40-1)

ORGANIZATION

To a rational mind, the question is not: Do we want organization or do we not? The question is: How much organization do we want, and where and when and of what kind? In spite of a temperamental leaning to anarchism, I am persuaded that an industrial world cannot maintain itself against internal disruptive forces without a great deal more organization than we have at present. (I 28-9)

ORGANIZATIONS

Force is no more admirable in the economic sphere than in dealings between states. In order to secure the maximum of freedom with the minimum of force, the universal principle is: *Autonomy within each politically important group, and a neutral authority for deciding questions involving relations between groups.* The neutral authority should, of course, rest on a democratic basis, but should, if possible, represent a constituency wider than that of the groups concerned. (PI 99)

ORGANIZATIONS, NEEDED
see CHARITY

ORPHICS

Whatever may have been the teaching of Orpheus (if he existed), the teaching of the Orphics is well known. They believed in the transmigration of souls; they taught that the soul hereafter might achieve eternal bliss or suffer eternal or temporary torment according to its way of life here on earth. They aimed at becoming "pure," partly by ceremonies of purification, partly by avoiding certain kinds of contamination. The most orthodox among them abstained from animal food, except on ritual occasions when they ate it sacramentally. (HWP 17)

ORTHODOXY

Orthodoxy is the grave of intelligence, no matter what orthodoxy it may be. And in this respect the orthodoxy of the radical is no better than that of the reactionary. (ESO 21)

OWEN, ROBERT

In other respects, however, there is still a very great deal to be said for Owen's parallelograms. Unlike his contemporaries, he did not think of life in terms of profit and loss; he remembered beauty, the cultivation of the senses and the intellect, and, above all children. In a communal life such as he planned, it is possible to have all the beauty of the Oxford and Cambridge Colleges; it is possible to have space, fine public rooms, freedom for children's work and play. All these things the family individualism to which we are accustomed makes impossible. It is only by combination that men who are not richer than any one should be can escape from squalor and enjoy the aesthetic delights belonging to spacious architecture and an abundance of air and sunshine. For children the modern urban world is a prison, unless they are poor enough to be allowed to play in the streets, and even then it is unhealthy and dangerous. Owen would have provided for important needs which are overlooked in an individualistic and competitive world. (FO 166)

OWNERSHIP, PUBLIC

I think the great difficulty of perfect control without public ownership—at least as I have seen it in Europe—is that it lands you in corruption; that it gives very rich men an enormous motive for corrupting the politician. (TEP 8)

P

PACIFISM, ABSOLUTE-LIMITS OF
see NON-VIOLENCE

PACIFISM, RELATIVE

"Relative Pacifism" is the doctrine that *very few* wars are worth fighting, and that the evils of war are *almost* always greater than they seem to excited populations at the moment when war breaks out. The doctrine may go further, and urge that a civilized and humane way of life can hardly survive where wars are frequent and serious. On this ground, the relative pacifist will urge, it is of immeasurable importance to create machinery that will diminish the likelihood of great wars. (FOP 8)

PACIFISM, RELATIVE POLITICAL

In considering the future of pacifism, we must distinguish according to the kind of pacifism concerned. I think myself that the most useful kind of pacifism, and also the one most likely to become influential, is relative political pacifism. (FOP 8)

PACIFIST, INDIVIDUAL

There is another important distinction, namely, that between individual and political pacifism. The individual pacifist says: No matter what my government may command, I myself will not fight. The political pacifist, on the contrary, is concerned to keep his government out of war. (FOP 8)

PACIFIST, POLITICAL
see PACIFIST, INDIVIDUAL

PARALLELISM, PSYCHO-PHYSICAL

The modern doctrine of psycho-physical parallelism is not appreciably different from this theory of the Cartesian school. Psycho-physical parallelism is the theory that mental and physical events each have causes in their own sphere, but run on side by side owing to the fact that every state of the brain coexists with a definite state of the mind, and vice versa. This view of the reciprocal causal independence of mind and matter has no basis except in metaphysical theory. (AM 35)

PARENTHOOD, HAPPINESS OF

For my own part, speaking personally, I have found the happiness of parenthood greater than any other that I have experienced. I believe that when circumstances lead men or women to forego this happiness, a very deep need remains ungratified, and that this produces a dissatisfaction and listlessness of which the cause may remain quite unknown. To be happy in this world, especially when youth is past, it is necessary to feel oneself not merely an isolated individual whose day will soon be over, but part of the stream of life flowing on from the first germ to the remote and unknown future. (CH 198)

PARMENIDES

What makes Parmenides historically important is that he invented a form of metaphysical argument that, in one form or another, is to be found in most subsequent metaphysicians down to and including Hegel. He is often said to have invented logic, but what he really invented was metaphysics based on logic. (HWP 48)

PAROCHIALISM

Our age is the most parochial since Homer. I speak not of any geographical parish: the inhabitants of Mudcombe-in-the-Meer are more aware than at any former time of what is being done and thought at Praha, at Gorki, or at Peiping. It is in the chronological sense that we are parochial: as the new names conceal the historic cities of Prague, Nijni-Novgorod, and Pekin, so new catchwords hide from us the thoughts and feelings of our ancestors, even when they differed little from our own. (UE 65)

PARTICULAR
see UNIVERSAL

PARTICULAR, BIOGRAPHY OF A

The sum-total of all the particulars that are (directly) either simultaneous with or before or after a given particular may be defined as the "biography" to which that particular belongs. (ML 141)

PARTICULARS

The definition of "particulars" is as follows: among sentences

containing no apparent variables or logical words (which we may call "atomic" sentences) there are words of two kinds. Some can only occur in atomic sentences of one certain form, others can occur in atomic sentences of any form. (The "form" of a sentence is the class of significant sentences derived from it by changing some or all of its component words.) The latter are called "proper names," and the objects they designate are called "particulars." A particular is part of the "stuff" of a mind if its name can occur in a sentence giving a datum for psychology. In the above I assume a syntactically correct language. At various points what has just been said needs amplification, but it may serve to indicate what I mean by "stuff." I think there could be a less linguistic definition of "particulars," but it would be difficult to make it precise. (RTC 698)
see INDIVIDUALS; MATTER

PASSIONS, COLLECTIVE

Men's collective passions are mainly evil; far the strongest of them are hatred and rivalry directed towards other groups. Therefore at present all that gives men power to indulge their collective passions is bad. That is why science threatens to cause the destruction of civilization. The only solid hope seems to lie in the possibility of world-wide domination by one group, say the United States, leading to the gradual foundation of an orderly economic and political world-government. (I 63)

PATRIOTISM, EXCESSIVE

But there are many good things in the world which are not American—for instance, Chinese art—and there are even some bad things which are American. It is impossible for a bystander not to feel a shiver of alarm when he encounters exaggerations of national pride such as those which I have quoted. Patriotism which has the quality of intoxication is a danger not only to its native land but to the world, and "My country never wrong" is an even more dangerous maxim than "My country, right or wrong." (CAB 58)

PATRIOTISM, TRUE

Those of us who do not wish to see our whole civilization go down in red ruin have a great and difficult duty to perform—to guard the door of our minds against patriotism. I mean, that we should view impartially any dispute between our own country and another, that we should teach ourselves not to believe our own country morally superior to others, and that even in time of war we should view the whole matter as a neutral might view it. This is part of the larger duty of pursuing truth; nationalism cannot survive without false beliefs. If we can learn to serve truth, to be truthful in our thoughts, to avoid the flattering myths in which we like to disguise our passions, we shall have done what we can to save our world from disaster. For this creed it is worth-while to suffer, and indeed those who have it must suffer, for persecution is as bitter as in the days of the Spanish Inquisition. But in the very suffering there is happiness, and a promise of better things in the time to come. (PNW 12)

PEACE

Our own planet, in which philosophers are apt to take a parochial and excessive interest, was once too hot to support life, and will in time be too cold. After ages during which the earth produced harmless trilobites and butterflies, evolution progressed to the point at which it generated Neros, Genghis Khans, and Hitlers. This, however, is a passing nightmare; in time the earth will become again incapable of supporting life, and peace will return. (UE 9)

PEACE, PSYCHOLOGY OF

The problem of making peace with our anarchic impulses is one which has been too little studied, but one which becomes more and more imperative as scientific technique advances. From the purely biological point of view it is unfortunate that the destructive side of technique has advanced so very much more rapidly than the creative side. (AAI 24)

PELAGIANISM

Pelagius was a Welshman, whose real name was Morgan, which means "man of the sea," as "Pelagius" does in Greek. He was a cultivated and agreeable ecclesiastic, less fanatical than many of his contemporaries. He believed in free will, questioned the doctrine of original sin, and thought that, when men act virtuously, it is by virtue of their own moral effort. If they act rightly, and are orthodox, they go to heaven as a reward for their virtues . . . These views, though they may now seem commonplace, caused, at the time, a great commotion, and were, through Saint Augustine's efforts, declared heretical. (HWP 364)

PERCEIVING

Since the stimulus differs for different observers, the reaction also differs; consequently, in all our perceptions of physical processes there is an element of subjectivity. If, therefore, physics is true in its broad outlines (as the above argument supposes), what we call "perceiving" a physical process is something private and subjective, at least in part, and is yet the only possible starting-point for our knowledge of the physical world. (OP 130)

PERCEPTION

In our environment it frequently happens that events occur together in bundles—such bundles as distinguish a cat from another kind of object. Any one of our senses may be affected by a stimulus arising from some characteristic of the bundle in question. Let us suppose the stimulus to be visual. Then physics allows us to infer that light of certain frequencies is proceeding from the object to our eyes. Induction allows us to infer that this pattern of light, which, we will suppose, looks like a cat, probably proceeds from a region in which the other properties of cats are also present. Up to a point, we can test this hypothesis by experiment: we can touch the cat, and pick it up by the tail to see if it mews. Usually the experiment succeeds; when it does not, its failure is easily accounted for without modifying the laws of physics. (It is in this respect that physics is superior to ignorant common sense.) But all this elaborate work of induction, in so far as it belongs to common sense rather than science, is performed spontaneously by habit, which transforms the mere sensation into a perceptive experience. Broadly speaking, a perceptive experience is a dogmatic belief in what physics and induction show to be probable; it is wrong in its dogmatism, but *usually* right in its content. (IMT 152)

When a mental occurrence can be regarded as an appearance of an object external to the brain, however irregular, or even as a confused appearance of several such objects, then we may regard it as having for its stimulus the object or objects in question, or their appearances at the sense-organ concerned. When, on the other hand, a mental occurrence has not sufficient connection with objects external to the brain to be regarded as an appearance of such objects, then its physical causation (if any) will have to be sought in the brain. In the former case it can be called a perception; in the latter it cannot be so called. But the distinction is one of

degree, not of kind. Until this is realized, no satisfactory theory of perception, sensation, or imagination is possible. (AM 136)
see SENSATION

PERCEPTION, NON-SENSATIONAL ELEMENTS IN

When we perceive any object of a familiar kind, much of what appears subjectively to be immediately given is really derived from past experience. When we see an object, say a penny, we seem to be aware of its "real" shape: we have the impression of something circular, not of something elliptical. In learning to draw, it is necessary to acquire the art of representing things according to the sensation, not according to the perception. And the visual appearance is filled out with feeling of what the object would be like to touch, and so on. (AM 81)

PERCEPTIVE PREMISSES

Speaking psychologically, a "perceptive premiss" may be defined as a belief caused, as immediately as possible, by a percept. If I believe there *will be* an eclipse because the astronomers say so, my belief is not a perceptive premiss; if I believe there *is* an eclipse because I see it, that is a perceptive premiss. (IMT 168)

PERCEPTS AND PHYSICS

The gulf between percepts and physics is not a gulf as regards intrinsic quality, for we know nothing of the intrinsic quality of the physical world, and therefore do not know whether it is, or is not, very different from that of percepts. The gulf is as to what we know about the two realms. We know the quality of percepts, but we do not know their laws so well as we could wish. We know the laws of the physical world, in so far as these are mathematical, pretty well, but we know nothing else about it. If there is any intellectual difficulty in supposing that the physical world is intrinsically quite unlike that of percepts, this is a reason for supposing that there is not this complete unlikeness. And there is a certain ground for such a view, in the fact that percepts are part of the physical world, and are the only part that we can know without the help of rather elaborate and difficult inferences. (AOM 264)

PERFECTION

I do not imagine that mankind can be made perfect; whatever may be done, some defects will survive, but a great many of the defects from which adults suffer are due to preventable mistakes in their education, and the most important of these mistakes is the inculcation of fear. (EDTF 219)

PERSPECTIVE
see PHYSICAL OBJECT

PERSPECTIVE, HISTORICAL

The military superiority of Europe to Asia is not an eternal law of nature, as we are tempted to think; and our superiority in civilization is a mere delusion. Our histories, which treat the Mediterranean as the center of the universe, give quite a wrong perspective. (PC 22)

PERSPECTIVE, INDIVIDUAL

For those to whom dogmatic religion can no longer bring comfort, there is need of some substitute, if life is not to become dusty and harsh and filled with trivial self-assertion. The world at present is full of angry self-centered groups, each incapable of viewing human life as a whole, each willing to destroy civilization rather than yield an inch. To this narrowness no amount of technical instruction will provide an antidote. The antidote, in so far as it is matter of individual psychology, is to be found in history, biology, astronomy, and all those studies which, without destroying self-respect, enable the individual to see himself in his proper perspective. (IPI 52)

PERSPECTIVES

The system consisting of all views of the universe perceived and unperceived, I shall call the system of "perspectives"; I shall confine the expression "private worlds" to such views of the universe as are actually perceived. Thus a "private world" is a perceived "perspective"; but there may be any number of unperceived perspectives. (KEW 93)

PESSIMISM

From a scientific point of view, optimism and pessimism are alike objectionable: optimism assumes, or attempts to prove, that the universe exists to please us, and pessimism that it exists to displease us. Scientifically, there is no evidence that it is concerned with us either one way or the other. The belief in either pessimism or optimism is a matter of temperament, not of reason. (HWP 759)

PHENOMENALISM

Intermediate between solipsism and the ordinary scientific view, there is a half-way house called "phenomenalism." This admits events other than those which I experience, but holds that all of them are percepts or other mental events. Practically, it means, when advocated by scientific men, that they will accept the testimony of other observers as to what they have actually experienced, but that they will not infer thence anything which no observer has experienced. It may be said, in justification of this position, that, while it employs analogy and induction, it refrains from assuming causality. But it may be doubted whether it can really abstain from causality. (AOM 399)

PHILO

The philosopher Philo, who was a contemporary of Christ, is the best illustration of Greek influence on the Jews in the sphere of thought. While orthodox in religion, Philo is, in philosophy, primarily a Platonist; other important influences are those of the Stoics and Neo-pythagoreans. While his influence among the Jews ceased after the fall of Jerusalem, the Christian Fathers found that he had shown the way to reconcile Greek philosophy with acceptance of the Hebrew Scriptures. (HWP 322)

PHILOSOPHER, STUDYING A

In studying a philosopher, the right attitude is neither reverence nor contempt, but first a kind of hypothetical sympathy, until it is possible to know what it feels like to believe in his theories, and only a revival of the critical attitude, which should resemble, as far as possible, the state of mind of a person abandoning opinions which he has hitherto held. (HWP 39)

PHILOSOPHERS

Most philosophers are extraordinarily dry and very dull; Descartes is neither dry nor dull, and that is very largely because he doesn't confine himself to strict logic, but puts in picturesque material of a biographical sort. (DDM 93)

PHILOSOPHERS, CHARACTERIZING

In attempting to characterize philosophers, no uniform method should be adopted. The method, in each case, should be such as to exhibit what the philosopher himself thinks important, and what, in the opinion of the critic, makes him worthy of study. (POS 453)

PHILOSOPHIC SPIRIT

A man imbued with the philosophic spirit, whether a professional philosopher or not, will wish his beliefs to be as true as he can make them, and will, in equal measure, love to know, and hate to be in error. This principle has a wider scope than may be apparent at first sight. (UE 30)

PHILOSOPHY

My purpose is to exhibit philosophy as an integral part of social and political life; not as the isolated speculations of remarkable individuals, but as both an effect and a cause of the character of the various communities in which different systems flourished. (HWP ix)

Philosophy, as I shall understand the word, is something intermediate between theology and science. Like theology, it consists of speculations on matters as to which definite knowledge has, so far, been unascertainable; but like science, it appeals to human reason rather than to authority, whether that of tradition or that of revelation. All *definite* knowledge—so I should contend—belongs to science; all *dogma* as to what surpasses definite knowledge belongs to theology. But between theology and science there is a No Man's Land, exposed to attack from both sides; this No Man's Land is philosophy. (HWP xiii)

Philosophy, as opposed to science, springs from a kind of self-assertion: a belief that our purposes have an important relation to the purpose of the universe, and that, in the long run, the course of events is bound to be, on the whole, such as we should wish. Science abandoned this kind of optimism, but is being led towards another: that we, by our intelligence, can make the world such as to satisfy a large proportion of our desires. This is a practical, as opposed to a metaphysical, optimism. I hope it will not seem to future generations as foolish as that of Dr. Pangloss. (UE 56-7)

Philosophy should be comprehensive, and should be bold in suggesting hypotheses as to the universe which science is not yet in a position to confirm or confute. But these should always be presented *as* hypotheses, not (as is too often done) as immutable certainties like the dogmas of religion. Although, moreover, comprehensive construction is part of the business of philosophy, I do not believe it is the most important part. The most important part, to my mind, consists in criticizing and clarifying notions which are apt to be regarded as fundamental and accepted uncritically. (LA 379)

The value of philosophy is, in fact, to be sought largely in its very uncertainty. The man who has no tincture of philosophy goes through life imprisoned in the prejudices derived from common sense, from the habitual beliefs of his age or his nation and from convictions which have grown up in his mind without the co-operation or consent of his deliberate reason. To such a man the world tends to become definite, finite, obvious; common objects rouse no questions, and unfamiliar possibilities are contemptuously rejected. As soon as we begin to philosophise, on the contrary, we find, as we saw in our opening chapters, that even the most everyday things lead to problems to which only very incomplete answers can be given. (PP 242-3)

PHILOSOPHY, AIMS OF

Philosophy has had from its earliest days two different objects which were believed to be closely interrelated. On the one hand, it aimed at a theoretical understanding of the structure of the world; on the other hand, it tried to discover and inculcate the best possible way of life. (UE 23)

PHILOSOPHY, FUNCTION OF

Apart from the attempt to understand the world, philosophy has other functions to fulfill. It can enlarge the imagination by the construction of a cosmic epic, or it can suggest a way of life less wayward and accidental than that of the unreflective. A philosopher who attempts either of these tasks must be judged by a standard of values, aesthetic or ethical, rather than by intellectual correctness. (POS 453)

Leaving aside, for the moment, all questions that have to do with ethics or with values, there are a number of purely theoretical questions, of perennial and passionate interest, which science is unable to answer, at any rate at present. Do we survive death in any sense, and if so, do we survive for a time or forever? Can mind dominate matter, or does matter completely dominate mind, or has each, perhaps, a certain limited independence? Has the universe a purpose? Or is it driven by blind necessity? Or is it a mere chaos and jumble, in which the natural laws that we think we find are only a fantasy generated by our love of order? If there is a cosmic scheme, has life more importance in it than astronomy would lead us to suppose, or is our emphasis upon life mere parochialism and self-importance? I do not know the answer to these questions, and I do not believe that anybody else does, but I think human life would be impoverished if they were forgotten, or if definite answers were accepted without adequate evidence. To keep alive the interest in such questions, and to scrutinize suggested answers, is one of the functions of philosophy. (UE 25-6)

PHILOSOPHY, HISTORY OF

The history of philosophy is a study which proposes to itself two somewhat different objects, of which the first is mainly historical, while the second is mainly philosophical. From this cause it is apt to result that, where we look for history *of* philosophy, we find rather history *and* philosophy. Questions concerning the influence of the times or of other philosophers, concerning the growth of a philosopher's system, and the causes which suggested his leading ideas—all these are truly historical: they require for their answer a considerable knowledge of the prevailing education, of the public to whom it was necessary to appeal, and of the scientific and political events of the period in question. But it may be doubted how far the topics dealt with in works where these elements predominate can be called properly philosophical. (PL xi)

PHILOSOPHY, INDUSTRIAL

The dominating belief of what may be called the industrial philosophy is that man is master of his fate, and need not submit tamely to the evils hitherto inflicted upon him by the niggardliness of inanimate nature or the follies of human nature. Man was in the past dependent upon the weather, which was beyond his control. This is still the case with peasants, who are usually pious, and still more so with fishermen, who are still more pious. It may be laid down broadly that the intensity of religious belief among sea-faring folk is inversely proportional to the size of their vessel. (S 67)

PHILOSOPHY, PLACE OF

But there is a second problem, less precise, and by some mistakenly regarded as unimportant—I mean the problem of how best to utilize our command over the forces of nature. This includes such burning issues as democracy versus dictatorship, capitalism versus socialism, international government versus international anarchy, free speculation versus authoritarian dogma. On such issues the laboratory can give no decisive guidance. The kind of knowledge that gives most help in solving such problems is a wide survey of human life, in the past as well as in the present, and an appreciation of the sources of misery or contentment as they appear in history. (UE 21)

PHILOSOPHY, PROFESSIONAL

"Philosophy" means "love of wisdom," and philosophy in this sense is what men must acquire if the new powers invented by technicians, and handed over by them to be wielded by ordinary men and women, are not to plunge mankind into an appalling cataclysm. But the philosophy that should be a part of general education is not the same thing as the philosophy of specialists. Not only in philosophy, but in all branches of academic study, there is a distinction between what has cultural value and what is only of professional interest. (UE 22)

PHILOSOPHY, SCIENTIFIC

A scientific philosophy such as I wish to recommend will be piecemeal and tentative like other sciences; above all, it will be able to invent hypotheses which, even if they are not wholly true, will yet remain fruitful after the necessary corrections have been made. This possibility of successive approximations to the truth is more than anything else, the source of the triumphs of science, and to transfer this possibility to philosophy is to ensure a progress in method whose importance it would be almost impossible to exaggerate. (ML 113)

PHILOSOPHY, STUDY OF

And since the philosophies of the past belong to one or other of a few great types—types which in our own day are perpetually recurring—we may learn, from examining the greatest representative of any type, what are the grounds for such a philosophy. (PL xii)

PHILOSOPHY, VALUE OF

It can give a habit of exact and careful thought, not only in mathematics and science, but in questions of large practical import. It can give an impersonal breadth and scope to the conception of the ends of life. It can give to the individual a just measure of himself in relation to society, of man in the present to man in the past and in the future, and of the whole history of man in relation to the astronomical cosmos. By enlarging the objects of his thoughts it supplies an antidote to the anxieties and anguish of the present, and makes possible the nearest approach to serenity that is available to a sensitive mind in our tortured and uncertain world. (UE 32-3)

PHYSICAL OBJECT

According to the view that I am suggesting, a physical object or piece of matter is the collection of all those correlated particulars which would be regarded by common sense as its effects or appearances in different places. On the other hand, all the happenings in a given place represent what common sense would regard as the appearances of a number of different objects as viewed from that place. All the happenings in one place may be regarded as the view of the world from that place. I shall call the view of the world from a given place a "perspective." (AM 101)

PHYSICS

Physics must be interpreted in a way which tends toward idealism, and perception in a way which tends towards materialism. I believe that matter is less material, and mind less mental, than is commonly supposed, and that, when this is realized, the difficulties raised by Berkeley largely disappear. (AOM 7)
see PSYCHOLOGY AND PHYSICS

PHYSICS AND PSYCHOLOGY

The laws which physics seeks can, broadly speaking, be stated by treating such systems of particulars as causal units. The laws which psychology seeks cannot be so stated, since the particulars themselves are what interests the psychologist. This is one of the fundamental differences between physics and psychology. . . .(AM 106)

PHYSICS, DATA OF
see DATA, PUBLIC AND PRIVATE

PHYSICS, MODERN

The extreme abstractness of modern physics makes it difficult to understand, but gives to those who can understand it a grasp of the world as a whole, a sense of its structure and mechanism, which no less abstract apparatus could possibly supply. The power of using abstractions is the essence of intellect, and with every increase in abstraction triumphs of science are enhanced. (SO 84)

PIETY, DEGREES OF
see PHILOSOPHY, INDUSTRIAL

PLACE

Indeed the whole notion that one is always in some definite "place" is due to the fortunate immovability of most of the large objects on the earth's surface. The idea of "place" is only a rough practical approximation: there is nothing logically necessary about it, and it cannot be made precise. (ABCR 7)

PLANNED SOCIETIES
see MORE'S UTOPIA

PLATO'S REPUBLIC

That Plato's Republic should have been admired, on its political side, by decent people is perhaps the most astonishing example of literary snobbery in all history. Let us consider a few points in this totalitarian tract. The main purpose of education, to which everything else is subordinated, is to produce courage in battle. To this end, there is to be a rigid censorship of the stories told by mothers and nurses to young children; there is to be no reading of Homer, because that degraded versifier makes heroes lament and gods laugh; the drama is to be forbidden, because it contains villains and women; music is to be only of certain kinds, which, in modern terms, would be "Rule Britannia" and "The British Grenadiers." (UE 7)

When we ask: what will Plato's Republic achieve? The answer is rather humdrum. It will achieve success in wars against roughly equal populations, and it will secure a livelihood for a certain small number of people. It will almost certainly produce no art or science, because of its rigidity; in this respect, as in others, it will be like Sparta. In spite of all the fine talk, skill in war and enough to eat is all that will be achieved. (HWP 115)

PLATO'S THEORY OF IDEAS

But if the word "cat" means anything, it means something which is not this or that cat, but some kind of universal cattyness. This is not born when a particular cat is born, and does not die when it dies. In fact, it has no position in space or time; it is "eternal." This is the logical part of the doctrine. The arguments in its favour, whether ultimately valid or not, are strong, and quite independent of the metaphysical part of the doctrine. (HWP 121)

Similarly with any other word which may be applicable to common facts such as "whiteness" for example. The word will be applicable to a number of particular things because they all participate in a common nature or essence. This pure essence is what Plato calls an "idea" or "form." (It must not be supposed that "ideas," in his sense, exist in minds, though they may be apprehended by minds.) The "idea" *justice* is not identical with anything that is just: it is something other than particular things, which particular things partake of. Not being particular, it cannot itself exist in the world of sense. Moreover it is not fleeting or changeable like the things of sense: it is eternally itself, immutable and indestructible. (PP 143-4)

PLAY

Men as well as children have need of play, that is to say, of periods of activity having no purpose beyond present enjoyment. But if play is to serve its purpose, it must be possible to find pleasure and interest in matters not connected with work. (IPI 45)

The games of later years differ from those of early childhood by the fact that they become increasingly competitive. At first, a child's play is solitary; it is difficult for an infant to join in the games of older brothers and sisters. But collective play, as soon as it becomes possible, is so much more delightful that pleasure in playing alone quickly ceases. English upper-class education has always attributed an enormous moral importance to school games. To my mind, there is some exaggeration in the conventional British view, although I admit that games have certain important merits. They are good for health, provided they are not too expert; if exceptional skill is too much prized the best players overdo it, while the others tend to lapse into spectators. They teach boys and girls to endure hurts without making a fuss, and to incur great fatigue cheerfully. But the other advantages which are claimed for them seem to me largely illusory. They are said to teach co-operation, but in fact they only teach it in its competitive form. (EEC 131-2)

PLEASURE

"Pleasure" is a property of a sensation or other mental occurrence, consisting in the fact that the occurrence in question either does not stimulate any voluntary or reflex movement, or, if it does, stimulates only such as tend to prolong the occurrence in question. (AM 71-2)

see BENTHAM

PLEASURE, CALCULUS OF

The intellectual conviction that pleasure is the sole good, together with a temperamental incapacity for experiencing it, was characteristic of Utilitarians. From the point of view of the calculus of pleasures and pains, their emotional poverty was advantageous: they tended to think that pleasure could be measured by the bank-account, and pain by fines or terms of imprisonment. Unselfish and stoical devotion to the doctrine that every man seeks only his own pleasure is a curious psychological paradox. (FO 98)

PLEBISCITES

Any constitutional change in any country therefore should in future be sanctioned by a plebiscite, not imposed by an armed minority; and any regional minority should have the power of presenting its grievances to an international authority, which should be empowered to conduct a plebiscite in the region concerned to determine whether or not it should be granted local autonomy. (ISIP 231)

PLOTINUS

Plotinus, however, is not *only* historically important. He represents, better than any other philosopher, an important type of theory. A philosophical system may be judged important for various different kinds of reasons. The first and most obvious is that we think it may be true. Not many students of philosophy at the present time would feel this about Plotinus; Dean Inge is, in this respect, a rare exception. But truth is not the only merit that a metaphysic can possess. It may have beauty, and this is certainly to be found in Plotinus. (HWP 285)

PLURALISM

Pluralism is the view of science and common sense, and is therefore to be accepted, if the arguments against it are not conclusive. For my part, I have no doubt whatever that it is the true view, and that monism is derived from a faulty logic inspired by mysticism. This logic dominates the philosophy of Hegel and his followers; it is also the essential basis of Bergson's system, although it is seldom mentioned in his writings. When it is rejected, ambitious metaphysical systems such as those of the past are seen to be impossible. (OP 253)

PLURALISM, ABSOLUTE
see LOGICAL ATOMISM

POPULAR SOVEREIGNTY
see MARSIGLIO

POSSIBILITY, SYNTACTIC

There is one sense of the word "possibility" which is connected with our present problem. We may say that whatever is asserted by a significant sentence has a certain kind of possibility. I will define this as "syntactic" possibility. It is perhaps narrower than logical possibility, but certainly wider than physical possibility. (IMT 214)

POSTERITY OF A GIVEN NATURAL NUMBER

We will define the "posterity" of a given natural number with respect to the relation "immediate predecessor" (which is the converse of "successor") as all those terms that belong to every hereditary class to which the given number belongs. (IMP 22)

POSTULATES

Science cannot dispense wholly with postulates, but as it advances their number decreases. I mean by a postulate something not very different from a working hypothesis, except that it is more general: it is something which we assume without sufficient evidence, in the hope that, by its help, we shall be able to construct a theory which the facts will confirm. It is by no means essential to science to assume that its postulates are true always or necessarily; it is enough if they are often true. (AOM 167)

POWER

The mere possession of power tends to produce a love of power, which is a very dangerous motive, because the only sure proof of power consists in preventing others from doing what they wish to do. The essential theory of democracy is the diffusion of power among the whole people, so that the evils produced by one man's possession of great power shall be obviated. But the diffusion of power through democracy is only effective when the voters take an interest in the question involved. (PI 85-6)

Power may be defined as ability to cause people to act as we wish, when they would have acted otherwise but for the effects of our desires; it includes also ability to prevent people from acting against our wishes, which is sometimes the utmost that we aim at achieving—for instance, in the case of a murderer who is executed. (PIC 190)

But unless the power of officials can be kept within bounds, socialism will mean little more than the substitution of one set of masters for another: all the former powers of the capitalist will be inherited by the official. (ISOS 37)

POWER, HORRORS OF NAKED

Most of the great abominations in human history are connected with naked power—not only those associated with war, but others equally terrible if less spectacular. Slavery and the slave trade, the exploitation of the Congo, the horrors of early industrialism, cruelty to children, judicial torture, the criminal law, prisons, workhouses, religious persecution, the atrocious treatment of the Jews, the merciless frivolities of despots, the unbelievable iniquity of the treatment of political opponents in Germany and Russia at the present day—all these are examples of the use of naked power against defenseless victims. (P 103-4)

POWER, KINDS OF

We may therefore distinguish, though not too sharply, three kinds of power: military, economic, and mental. The power of armies and navies is military, the power of trust magnates is economic, and the power of the Catholic church is mental. (PIC 191-2)

POWER, NAKED AND TRADITIONAL

As the beliefs and habits which have upheld traditional power decay, it gradually gives way either to power based upon some new belief, or to "naked" power, i.e., to the kind that involves no acquiescence on the part of the subject. Such is the power of the butcher over the sheep, of an invading army over a vanquished nation, and of the police over detected conspirators. The power of the Catholic Church over Catholics is traditional, but its power over heretics who are persecuted is naked. The power of the State over loyal citizens is traditional, but its power over rebels is naked. (P 83)

POWER, PROPER USE OF

There must be power, either that of governments, or that of anarchic adventurers. There must even be naked power, so long as there are rebels against governments, or even ordinary criminals. But if human life is to be, for the mass of mankind, anything better than a dull misery punctuated with moments of sharp horror, there must be as little naked power as possible. The exercise of power, if it is to be something better than the infliction of wanton torture, must be hedged round by safeguards of law and custom, permitted only after due deliberation, and entrusted to men who are closely supervised in the interests of those who are subjected to them. I do not pretend that this is easy. (P 104)

POWER, UNRESTRICTED

Soviet imperialism, Soviet bad faith, Soviet refusal to prevent an atomic armament race—all these things are bad, but they are not so new as the internal evils. In Russia, as in a vast human laboratory, the student can see the result of allowing the power impulse unrestricted scope in a modern monolithic state. It is a terrible spectacle, and it all springs from mistakes in Lenin's thinking. (CTR 37)

POWER, USE OF

The ultimate aim of those who have power (and we all have some) should be to promote social co-operation, not in one group as against another, but in the whole human race. The chief obstacle to this end at present is the existence of feelings of unfriendliness and desire for superiority. Such feelings can be diminished either directly by religion and morality, or indirectly by removing the political and economic circumstances which at present stimulate them—notably the competition for power between States and the connected competition for wealth between large national industries. Both methods are needed: they are not alternatives, but supplement each other. (P 271)

PRAGMATISM

Pragmatism muddles up the practical and philosophical in a way I don't like; I am an admirer of certain passions, but I don't admire a philosophy made up, like pragmatism, of unduly practical theory and unduly theoretical practice. (TWW 17)

Although pragmatism may not contain ultimate philosophical truth, it has certain important merits. First, it realizes that the truth that *we* can attain to is merely human truth, fallible and changeable like everything human. What lies outside the cycle of human occurrences is not truth, but fact (of certain kinds). Truth is a property of beliefs, and beliefs are psychical events. Moreover their relation to facts does not have the schematic simplicity which logic assumes; to have pointed this out is a second merit in pragmatism. (SE 63)

PREACHING

And everybody who has ever had to do with children knows that a suitable diet does more to make them virtuous than the most eloquent preaching in the world. (RUC 21-2)

PREDECESSOR, IMMEDIATE
see POSTERITY OF A GIVEN NATURAL NUMBER

PREDICATE
see SUBJECT

PREJUDICE
see MIND, ADVOCACY OF THE OPEN

PRIVATE WORLDS
see PERSPECTIVES

PROBABILITY

The theory of probability is in a very unsatisfactory state, both logically and mathematically; and I do not believe that there is any alchemy by which it can produce regularity in large numbers out of pure caprice in each single case. If the penny really chose by caprice whether to fall heads or tails, have we any reason to say that it would choose one about as often as the other? Might not caprice lead just as well always to the same choice? This is no more than a suggestion, since the subject is too obscure for dogmatic statements. (RAS 168)

It is therefore necessary to examine what is meant by "probability." It will be found that there are two different concepts that may be meant. On the one hand, there is mathematical probability: If a class has n members, and m of them have a certain characteristic, the mathematical probability that an unspecified member of this class will have the characteristic in question is m/n. On the other hand, there is a wider and vaguer concept, which I call "degree of credibility," which is the amount of credence that it is rational to assign to a more or less uncertain proposition. Both kinds of probability are involved in stating the principles of scientific inference. (HK xiii)

I suggest, as a principle of inference used unconsciously by common sense but consciously in science and law, the following postulate: "When a group of complex events in more or less the same neighborhood all have a common structure, and appear to be grouped about a central event, it is probable that they have a common causal ancestor." I am using "probable" here in the sense of frequency; I mean that this happens in most cases. (HK 464-5)

For this reason the inductive principle cannot be proved or disproved by experience. We might prove validly that such and such a conclusion was enormously probable, and yet it might not happen. We might prove invalidly that it was probable, and yet it might happen. What happens affects the probability of proposition, since it is relevant evidence; but it never alters the probability relative to the previously available evidence. The whole subject of probability, therefore, on Mr. Keynes's theory, is strictly *a priori* and independent of experience. (OP 274-5)

PRODUCTION, INTERNATIONAL

If nations had sense, they would arrange, by international agreement, which nation was to produce what, and would no more attempt to produce everything than individuals do. No individual tries to make his own clothes, his own shoes, his own food, his own house, and so on; he knows quite well that, if he did, he would have to be content with a very low level of comfort. But nations do not yet understand the principle of division of labor. (IPI 78)

PROGRESS
see CHANGE

PROGRESSION

A series of the form

$$x_0, x_1, x_2, \ldots \ldots x_n, \ldots \ldots$$

in which there is a first term, a successor to each term (so that there is no last term), no repetitions, and every term can be reached from the start in a finite number of steps, is called a *progression*. (IMP 8)

PROLETARIAT
see DICTATORSHIP

PROPAGANDA

We are beginning to understand the art of manufacturing opinions wholesale as we manufacture pins. The technique is not yet quite perfect, but it may be confidently hoped that within another hundred years almost every citizen of a state will have, on almost every subject, the opinions which the Government of that state wishes him to have. (SSI 18)

Propaganda is only successful when it is in harmony with something in the patient: his desire' for an immortal soul, for health, for the greatness of his nation, or what not. Where there is no such fundamental reason for acquiescence, the assertions of authority are viewed with cynical skepticism. (P 141)

The art of propaganda, as practised by modern politicians and Governments, is derived from the art of advertisement. The science of psychology owes a great deal to advertisers. In former days most psychologists would probably have thought that a man could not convince many people of the excellence of his own wares by merely stating emphatically that they were excellent. Experience shows, however, that they were mistaken in this. (FT 36-7)

Propaganda may be defined as any attempt, by means of persuasion, to enlist human beings in the service of one party to any dispute. It is thus distinguished from persecution by its method, which is one that eschews force, and from instruction by its motive, which is not the dissemination of knowledge, but the generating of some kind of party feeling. (ESO 207)

PROPAGANDA, BASIS FOR CURRENT

I think a great deal more could be achieved by propaganda than is being achieved at present. The gradual russification of satellite nations should be emphasized, and so should the bad economic conditions of the workers under Soviet rule. Tito should be vigorously supported, and so should every beginning of a similar movement in Poland, Bulgaria, and Hungary. Truman's Fourth Point should be implemented to the extreme of what is financially possible. Vigorous young intellectuals from doubtful regions—e.g. the Near East—should be trained in England or America, as young communists are trained in Moscow. And much more should be done than is done at present to make clear positively what the West stands for, and what will be lost to mankind if Moscow triumphs. (TWI 13)

PROPAGANDA, GOVERNMENT

But it is only in recent years that Governments, and even single departments, have instituted regularly organised propaganda bureaus, for the purpose of giving publicity to their own virtues and to the vices of their opponents. (GBP 380)

PROPAGANDA, TECHNIQUE OF

The technique of Government propaganda, as applied to adults, is derived from the practice of advertisers. Commercial competition has provided data as to the kind of advertisements that are successful; in America, the psychology of advertising has been carefully studied by eminent psychologists. Advertising is the art of producing belief by reiterated and striking assertions, wholly divorced from all appeal to reason. Experience shows that the average man, if he is told a hundred times a day that A's soap is the best, and fifty times a day that B's is the best, will buy A's, although he knows that A is making the assertion for the sake of his own pocket, not from a disinterested love of truth. (GBP 384)

PROPERTY

The essence of private property is legal possession, secured to some person or group within the state, together with the rights built upon that possession. It is not essential that the possessor should be an individual. (PIC 43)

PROPHECIES

I have spoken of a two-fold movement in past history, but I do not consider that there is anything either certain or inevitable about such laws of historical development as we can discover. New knowledge may make the course of events completely different from what it would otherwise have been; this was, for instance, a result of the discovery of America. New institutions also may have effects that could not have been foreseen: I do not see how any Roman at the time of Julius Caesar could have predicted anything at all like the Catholic Church. And no one in the nineteenth century, not even Marx, foresaw the Soviet Union. For such reasons, all prophecies as to the future of mankind should be treated only as hypotheses which may deserve consideration. (AAI 43)

PROPOSITION

We mean by a "proposition" primarily a form of words which expresses what is either true or false. I say "primarily," because I do not wish to exclude other than verbal symbols, or even mere thoughts if they have a symbolic character. But I think the word "proposition" should be limited to what may, in some sense, be called "symbols," and further to such symbols as give expression to truth and falsehood. (IMP 155)

A proposition is something which may be said in any language: "Socrates is mortal" and "Socrate est mortel" express the same proposition. In a given language it may be said in various ways: the difference between "Caesar was killed on the Ides of March" and "it was on the Ides of March that Caesar was killed" is merely rhetorical. It is thus possible for two forms of words to "have the same meaning." We may, at least for the moment, define a "proposition" as "all the sentences which have the same meaning as some given sentence." (IMT 10)

A form of words which must be either true or false, I shall call a *proposition*. (KEW 55)

PROPOSITION, ATOMIC

A proposition which expresses what we have called a fact, i.e. which, when asserted, asserts that a certain thing has a certain quality, or that certain things have a certain relation, will be called an atomic proposition, because as we shall see immediately, there are other propositions into which atomic propositions enter in a way analogous to that in which atoms enter into molecules. (KEW 55-6)

PROPOSITION, GENERAL

The next kind of propositions we have to consider are *general* propositions, such as "all men are mortal," "all equilateral triangles are equiangular." And with these belong propositions in which the word "some" occurs, such as "some men are philosophers" or "some philosophers are not wise." (KEW 58)

General propositions may thus form part of our thinking from the start. Such general propositions are merely the verbal expression of habits. The hand-eye co-ordination becomes firmly fixed as a motor habit, and then, when we think, we conclude that what can be seen can often be touched—in fact, that it can be touched in circumstances which we know in practice, though we might have difficulty in formulating them exactly. Such general propositions are synthetic, and are in a certain sense *a priori*; for, though experience has *caused* them, they are not obtained by inference from other propositions, but by rationalizing and verbalizing our habits; that is to say, their antecedents are pre-intellectual. (AOM 185)

PROPOSITION, MOLECULAR

"Molecular" propositions are such as contain conjunctions—*if, or, and, unless*, etc.—and such words are the marks of a molecular proposition. Consider such an assertion as, "If it rains, I shall bring my umbrella." (KEW 57)

PROPOSITION, NEGATIVE AND POSITIVE GENERAL

We will call propositions containing the word "some" *negative* general propositions, and those containing the word "all" *positive* general propositions. (KEW 58)

PROPOSITIONAL ATTITUDES

There is another very important class of words that must be at least provisionally excluded, namely such words as "believe," "desire," "doubt," all of which, when they occur in a sentence, must be followed by a subordinate sentence telling what it is that is believed or desired or doubted. Such words, so far as I have been able to discover, are always psychological, and involve what I call "propositional attitudes." For the present, I will merely point out that they differ from such words as "or" in an important respect, namely that they are necessary for the description of observable phenomena. (IMT 79)

PROPOSITIONAL FUNCTION

"A propositional function" is an expression containing one or more undetermined constituents x, y, . . . , and such that, if we settle what these are to be, the result is a proposition. Thus "x is a man" is a propositional function, because, if you decide on a value for x, the result is a proposition—a true proposition if you define that x is to be Socrates or Plato, a false proposition if x is to be Cerberus or Pegasus. The values for which it is true constitute the class of men. Every propositional function determines a class, namely the class of values of the variable for which it is true. (IMT 326)

PROPOSITIONS
see WORDS AND PROPOSITIONS

PROPOSITIONS, ANALYSIS OF

That all sound philosophy should begin with an analysis of propositions, is a truth too evident, perhaps, to demand a proof. (PL 8)

PROPOSITIONS, BASIC

"Basic propositions," as I wish to use the term, are a sub-class of epistemological premises, namely those which are caused, as immediately as possible, by perceptive experiences. This excludes the premisses required for inference, whether demonstrative or probable. (IMT 171)

PROPOSITIONS, EQUIVALENT

Two *propositions* are "equivalent" when both are true or both false. . . . (IMP 183-184)
see TRUTH-FUNCTION, THEORY OF

PROPOSITIONS, NEGATIVE

Let us consider, in like manner, negative propositions which seem to have an immediate relation to experience. Suppose you are told "there is butter in the larder, but no cheese." Although they seem equally based upon sensible experience in the larder, the two statements "there is butter" and "there is not cheese" are really on a very different level. There was a definite occurrence which was seeing butter, and which might have put the word "butter" into your mind even if you had not been thinking of butter. (IMT 89)

PROSTITUTION

Prostitution as it exists at present is obviously an undesirable kind of life. The risk of disease in itself renders prostitution a dangerous trade, like working in white lead, but apart from that the life is a demoralizing one. It is idle; and tends to excessive drinking. It has the grave drawback that the prostitute is generally despised, and is probably thought ill of even by her clients. It is a life against instinct—quite as much against instinct as the life of a nun. For all these reasons prostitution, as it exists in Christian countries, is an extraordinarily undesirable career. (MM 150)

PROSTITUTION, SACRED

Sacred prostitution is another institution which was very widespread in antiquity. In some places ordinary respectable women went to a temple and had sexual intercourse either with a priest or with a casual stranger. In other cases, the priestesses themselves were sacred harlots. Probably all such customs arose out of the attempt to secure the fertility of women through the favour of the gods, or the fertility of the crops by sympathetic magic. (MM 37)

PROTAGORAS

He is chiefly noted for his doctrine that "Man is the measure of all things, of things that are that they are, and of things that are not that they are not." This is interpreted as meaning that *each* man is the measure of all things, and that, when men differ, there is no objective truth in virtue of which one is right and the other wrong. The doctrine is essentially sceptical, and is presumably based on the "deceitfulness" of the senses. (HWP 77)

PROTECTION

It was the German economist List who first (in 1841) provided a theoretical defence of protectionism. This was the famous "infant industries" argument. Take, say, steel. It may be that a country is well suited by nature to the development of a great steel industry, but that, owing to foreign competition, the initial expenses are prohibitive, unless government assistance is obtainable. This situation existed in Germany when List wrote and for some time after that. But experience has shown that protection, once granted, cannot be withdrawn even when the infant has grown into a giant. (FO 142)

PSYCHICAL RESEARCH
see IMMORALITY

PSYCHO-ANALYSIS

Psycho-analysis, though no doubt it has its exaggerations, and even perhaps absurdities, has taught us a great deal that is true and valuable. It is an old saying that even if you expel nature with a pitchfork it will still come back, but psycho-analysis has supplied the commentary to this text. We now know that a life which goes excessively against natural impulse is one which is likely to involve effects of strain that may be quite as bad as indulgence in forbidden impulses would have been. People who live a life which is unnatural beyond a point are likely to be filled with envy, malice and uncharitableness. (AAI 20-1)

Whatever may be thought of psycho-analysis, there is one point in which it is unquestionably in the right, and that is in the enormous stress which it lays upon the emotional life. Given the right emotional development, both character and intelligence ought to develop spontaneously. It is, therefore, to the emotions above all that the scientific educator should direct his attention. (SAE 88)

For our purposes, the essential discovery of psycho-analysis is this: that an impulse which is prevented, by behaviourist methods, from finding overt expression in action, does not necessarily die, but is driven underground, and finds some new outlet which has not been inhibited by training. Often the new outlet will be more harmful than the one that has been prevented, and in any case the deflection involves emotional disturbance and unprofitable expenditure of energy. (ESO 55)

Psycho-analysis, as every one knows, is primarily a method of understanding hysteria and certain forms of insanity; but it has been found that there is much in the lives of ordinary men and women which bears a humiliating resemblance to the delusions of the insane. The connection of dreams, irrational beliefs and foolish actions with unconscious wishes has been brought to light, though with some exaggeration, by Freud and Jung and their followers. As regards the nature of these unconscious wishes it seems to me—though as a layman I speak with diffidence—that many psycho-analysts are unduly narrow; no doubt the wishes they emphasize exist, but others, e.g. for honour and power, are equally operative and equally liable to concealment. (AM 32-3)

PSYCHOLOGY
see PHYSICS AND PSYCHOLOGY

PSYCHOLOGY AND PHYSICS
It follows that if physics is an empirical science, whose statements can be confirmed or confuted by observation, then physics must be supplemented by laws connecting stimulus and sensation. Now such laws belong to psychology. Therefore what is empirically verifiable is not pure physics in isolation, but physics plus a department of psychology. Psychology, accordingly, is an essential ingredient in every part of empirical science. (HK 49)

PSYCHOLOGY, CHILD
If you could take children more naturally and spontaneously and not bother so much about child psychology, it would be very much better I think. (CAW 217)

PSYCHOLOGY, DATA OF
see DATA, PUBLIC AND PRIVATE

PSYCHOTHERAPY
Such a desire is generally, in morbid cases, of a sort which the patient would consider wicked; if he had to admit that he had the

desire, he would loathe himself. Yet it is so strong that it must force an outlet for itself; hence it becomes necessary to entertain whole systems of false beliefs in order to hide the nature of what is desired. The resulting delusions in very many cases disappear if the hysteric or lunatic can be made to face the facts about himself. The consequence of this is that the treatment of many forms of insanity has grown more psychological and less physiological than it used to be. (AM 33-4)

PUBLIC DEFENDER

If law-abiding citizens are to be protected against unjust persecution by the police, there must be two police forces and two Scotland Yards, one designed, as at present, to prove guilt, the other to prove innocence. . . . . (P 283-4)

PUBLIC OPINION, INTERNATIONAL

No mechanism, however perfect, will work unless it is supported by a strong public opinion. The establishment of an international government will not be successful unless most of the civilized nations have become persuaded that unrestricted national sovereignty involves disaster. (WWP 84)

PUBLIC OWNERSHIP, CONTROL OF

While, therefore, public ownership and control of all large-scale industry and finance is a *necessary* condition for the training of power, it is far from being a *sufficient* condition. It needs to be supplemented by a democracy more thoroughgoing, more carefully safeguarded against official tyranny, and with more deliberate provision for freedom of propaganda, than any purely political democracy that ever existed. (P 290)

PUNCTUALITY

Another rather humble virtue which is not likely to be produced by a wholly free education is punctuality. Punctuality is a quality the need of which is bound up with social co-operation. It has nothing to do with the relation of the soul to God, or with mystic insight, or with any of the matters with which the more elevated and spiritual moralists are concerned. One would be surprised to find a saint getting drunk, but one would not be surprised to find him late for an engagement. And yet in the ordinary business of life punctuality is absolutely necessary. (ESO 34-5)

PUNISHMENT

For my part, I believe that punishment has a certain very minor place in education; but I doubt whether it need ever be severe. I include speaking sharply or reprovingly among punishments. The most severe punishment that ought ever to be necessary is the natural spontaneous expression of indignation. On a few occasions when my boy has been rough with his younger sister, his mother has expressed anger by an impulsive exclamation. The effect has been very great. (EEC 167)

PUNISHMENT, PHYSICAL

Physical punishment, I believe to be never right. In mild forms, it does little harm, though no good; in severe forms, I am convinced that it generates cruelty and brutality. It is true that it often produces no resentment against the person who inflicts it; where it is customary, boys adapt themselves to it and expect it as part of the course of nature. But it accustoms them to the idea that it may be right and proper to inflict physical pain for the purpose of maintaining authority—a peculiarly dangerous lesson to teach to those who are likely to acquire positions of power. (EEC 176)

PURITANISM

My point is that the pleasures which remain possible after the Puritan has done his utmost are more harmful than those he condemns. Next to enjoying ourselves, the next greatest pleasure consists in preventing others from enjoying themselves, or, more generally, in the acquisition of power. Consequently those who live under the dominion of Puritanism become exceedingly desirous of power. Now love of power does far more harm than love of drink or any of the other vices against which Puritans protest. (SE 130)

PYTHAGORAS

Pythagoras is one of the most interesting and puzzling men in history. Not only are the traditions concerning him an almost inextricable mixture of truth and falsehood, but even in their barest and least disputable form they present us with a very curious psychology. He may be described, briefly, as a combination of Einstein and Mrs. Eddy. (HWP 31)
see DICTATORSHIP

Q

QUALITIES
Next come qualities—red, blue, hard, soft, hot, cold, etc. Many of these are usually learned ostensively, but the less common ones, such as vermilion, may be described by their similarities and differences. (HK 69)

Let us give the name "qualities" to specific shades of colour, specific degrees of hardness, sounds completely defined as to pitch and loudness and every other distinguishable characteristic, and so on. (IMT 121)

QUANTA THEORY
Planck's principle in its original form is as follows. If a body is undergoing any kind of vibration or periodic motion of frequency v (i.e. the body goes through its whole period v times in a second), then there is a certain fundamental constant h such that the energy of the body owing to this periodic motion is hv or some exact multiple of hv. That is to say, hv is the smallest amount of energy that can exist in any periodic process whose frequency is v, and if the energy is greater than hv it must be exactly twice as great, or three times as great, or four times as great, or etc. (ABCA 60-1)

QUANTITATIVE TEST IN EDUCATION
One of the characteristics of the scientific method is that it is quantitative and aims at discovering the just balance of the different ingredients required to produce a good result, whereas pre-scientific methods consider some things good and some bad without regard to quantity. Take, for example, the question of the quantity of adult attention that is best for a child. In old days most children got less of this than they should have had; nowadays, most children of the well-to-do get more. (SAE 94)

QUANTUM MECHANICS

According to quantum mechanics, it cannot be known what an atom will do in given circumstances; there are a definite set of alternatives open to it, and it chooses sometimes one, sometimes another. We know in what proportion of cases one choice will be made, in what proportion a second, or a third, and so on. But we do not know any law determining the choice in an individual instance. We are in the same position as a booking-office clerk at Paddington, who can discover, if he chooses, what proportion of travellers from that station go to Birmingham, what proportion to Exeter, and so on, but knows nothing of the individual reasons which lead to one choice in one case and another in another. (RAS 158-9)

R

R-ANCESTOR

A term x is said to be an "R-ancestor" of the term y if y has every R-hereditary property that x has, provided x is a term which has the relation R to something or to which something has the relation R. (This is only to exclude trivial cases.) (IMP 25)

R-HEREDITARY

A property is called "R-hereditary" when, if it belongs to a term x, and x has the relation R to y, then it belongs to y. A class is R-hereditary when its defining property is R-hereditary. (IMP 25)

R-POSTERITY

The "R-posterity" of x is all the terms of which x is an R-ancestor. (IMP 26)

RACE

About race, if politics were not involved, it would be enough to say that nothing politically important is known. It may be taken as probable that there are genetic mental differences between races; but it is certain that we do not yet know what these differences are. In an adult man, the effects of environment mask those of heredity. (IPI 113)

There is a special absurdity in applying racial theories to the various populations of Europe. There is not in Europe any such thing as a pure race. Russians have an admixture of Tartar blood, Germans are largely Slavonic, France is a mixture of Celts, Germans, and people of Mediterranean race, Italy the same with the addition of the descendants of slaves imported by the Romans. The English are perhaps the most mixed of all. There is no evidence that there is any advantage in belonging to a pure race. The purest races now in existence are the Pygmies, the Hottentots, and the Australian aborigines; the Tasmanians, who were probably even purer, are extinct. (UE 89-90)

RADICALISM

Radicalism, unlike Liberalism, was a doctrine inspired by economic considerations, especially such as were suggested by nascent industrialism. Radicals were even more individualistic than Liberals, since they took no interest in nations. As individuals they may have been liable to patriotism, but as theorists they were cosmopolitan. They believed in free trade, free competition, free individual initiative within the limits of the criminal law. They did not object to the power of property, so long as the property had been acquired by personal effort, not by privilege or inheritance. (FO 448)

RADICALS

see EVILS, CONSCIOUSNESS OF

RADICALS, THE PHILOSOPHICAL

The Philosophical Radicals, as a school, had certain important merits which, in our day, are apt to be overlooked. They applied to all existing institutions the test of utility, and accepted nothing on the mere ground of historical prescription.   By this test, they found no justification for monarchy, aristocracy, religion, war, or empire. Liberals had a rhetorical and sentimental objection to some of these, but the objections of Philosophical Radicals were argumentative, calm and apparently derived from the inexorable voice of Reason. (FO 449)

RAGE

Then again, take rage: both rage and fear, as we know from the work of Cannon, are due to secretion of adrenalin in the blood. Presumably, anything that makes the adrenal gland more active will make people more prone to these emotions, of which the one or the other is felt according to the nature of the external situation. Perhaps we shall learn to eliminate both emotions by regulating the action of the adrenal gland or by administering an antidote. (SAE 91)

RATIONAL REAL NUMBER

A "rational real number" is a segment of the series of ratios which has a boundary. (IMP 72)

RATIONALISM

Rationalism and anti-rationalism have existed side by side since the beginning of Greek civilization, and each, when it had seemed likely to become completely dominant, has always led, by reaction, to a new outburst of its opposite. (IPI 102)

RATIONALISTS

. . .the rationalists—who are represented by the Continental philosophers of the seventeenth century, especially Descartes and Leibniz—maintained that, in addition to what we know by experience, there are certain "innate ideas" and "innate principles," which we know independently of experience. (PP 114-5)

RATIONALITY

Rationality in practice may be defined as the habit of remem bering all our relevant desires, and not only the one which happens at the moment to be strongest. Like rationality in opinion, it is a matter of degree. Complete rationality is no doubt an unattainable ideal, but so long as we continue to classify some men as lunatics it is clear that we think some men more rational than others. I believe that all solid progress in the world consists of an increase in rationality, both practical and theoretical. (SE 54)

RATIONALIZING

Freudians have accustomed us to "rationalizing", i.e., the process of inventing what seem to ourselves rational grounds for a decision or opinion that is in fact quite irrational. But there is, especially in English-speaking countries, a converse process which may be called "irrationalizing." A shrewd man will sum up, more or less subconsciously, the pros and cons of a question from a selfish point of view. (Unselfish considerations seldom weigh subconsciously except where one's children are concerned.) Having come to a sound egoistic decision by the help of the unconscious, a man proceeds to invent, or adopt from others, a set of high-sounding phrases showing how he is pursuing the public good at immense personal sacrifice. (SE 20-1)

REACTIONS, SUSPENDED

Sentences are needed to distinguish between these various uses of words. They are needed also—and this is perhaps their main use—to express what may be called "suspended reactions." Suppose you intend to take a railway journey tomorrow, and you look up your train today; you do not propose, at the moment, to take any further action on the knowledge you have acquired, but when the time comes you will behave in the appropriate manner. Knowledge, in the sense in which it does not merely register present sensible impressions, consists essentially of preparations for such delayed reactions. Such preparations may in all cases be called "beliefs," but they are only to be called "knowledge" when they prompt *successful* reactions, or at any rate show themselves related to the facts with which they are concerned in some way which distinguishes them from preparations that would be called "errors." (HK 94)

READING

The competitive habit of mind easily invades regions to which it does not belong. Take, for example, the question of reading. There are two motives for reading a book: one, that you enjoy it; the other, that you can boast about it. It has become the thing in America for ladies to read (or seem to read) certain books every month; some read them, some read the first chapter, some read the reviews, but all have these books on their tables. They do not, however, read any old masterpieces. There has never been a month when "Hamlet" or "King Lear" has been selected by the book clubs; there has never been a month when it has been necessary to know about Dante. (CH 52)

REAL

The supposed "real" table underlying its appearances is, in any case, not itself perceived, but inferred, and the question whether such-and-such a particular is an "aspect" of this table is only to be settled by the connection of the particular in question with the one or more particulars by which the table is "defined." That is to say, even if we assume a "real" table, the particulars which are its aspects have to be collected together by their relations to each other, not to it, since it is merely inferred from them. (AM 98)

REAL NUMBER

A "real number" is a segment of the series of ratios in order of magnitude. (IMP 72)

REAL OBJECTS

Objects of sense are called "real" when they have the kind of connection with other objects of sense which experience has led us to regard as normal; when they fail in this, they are called "illusions." (KEW 90)

REALISM

I think Pierce was right in regarding the realist-nominalist controversy as one which is still undecided, and which is as important as at any former time. (FPF xv)

The view which I should wish to advocate is that objects of perception do not persist unchanged at times when they are not perceived, although probably objects more or less resembling them do exist at such times, that objects of perception are part, and the only empirically knowable part, of the actual subject-matter of physics, and are themselves properly to be called physical; that purely physical laws exist determining the character and duration of objects of perception without any reference to the fact that they are perceived; and that in the establishment of such laws the propositions of physics do not presuppose any propositions of psychology or even the existence of mind. I do not know whether realists would recognize such a view as realism. All that I should claim for it is, that it avoids difficulties which seem to me to beset both realism and idealism as hitherto advocated, and that it avoids the appeal which they have made to ideas which logical analysis shows to be ambiguous. (ML 123)
see IDEALISM

REALISM, SCHOLASTIC

Scholastic realism was a metaphysical theory, but every metaphysical theory has a technical counterpart. I had been a realist in the scholastic or Platonic sense; I had thought that cardinal integers, for instance, have a timeless being. When integers were reduced to classes of classes, this being was transferred to classes. Meinong, whose work interested me, applied the argument of realism to descriptive phrases. Everyone agrees that "the golden mountain does not exist" is a true proposition. But it has, apparently, a subject, "the golden mountain," and if this subject did not designate some object, the proposition would seem to be meaningless. Meinong inferred that there is a golden mountain which is golden and a mountain, but does not exist. He even thought that the existent golden mountain is existent, but does not exist. This did not satisfy me, and the desire to avoid Meinong's unduly populous realm of being led me to the theory of descriptions. What was of importance in this theory was the discovery that, in analysing a significant sentence, one must not assume that each separate word or phrase has significance on its own account. "The golden mountain" can be part of a significant sentence, but is not significant in isolation. It soon appeared that class-symbols could be treated like descriptions. . . (MMD 13-4)

REALITY

The question we have therefore to consider is the question as to what can be meant by assigning "reality" to some but not all of the entities that make up the world. Two elements, I think, make up what is felt rather than thought when the word "reality" is used in this sense. A thing is real if it persists at times when it is not perceived; or again, a thing is real when it is correlated with other things in a way which experience has led us to expect. It will be seen that reality in either of these senses is by no means necessary to a thing, and that in fact there might be a whole world in which nothing was real in either of these senses. It might turn out that the objects of perception failed of reality in one or both of these respects, without its being in any way deducible that they are not parts of the external world with which physics deals. (ML 121-2)

REASON

I do not mean by "reason" any faculty of determining the ends of life. The ends which a man will pursue are determined by his desires; but he may pursue them wisely or unwisely. We may assume that the kaiser hoped to increase his power by the war, and that the czar hoped to avert revolution; neither of them showed wisdom in the choice of means to these ends. When I speak of "reason," I mean merely the endeavor to find out the truth about any matter with which we are concerned, as opposed to the endeavor to prove to ourselves that what we desire is true. (PIC 225)

Reason is a harmonising, controlling force rather than a creative one. Even in the most purely logical realm, it is insight that first arrives at what is new. (ML 13)

I think that what we mean in practice by reason can be defined by three characteristics. In the first place, it relies upon persuasion rather than force; in the second place, it seeks to persuade by means of arguments, which the man who uses them believes to be completely valid; and in the third place, in forming opinions, it uses observation and induction as much as possible and intuition as little as possible. (IPI 99-100)

The power of reason is thought small in these 'days, but I remain an unrepentant rationalist. Reason may be a small force, but it is constant, and works always in one direction, while the forces of unreason destroy one another in futile strife. Therefore every orgy of unreason in the end strengthens the friends of reason, and shows afresh that they are the only true friends of humanity. (SE 123)

For my part, I prefer the ontological argument, the cosmological argument, and the rest of the old stock-in-trade, to the sentimental illogicality that has sprung from Rousseau. The old arguments at least were honest; if valid, they proved their point; if invalid, it was open to any critic to prove them so. But the new theology of the heart dispenses with argument; it cannot be refuted, because it does not profess to prove its points. At bottom, the only reason offered for its acceptance is that it allows us to indulge in pleasant dreams. This is an unworthy reason, and if I had to choose between Thomas Aquinas and Rousseau, I should unhesitatingly choose the Saint. (HWP 694)
see JOHN SCOTUS

REASON, NEW AGE OF

The eighteenth century—the age of reason—was a period of relaxation after the excitements of the wars of religion. So, I doubt not, the modern wars of ideologies will be succeeded by another age of reason, in which, once more, people will not be willing to persecute in the name of beliefs for which there is no evidence. (LPR 410)

REASON, PRINCIPLE OF SUFFICIENT

This brings me to the principle of sufficient reason. This principle is usually supposed to be, by itself, adequate to the deduction of what actually exists. To this supposition, it must be confessed, Leibniz's words often lend colour. But we shall find that there are really two principles included under the same name, the one general, and applying to all possible worlds, the other special, and applying only to the actual world. Both differ from the law of contradiction, by the fact that they apply specially—the former, however, not exclusively—to existents, possible or actual. (PL 30)

REBELLION

I do not mean to be understood as an advocate of rebellion.

Rebellion in itself is no better than acquiescence in itself, since it is equally determined by relation to what is outside ourselves rather than by a purely personal judgment of value. Whether rebellion is to be praised or deprecated depends upon that against which a person rebels, but there should be the possibility of rebellion on occasion, and not only a blind acquiescence produced by a rigid education in conformity. And what is perhaps more important than either rebellion or acquiescence, there should be the capacity to strike out a wholly new line, as was done by Pythagoras when he invented the study of geometry. (ESO 14)

Without rebellion, mankind would stagnate, and injustice would be irremediable. The man who refuses to obey authority has, therefore, in certain circumstances, a legitimate function, provided his disobedience has motives which are social rather than personal. But the matter is one as to which, by its very nature, it is impossible to lay down rules. (P 252)

REFERENCE, EXTERNAL

That which has external reference—the belief or idea or bodily movement—is in some cases public and in others private. It is public when it consists in overt behavior, including speech; it is private when it consists of images or "thoughts." (The meaning of "public" and "private" in this connection will be explained in Part Three.) When an occurrence in an organism has external reference, the only feature *always* present is the causal one explained in the last paragraph, namely, that the occurrence has some of the effects that would result from the sensible presence of that which is its external reference. We will give the name "representational occurrence" to anything that happens in an organism and has external reference. (HK 114)

REFLEX, LAW OF CONDITIONED AND UNCONDITIONED

The fundamental law in this subject is the law of conditioned reflexes; when the stimulus to an unconditioned reflex has been repeatedly accompanied, or immediately preceded, by some other stimulus, this other stimulus alone will, in time, equally produce the response which was originally called forth by the stimulus to the unconditioned reflex. (SO 49)

REFLEXIVE

A number is said to be *reflexive* when it is not increased by adding 1 to it. It follows at once that any finite number can be added to a reflexive number without increasing it. This property of infinite numbers was always thought, until recently, to be self-contradictory; but through the work of Georg Cantor it has come to be recognised that, though at first astonishing, it is no more self-contradictory than the fact that people at the antipodes do not tumble off. (KEW 206)

REFORM

The method of gradual reform has many merits as compared to the method of revolution, and I have no wish to preach revolution. (PI 74)

REFORM, PENAL

I do not wish, however, to embark upon the subject of Penal Reform. I merely wish to suggest that we should treat the criminal as we treat a man suffering from plague. Each is a public danger, each must have his liberty curtailed until he has ceased to be a danger. But the man suffering from plague is an object of sympathy and commiseration, whereas the criminal is an object of execration. (WIB 54)

REFORMATION

From the sixteenth century onward, the history of European thought is dominated by the Reformation. The Reformation was a complex many-sided movement, and owed its success to a variety of causes. In the main, it was a revolt of the northern nations against the renewed dominion of Rome. Religion was the force that had subdued the North, but religion in Italy had decayed: the papacy remained as an institution, and extracted a huge tribute from Germany and England, but these nations, which were still pious, could feel no reverence for the Borgias and Medicis, who professed to save souls from purgatory in return for cash which they squandered on luxury and immorality. National motives, economic motives, and moral motives all combined to strengthen the revolt against Rome. (HWP xix-xx)

REGION, MINIMAL

We will define a set of compresent events as a "minimal region." We find that minimal regions form a four-dimensional manifold, and that, by a little logical manipulation, we can construct from them the manifold of space-time that physics requires. (LA 381)

RELATION, ASYMMETRICAL

A relation is called *asymmetrical* when, if it holds between A and B, it *never* holds between B and A. Thus husband, father, grandfather, etc. are asymmetrical relations. So are *before, after, greater, above, to the right of*, etc. All the relations that give rise to series are of this kind. (KEW 50)

RELATION, INTRANSITIVE

A relation is said to be *intransitive* when, if A has the relation to B, and B to C, A never has it to C. Thus "father" is intransitive. So is such a relation as "one inch taller" or "one year later." (KEW 51)

RELATION, NON-SYMMETRICAL

All relations that are not symmetrical are called *non-symmetrical*. Thus "brother" is non-symmetrical, because, if A is a brother of B it may happen that B is a *sister* of A. (KEW 50)

RELATION, NON-TRANSITIVE

A relation is said to be *non-transitive*, whenever it is not transitive. Thus "brother" is non-transitive, because a brother of one's brother may be oneself. All kinds of dissimilarity are non-transitive. (KEW 51)

RELATION-NUMBERS

"Relation-numbers" are the set of all those classes of relations that are relation-numbers of various relations; or, what comes to the same thing, a relation number is a class of relations consisting of all those relations that are similar to one member of the class. (IMP 56)

RELATION, SQUARE OF A

The *square* of a relation is that relation which holds between two terms x and z when there is an intermediate term y such that the given relation holds between x and y and between y and z. Thus "paternal grandfather" is the square of "father," "greater by 2" is the square of "greater by 1," and so on. (IMP 32)

RELATION, SYMMETRICAL
see SYMMETRICAL RELATION

RELATION, TRANSITIVE

A relation is said to be *transitive*, if, whenever it holds between A and B and also between B and C it holds between A and C. Thus *before, after, greater, above* are transitive. All relations giving rise to series are transitive, but so are many others. The transitive relations just mentioned were asymmetrical, but many transitive relations are symmetrical—for instance, equality in any respect, exact identity of colour, being equally numerous (as applied to collections), and so on. (KEW 51)

RELATIONS, DYADIC, TRIADIC AND MONADIC

Thus "yellow" demands one proper name, "earlier" demands two, and "between" demands three. Such terms are called predicates, dyadic relation, triadic words, etc. Sometimes for the sake of uniformity, predicates are called monadic relation words. (IMT 54)

RELATIVITY

A certain type of superior person is fond of asserting that "everything is relative." This is, of course, nonsense, because if *everything* were relative, there would be nothing for it to be relative to. However, without falling into metaphysical absurdities it is possible to maintain that everything in the physical world is relative to an observer. (ABCR 14)

Two events in distant places may appear simultaneous to one observer who has taken all due precautions to insure accuracy (and, in particular, has allowed for the velocity of light), while another equally careful observer may judge that the first event preceded the second, and still another may judge that the second preceded the first. This would happen if the three observers were all moving rapidly relatively to each other. (ABCR 43)

For philosophy, far the most important thing about the theory of relativity is the abolition of the one cosmic time and one persistent space, and the substitution of space-time in place of both. This is a change of quite enormous importance, because it alters fundamentally our notion of the structure of the physical world, and has, I think, repercussions in psychology. It would be useless, in our day, to talk about philosophy without explaining this matter. (OP 108)

RELATIVITY, GENERAL THEORY OF

The general theory of relativity—published in 1915, ten years after the special theory—was primarily a geometrical theory of gravitation. This part of the theory may be considered firmly established. But it has also more speculative features. It contains, in its equations, what is called the "cosmic constant," which determines the size of the universe at any time. This part of the theory, as I mentioned before, is held to show that the universe is growing either continually larger or continually smaller. (HK 19)

The general theory of relativity has a much wider sweep than the special theory, and a greater philosophic interest, apart from the one matter of the substitution of space-time for space and time. The general theory demands an abandonment of all direct relations between distant events, the relations upon which space-time depends being primarily confined to very small regions, and only extended, where they can be extended, by means of integration. All the old apparatus of geometry—straight lines, circles, ellipses, etc.—is gone. (AOM 55)

RELATIVITY, THE SPECIAL THEORY OF

The special theory set itself the task of making the laws of physics the same relatively to any two co-ordinate systems in uniform rectilinear relative motion. There were two sets of equations to be considered: those of Newtonian dynamics, and Maxwell's equations. The latter are unaltered by a Lorenz transformation, but the former require certain adaptations. These, however, are such as experimental results had already suggested. Thus the solution of the problem in hand was complete, but of course it was obvious from the first that the real problem was more general. There could be no reason for confining ourselves to two co-ordinate systems in uniform rectilinear motion; the problem ought to be solved for any two co-ordinate systems, no matter what the nature of their relative motion. This is the problem which has been solved by the general theory of relativity. (AOM 53-54)

Einstein showed how to avoid Newton's conclusions, and make spatio-temporal position purely relative. But his theory of relativity did much more than this. In the special theory of relativity he showed that between two events there is a relation, which may be called "interval," which can be divided in many different ways into what we should regard as a spatial distance and what we should regard as a lapse of time. All these different ways are equally legitimate; there is not one way which is more "right" than the others. The choice between them is a matter of pure convention, like the choice between the metric system and the system of feet and inches. (HK 19)

The special theory of relativity, which we have been considering hitherto, solved completely a certain definite problem: to account for the experimental fact that, when two bodies are in uniform relative motion, all the laws of physics, both those of ordinary dynamics and those connected with electricity and magnetism, are exactly the same for the two bodies. "Uniform" motion, here, means motion in a straight line with constant velocity. (ABCR 91)

RELIABLE

An instrument is "reliable" with respect to a given set of stimuli when to stimuli which are not relevantly different it gives always responses which are not relevantly different. (AM 183)

RELIGION

"Religion" is a word which has many meanings and a long history. In origin, it was concerned with certain rites, inherited from a remote past, performed originally for some reason long since forgotten, and associated from time to time with various myths to account for their supposed importance. Much of this lingers still. (PSR 223)

By a religion, I mean a set of beliefs held as dogmas, dominating the conduct of life, going beyond or contrary to evidence, and inculcated by methods which are emotional or authoritarian, not intellectual. By this definition, Bolshevism is a religion: that its dogmas go beyond or contrary to evidence, I shall try to prove in what follows. Those who accept Bolshevism become impervious to scientific evidence, and commit intellectual suicide. Even if all the doctrines of Bolshevism were true, this would still be the case, since no unbiased examination of them is tolerated. One who believes, as I do, that the free intellect is the chief engine of human progress, cannot but be fundamentally opposed to Bolshevism, as much as to the Church of Rome. (PTB 117-8)
see CRUELTY AND RELIGION; FEAR AND RELIGION

RELIGION AND EVOLUTION

Religion, in our day, has accommodated itself to the doctrine of evolution, and has even derived new arguments from it. We are told that "through the ages one increasing purpose runs," and that evolution is the unfolding of an idea which has been in the mind of God throughout. It appears that during those ages which so troubled Hugh Miller, when animals were torturing each other with ferocious horns and agonizing stings, Omnipotence was quietly waiting for the ultimate emergence of man, with his still more exquisite powers of torture and his far more widely diffused cruelty. Why the Creator should have preferred to reach His goal by a process, instead of going straight to it, these modern theologians do not tell us. (RAS 81)

RELIGION, ELEMENTS OF

The three elements of religion, namely worship, acquiescence, and love, are intimately interconnected; each helps to produce the others, and all three together form a unity in which it is impossible to say which comes first, which last. All three can exist without dogma, in a form which is capable of dominating life and of giving infinity to action and thought and feeling; and life in the infinite, which is the combination of the three, contains all that is essential to religion, in spite of its absence of dogmatic beliefs. (ER 59)

RELIGION, ORGANIZED

The immense majority of ministers of religion support war whenever it occurs, though in peace time they are often pacifists; in supporting war, they give emphatic utterance to their conviction that God is on their side, and lend religious support to the persecution of men who think wholesale slaughter unwise. While slavery existed, religious arguments were found in support of it; now-a-days, similar arguments are found in support of capitalistic exploitation. Almost all traditional cruelties and injustices have been supported by organised religion until the moral sense of the lay community compelled a change of front. (ESO 107)

RELIGION, PSYCHOLOGY OF

It would seem, therefore, that the three human impulses embodied in religion are fear, conceit, and hatred. The purpose of religion, one may say, is to give an air of respectability to these passions provided they run in certain channels. It is because these passions make on the whole for human misery that religion is a force for evil, since it permits men to indulge these passions without restraint, where but for its sanction they might, at least to a certain degree, control them. (RUC 26)

RELIGION, THE ESSENCE OF

Sudden beauty in the midst of strife, uncalculating love, or the night-wind in the trees, seem to suggest the possibility of a life free from the conflicts and pettinesses of our everyday world, a life where there is peace which no misfortune can disturb. The things which have this quality of infinity seem to give an insight deeper than the piecemeal knowledge of our daily life. A life dominated by this insight, we feel, would be a life free from struggle, a life in harmony with the whole, outside the prison-walls built by the instinctive desires of the finite self. (ER 48-9)

RENAISSANCE

The main motive of the Renaissance was mental delight, the restoration of a certain richness and freedom in art and speculation which had been lost while ignorance and superstition kept the mind's eye in blinkers. (IPI 38)

The Renaissance was not a period of great achievement in philosophy, but it did certain things which were essential preliminaries to the greatness of the seventeenth century. In the first place, it broke down the rigid scholastic system, which had become an intellectual strait jacket. It revived the study of Plato, and thereby demanded at least so much independent thought as was required for choosing between him and Aristotle. In regard to both, it promoted a genuine and first-hand knowledge, free from the glosses of Neoplatonists and Arabic commentators. More important still, it encouraged the habit of regarding intellectual activity as a delightful social adventure, not a cloistered meditation aiming at the preservation of a predetermined orthodoxy. (HWP 500)

RENT, RICARDO'S THEORY OF

Ricardo's theory of rent is simple, and in suitable circumstances perfectly valid. In considering it, let us, to begin with, confine ourselves to agricultural land. Some land is more fertile, some less; at any given moment, there must be some land on the margin of cultivation, which is only just worth cultivating. That is to say, it just yields a return to the farmer's capital which is equal to what the same capital would yield if otherwise invested. If the landlord were to demand rent for this land, the farmer would no longer find it worth cultivating; such land, therefore, will yield no rent to the landlord. On more fertile land, on the contrary, a given amount of capital yields more than the usual rate of profit; therefore the farmer is willing to pay the landlord for the right to cultivate it. What he is willing to pay is the excess of the produce above what is yielded by the same amount of the worst land in cultivation. Thus the rent of an acre of land is the amount by which the value of the crop that can be raised on it exceeds the value of the crop that can be raised on an acre of the worst land in cultivation. (FO 103-4)

REPRESENTATIVE GOVERNMENT, DEMOCRATIC

I am a firm believer in democratic representative government as the best form for those who have the tolerance and self-restraint that is required to make it workable. But its advocates make a mistake if they suppose that it can be at once introduced into countries where the average citizen has hitherto lacked all training in the give-and-take that it requires. In a Balkan country, not so many years ago, a party which had been beaten by a narrow margin in a general election retrieved its fortunes by shooting a sufficient number of the representatives of the other side to give it a majority. People in the West thought this characteristic of the Balkans, forgetting that Cromwell and Robespierre had acted likewise. (UE 140)

RESIGNATION

Resignation, however, has also its part to play in the conquest of happiness, and it is a part no less essential than that played by effort. The wise man, though he will not sit down under preventable misfortunes, will not waste time and emotion upon such as are unavoidable, and even such as are in themselves avoidable he will submit to if the time and labor required to avoid them would interfere with the pursuit of some more important object. (CH 236)

REVELATION
see JOHN SCOTUS

REVERENCE

Those who realize the harm that can be done to others by any use of force against them, and the worthlessness of the goods that can be acquired by force, will be very full of respect for the liberty of others; they will not try to bind them or fetter them; they will be slow to judge and swift to sympathize; they will treat every human being with a kind of tenderness, because the principle of good in him is at once fragile and infinitely precious. They will not condemn those who are unlike themselves; they will know and feel that individuality brings differences and uniformity means death. They will wish each human being to be as much a living thing and as little a mechanical product as it is possible to be; they will cherish in each one just those things which the harsh usage of a ruthless world would destroy.

In one word, all their dealings with others will be inspired by a deep impulse of *reverence*. (PI 12-3)

REVOLUTION

In my mind, I should not think any gain worth civil war or armed rebellion. I do not think any good comes of that and I think we must rely on persuasion and peaceful propaganda. Otherwise, we shall get nowhere. (TEP 11)

Apart from all arguments of detail, there are two broad objections to violent revolution in a democratic community. The first is that, when once the principle of respecting majorities as expressed at the ballot-box is abandoned, there is no reason to suppose that victory will be secured by the particular minority to which one happens to belong. There are many minorities besides Communists: religious minorities, teetotal minorities, militarist minorities, capitalist minorities. Any one of these could adopt the method of obtaining power advocated by the Bolsheviks, and any one would be just as likely to succeed as they are. (PTB 146-7)

The right to revolution in certain circumstances has been, and still is, an important right. We should be glad to see a revolution against the Nazis in Germany, or against Vichy in France. Very few people would maintain that France ought still to be under the Bourbons, or Russia under the Romanovs, yet neither could have been got rid of except by revolution. At the same time, there are bad revolutions as well as good ones; Mussolini, Hitler, and Franco afford the visible proof. An international government would not be very satisfactory if it allowed Fascist revolutions in the various countries over which it had nominal authority. I think we may say that a justifiable revolution is one which has the support of the majority, while an unjustifiable one is one which aims at establishing the tyranny of a minority. (FOP 10)

I do not wish to suggest that revolutions are never necessary, but I do wish to suggest that they are not short cuts to the millennium. There is no short cut to the good life, whether individual or social. To build up the good life, we must build up intelligence, self-control, and sympathy. (WIB 63-4)

And I do find a lack of that in the philosophy which believes that by sudden revolutions everything can be effected. By sudden revolutions you can change the names of things, but you cannot change people's whole habits and movements. And you find that the old

things come back with the new names. And that has always been the danger with revolutions. (BW 76)
see LIBERTY; REFORM

RICARDO
see RENT, RICARDO'S THEORY OF; VALUE, RICARDO'S THEORY OF

RIGHTEOUSNESS
Righteousness cannot be born until self-righteousness is dead. (JWT 202)

RIVALRY
Rivalry is, with most well-to-do energetic people, a stronger motive than love of money. Successful rivalry requires organization of rival forces; the tendency is for a business such as oil, for example, to organize itself into two rival groups, between them covering the world. They might, of course, combine, and they would no doubt increase their wealth if they did so. But combination would take the zest out of life. (I 34-5)

ROBESPIERRE
see DICTATORSHIP

ROMAN PHILOSOPHY
Latin philosophers took over Greek theories. To the end, Rome was culturally parasitic on Greece. The Romans invented no art forms, constructed no original system of philosophy, and made no scientific discoveries. They made good roads, systematic legal codes, and efficient armies; for the rest they looked to Greece. (HWP 278)

ROMANS
The Romans discovered how to carry on the government of a great empire by means of a civil service and a body of law. (IPI 186)

ROMANTICISM
The Romantic Movement was essentially a protest in the name of the emotions against the previous undue emphasis upon the will. The Romantic Movement achieved something as regards the treatment of very young children, but in the main the educational authorities were too firmly entrenched and too much habituated to command to be appreciably affected by the softer ideals of the Romantics. (ESO 30)

The romantic movement is characterized, as a whole, by the

substitution of aesthetic, for utilitarian standards. The earth-worm is useful, but not beautiful; the tiger is beautiful, but not useful. Darwin (who was not a romantic) praised the earth-worm; Blake praised the tiger. The morals of the romantics have primarily aesthetic motives. But in order to characterize the romantics, it is necessary to take account, not only of the importance of aesthetic motives, but also of the change of taste which made their sense of beauty different from that of their predecessors. (HWP 678)

ROMANTICISM, CRITICISM OF

It is not the psychology of the romantics that is at fault; it is their standard of values. They admire strong passions, of no matter what kind, and whatever may be their social consequences. Romantic love, especially when unfortunate, is strong enough to win their approval, but most of the strongest passions are destructive—hate and resentment and jealousy, remorse and despair, outraged pride and the fury of the unjustly oppressed, martial ardour and contempt for slaves and cowards. Hence the type of man encouraged by romanticism, especially of the Byronic variety, is violent and anti-social, an anarchic rebel or a conquering tyrant. (HWP 681)

ROUSSEAU

Rousseau appealed to the already existing cult of sensibility, and gave it a breadth and scope that it might not otherwise have possessed. He was a democrat, not only in his theories, but in his tastes. For long periods of his life, he was a poor vagabond, receiving kindness from people only slightly less destitute than himself. He repaid this kindness, in action, often with the blackest ingratitude, but in emotion his response was all that the most ardent devotee of sensibility could have wished. Having the tastes of a tramp, he found the restraints of Parisian society irksome. From him the romantics learned a contempt for the trammels of convention—first in dress and manners, in the minuet and the heroic couplet, then in art and love, and at last over the whole sphere of traditional morals. (HWP 676)
see WILL, THE GENERAL

ROUTINE

Another respect in which, to my mind, many apostles of freedom go astray, is that they fail to recognize sufficiently the importance of routine in the life of the young. I do not mean that a routine should be rigid and absolute: there should be days when it is varied, such as Christmas Day and holidays. But even these variations should, on the whole, be expected by the child. A life of uncertainty is nervously exhausting at all times, but especially in youth. The child derives a sense of security from knowing more or less what is going to happen day by day. (ESO 37)

S

SABELLIANISM

The view which finally prevailed was that the Father and Son were equal, and of the same substance; they were, however, distinct Persons. The view that they were not distinct, but only different aspects of one Being, was the Sabellian heresy, called after its founder Sabellius. (HWP 333)

SABOTAGE

Sabotage is the practice of doing bad work, or spoiling machinery or work which has already been done, as a method of dealing with employers in a dispute when a strike appears for some reason undesirable or impossible. (RF 66)

SANCTIONS, MORAL

It is through the operation of praise and blame that the positive morality of a community becomes socially effective. (LAM 107)

SCAPEGOATS

The most curious form of this kind of transferred hatred is the habit of looking for scapegoats. In this case it is ourselves that we hate, but as this emotion is uncomfortable, we manage to heap all our own feelings of guilt upon some unfortunate victim. In the Old Testament the victim is a goat. This represents a humanitarian reform, because at an earlier time the victim had been human. (TFD 42)

SCEPTICISM

The scepticism that I advocate amounts only to this: (1) that when the experts are agreed, the opposite opinion cannot be held to be certain; (2) that when they are not agreed, no opinion can be regarded as certain by a non-expert; and (3) that when they all hold that no sufficient grounds for a positive opinion exist, the ordinary man would do well to suspend his judgment. (SE 12-3)

Scepticism, while logically impeccable, is psychologically impossible, and there is an element of frivolous insincerity in any philosophy which pretends to accept it. Moreover, if scepticism is to be theoretically defensible, it must reject *all* inferences from what is experienced; a partial scepticism, such as the denial of physical events experienced by no one, or a solipsism which allows events in my future or in my unremembered past, has no logical justification since it must admit principles of inference which lead to beliefs that it rejects. (HK xi)

Scepticism with regard to the senses had troubled Greek philosophers from a very early stage; the only exceptions were those who, like Parmenides and Plato, denied the cognitive value of perception, and made their denial into an opportunity for an intellectual dogmatism. The Sophists, notably Protagoras and Gorgias, had been led by the ambiguities and apparent contradictions of sense-perception to a subjectivism not unlike Hume's. Pyrrho seems (for he very wisely wrote no books) to have added moral and logical scepticism to scepticism as to the senses. (HWP 233)

Gradually, however, more especially during the last thirteen years, the best men of science, as a result of technical progress, have been led more and more to a form of scepticism closely analogous to Hume's. Eddington, in expounding the theory of relativity, tends to the view that most so-called scientific laws are human conventions. (S 65)
see DOGMATISM; VERIFICATION

SCEPTICISM, LIBERAL

It is therefore important, if democracy is to be preserved, both to avoid the circumstances that produce general excitement, and to educate in such a way that the population shall be little prone to moods of this sort. Where a spirit of ferocious dogmatism prevails, any opinion with which men disagree is liable to provoke a breach of the peace. Schoolboys are apt to ill-treat a boy whose opinions are in any way odd, and many grown men have not got beyond the mental age of schoolboys. A diffused liberal sentiment, tinged with skepticism, makes social co-operation much less difficult, and liberty correspondingly more possible. (P 295)

SCHOLASTICISM

Scholasticism, in its narrower sense, begins early in the twelfth century. As a philosophical school, it has certain definite character- istics. First, it is confined within the limits of what appears to the writer to be orthodoxy; if his views are condemned by a council, he is usually willing to retract. This is not to be attributed entirely to cowardice; it is analogous to the submission of a judge to the decision of a Court of Appeal. Second, within the limits of ortho- doxy, Aristotle, who gradually became more fully known during the twelfth and thirteenth centuries, is increasingly accepted as the su- preme authority; Plato no longer holds the first place. Third, there is a great belief in "dialectic" and in syllogistic reasoning; the gen- eral temper of the scholastics is minute and disputatious rather than mystical. Fourth, the question of universals is brought to the fore by the discovery that Aristotle and Plato do not agree about it; it would be a mistake to suppose, however, that universals are the main concern of the philosophers of this period. (HWP 435)

SCHOLASTICISM, DEFECTS OF

The defects of the scholastic method are those that inevitably result from laying stress on "dialectic." These defects are: indiffer- ence to facts and science, belief in reasoning in matters which only observation can decide, and an undue emphasis on verbal distinc- tions and subtleties. (HWP 435)

SCHOPENHAUER

His appeal has always been less to professional philosophers, than to artistic and literary people in search of a philosophy that they could believe. He began the emphasis upon Will which is char- acteristic of much nineteenth and twentieth-century philosophy; but for him Will, though metaphysically fundamental, is ethically evil— an opposition only possible for a pessimist. He acknowledged three sources of his philosophy, Kant, Plato, and the Upanishads, but I do not think he owes as much to Plato as he thinks he does. His outlook has a certain temperamental affinity with that of the Hellenistic age; it is tired and valetudinarian, valuing peace more than victory, and quietism more than attempts at reform, which he regards as in- evitably futile. (HWP 753)
see NIETZSCHE

SCIENCE

The sudden change produced by science has upset the balance between our instincts, and our circumstances, but in directions not sufficiently noticed. Over-eating is not a serious danger, but over-fighting is. The human instincts of power and rivalry, like the dog's wolfish appetite, will need to be artificially curbed, if industrialism is to succeed. (I 13)

Science can, if it chooses, enable our grandchildren to live the good life, by giving them knowledge, self-control and characters productive of harmony rather than strife. At present it is teaching our children to kill each other, because many men of science are willing to sacrifice the future of mankind to their own momentary prosperity. But this phase will pass when men have acquired the same domination over their own passions that they already have over the physical forces of the external world. Then at last we shall have won our freedom. (WIB 87)

These various forms of madness—communism, nazism, Japanese imperialism—are the natural result of the impact of science on nations with a strong pre-scientific culture. The effects in Asia are still at an early stage. The effects upon the native races of Africa have hardly begun. It is therefore unlikely that the world will recover sanity in the near future. (STS 31)

Science, as its name implies, is primarily knowledge; by convention it is knowledge of a certain kind, the kind, namely, which seeks general laws connecting a number of particular facts. Gradually, however, the aspect of science as knowledge is being thrust into the background by the aspect of science as the power of manipulating nature. It is because science gives us the power of manipulating nature that it has more social importance than art. Science as the pursuit of truth is the equal, but not the superior, of art. Science as a technique, though it may have little intrinsic value, has a practical importance to which art cannot aspire. (SO viii-ix)

A man of science is a man who is—I don't mean each particular man of science, for there are many of them who are not scientific— but the man of science as he should be is a man who is careful, cautious, piecemeal, empirical in his conclusions, who is not ready with sweeping generalizations, who will not accept some large doctrine merely because it is fine and symmetrical and synthetic, but will examine it in its detail and its application. (BW 43)

Men sometimes speak as though the progress of science must necessarily be a boon to mankind, but that, I fear, is one of the comfortable nineteenth-century delusions which our more disillusioned age must discard. Science enables the holders of power to realize their purposes more fully than they could otherwise do. (I 57)

From what has been said about substance, I draw the conclusion that science is concerned with groups of "events," rather than with "things" that have changing "states." This is also the natural conclusion to draw from the substitution of space-time for space and time. The old notion of substance had a certain appropriateness so long as we could believe in one cosmic time and one cosmic space; but it does not fit in so easily when we adopt the four-dimensional space-time framework. (AOM 286)

Short of a relapse into a pre-scientific society—which could only take place by a process involving wide-spread starvation and appalling misery—the only cure for this diversion of science to methods of destruction is the creation of a single superstate strong enough to make serious wars impossible. But this is a problem for the politicians, not for the men of science. (BOD 15)

see EMPIRICISM; ETHICS, SCIENCE AND; MYSTICISM AND SCIENCE

SCIENCE AND VALUES

The sphere of values lies outside science, except in so far as science consists in the pursuit of knowledge. Science as the pursuit of power must not obtrude upon the sphere of values, and scientific technique, if it is to enrich human life, must not outweigh the ends which it should serve. (SO 266)

SCIENCE, FAITH OF

It seems to me that what may be called the "faith" of science, is more or less of the following sort: There are formulas (causal laws) connecting events, both perceived and unperceived; these formulas exhibit spatio-temporal continuity; i.e., involve no direct unmediated relation between events at a finite distance from each other. A suggested formula having the above characteristics becomes highly probable if, in addition to fitting in with all past observations, it enables us to predict others which are subsequently confirmed and which would be very improbable if the formula were false. (HK 314)

SCIENCE, PROGRESS OF

Einstein's theory involves only very minute corrections of Newtonian results. These very minute corrections, so far as they are measurable, have been empirically verified; but while the practical change is small, the intellectual change is enormous, since our whole conception of space and time has had to be revolutionized. The work of Einstein has emphasized the difficulty of permanent achievement in science. Newton's law of gravitation had reigned so long, and explained so much, that it seemed scarcely credible that it should stand in need of correction. Nevertheless, such correction has at last proved necessary, and no one doubts that the correction will, in its turn, have to be corrected. (SO 40)

SCIENTIFIC METHOD

Scientific method, although in its more refined forms, it may seem complicated, is in essence remarkably simple. It consists in observing such facts as will enable the observer to discover general laws governing facts of the kind in question. (SO 13)

There are in science immense numbers of different methods, appropriate to different classes of problems; but over and above them all, there is something not easily definable, which may be called *the* method of science. It was formerly customary to identify this with the inductive method, and to associate it with the name of Bacon. But the true inductive method was not discovered by Bacon, and the true method of science is something which includes deduction as much as induction, logic and mathematics as much as botany and geology. (ML 41-2)

SCIENTIFIC SPIRIT

The opposition between Russia and the West, therefore, though fundamentally economic, may be expected to extend over the whole sphere of belief. When I speak of belief I mean dogmatic opinions on matters as to which the truth is not known. The whole evil could, of course, be avoided by the spread of the scientific spirit, that is to say, by the habit of forming opinions on evidence rather than on prejudice; but although scientific technique is necessary to industrialism, the scientific spirit belongs rather to commerce, since it is necessarily individualistic and uninfluenced by authority. (SE 234)

The scientific state of mind is neither sceptical nor dogmatic. The sceptic holds that the truth is undiscoverable, while the dogmatist holds that the truth is already discovered. The man of science holds that the truth is discoverable though not discovered, at any rate in the matters which he is investigating. But even to say that the truth is discoverable is to say rather more than the genuine man of science believes, since he does not conceive his discoveries as final and absolute. Absence of finality is of the essence of the scientific spirit. (ESO 22)

SCIENTIFIC TEMPER

The temper required to make a success of democracy is, in the practical life, exactly what the scientific temper is in the intellectual life; it is a halfway house between skepticism and dogmatism. (P 299)

My plea throughout this address has been for the spread of the scientific temper, which is an altogether different thing from the knowledge of scientific results. The scientific temper is capable of regenerating mankind and providing an issue for all our troubles. The results of science, in the form of mechanism, poison gas, and the yellow press, bid fair to lead to the total downfall of our civilization. (FT 55)
see MYSTICISM

SCIENTIFIC TRUTHFULNESS

In the welter of conflicting fanaticisms, one of the few unifying forces is scientific truthfulness, by which I mean the habit of basing our beliefs upon observations and inferences as impersonal, and as much divested of local and temperamental bias, as is possible for human beings. To have insisted upon the introduction of this virtue into philosophy, and to have invented a powerful method by which it can be rendered fruitful, are the chief merits of the philosophical school of which I am a member. (HWP 836)

You cannot possibly get security in the world unless people are so educated that their desires will be non-competitive. If we desire to be rich, we could conceivably all be rich; but if your desire is to be richer than your neighbor, that is impossible for everybody. (ISI 5)

SECURITY, COLLECTIVE

It is clear that collective security, as a method of preventing war, cannot succeed unless there is an international armed force, under the orders of an international authority, and sufficiently strong to be able to defeat easily any probable combination of rebel States. (WWP 80)

SECURITY, SENSE OF

I do not deny that something will be lost in the process of unification, but more will be preserved, and something of great value—namely a sense of security—will be gained. It is to such a consummation that our imagination and our long range political thinking must be directed. (KF 55)

SELF-FORGETFULNESS

I have spoken of men who were eminent in one way or another. But in actual fact I have been quite as often impressed by men and women of no eminence. What I have found most unforgettable is a certain kind of moral quality, a quality of self-forgetfulness, whether in private life, in public affairs, or in the pursuit of truth. (UE 171)

SELF-GOVERNMENT

But it is a great misfortune if, from a confusion of ideas, men come to think that, because Parliaments are imperfect, there is no reason why there should be self-government. The grounds for advocating self-government are very familiar: first, that no benevolent despot can be trusted to know or pursue the interests of his subjects; second, that the practice of self-government is the only effective method of political education; third, that it tends to place the preponderance of force on the side of the constitution, and thus to promote order and stable government. Other reasons could be found, but I think these are the chief. (PTB 188)

SELF-INTEREST

Bentham supposed that the whole of morality could be derived from "enlightened self-interest," and that a person who always acted with a view to his own maximum satisfaction in the long run would always act rightly. I cannot accept this view. Tyrants have existed who derived exquisite pleasure from watching the infliction of torture; I cannot praise such men when prudence led them to spare their victim's lives with a view to further sufferings another day. (WIB 35-6)

SELLING, PSYCHOLOGY OF

The ultimate psychological source of our preference for selling over buying is that we prefer power to pleasure. This is not a universal characteristic; there are spendthrifts, who like a short life and a merry one. But it is a characteristic of the energetic, successful individuals who give the tone to a competitive age. (IPI 86)

SENSATION

We shall give the name "sensation" to the experience of being immediately aware of these things. Thus, whenever we see a colour, we have a sensation *of* the colour, but the colour itself is a sense-datum, not a sensation. (PP 17)

And finally it is by no means certain that the peculiar causal laws which govern mental events are not really physiological. The law of habit, which is one of the most distinctive, may be fully explicable in terms of the peculiarities of nervous tissue, and these peculiarities, in turn, may be explicable by the laws of physics. It seems, therefore, that we are driven to a different kind of definition. It is for this reason that it was necessary to develop the definition of perception. With this definition, we can define a sensation as the non-mnemic elements in a perception. (AM 139)

I believe that sensations (including images) supply all the "stuff" of the mind, and that everything else can be analysed into groups of sensations related in various ways, or characteristics of sensations or of groups of sensations. (AM 69)

Sensations are what is common to the mental and physical worlds; they may be defined as the intersection of mind and matter. (AM 144)
see PERCEPTION

SENSE-DATA

If we have been right in our contentions, sense-data are merely those among the ultimate constituents of the physical world of which we happen to be immediately aware; they themselves are purely physical, and all that is mental in connection with them is our awareness of them, which is irrelevant to their nature and to their place in physics. (ML 143)

Let us give the name of "sense-data" to the things that are immediately known in sensation: such things as colours, sounds, smells, hardnesses, roughnesses, and so on. (PP 17)

SENSIBILIA

I shall give the name *sensibilia* to those objects which have the same metaphysical and physical status as sense-data, without necessarily being data to any mind. Thus the relation of a *sensibile* to a sense-datum is like that of a man to a husband: a man becomes a husband by entering into the relation of marriage, and similarly a *sensibile* becomes a sense-datum by entering into the relation of acquaintance. (ML 148-9)

SENSITIVENESS

A purely theoretical definition would be that a person is emotionally sensitive when many stimuli produce emotions in him; but taken thus broadly the quality is not necessarily a good one. If sensitiveness is to be good, the emotional reaction must be in some sense *appropriate:* mere intensity is not what is needed. The quality I have in mind is that of being affected pleasurably or the reverse by many things, and by the right things. (EEC 69-70)

SENTENCE, A SINGLE

A single sentence, for our purposes, must be one which says something that cannot be said in two separate simpler sentences. (IMT 35)

SENTENCE, VERIFIER AND FALSIFIER OF THE

When an indicative sentence is asserted, there are three things concerned. There is the cognitive attitude of the assertor-belief, disbelief and hesitation, in the cases so far considered; there is the content or contents denoted by the sentence; and there is the fact or facts in virtue of which the sentence is true or false, which I will call the "verifier" or "falsifier" of the sentence. (HK 128)

SENTENCES

Thus the correct use of relational words, i.e. of sentences, involves what may be correctly termed "perception of form", i.e. it involves a definite reaction to a stimulus which is a form. Suppose, for example, that a child has learnt to say that one thing is "above" another when this is in fact the case. The stimulus to the use of the word "above" is a relational feature of the environment, and we may say that this feature is "perceived" since it produces a definite reaction. It may be said that the relation *above* is not very like the word "above." That is true; but the same is true of ordinary physical objects. A stone, according to the physicists, is not at all like what we see when we look at it, and yet we may be correctly said to "perceive" it. This, however, is to anticipate. The definite point which has emerged is that, when a person can use sentences correctly, that is a proof of sensitiveness to formal or relational stimuli. (OP 56)

We must now define "sentence" and "having the same meaning." Ignoring the latter for the moment, what is a sentence? It may be a single word, or, more usually, a number of words put together according to the laws of syntax; but what distinguishes it is that it expresses something of the nature of an assertion, a denial, an imperative, a desire, or a question. What is more remarkable about a sentence, from our point of view, is that we can understand what it expresses if we know the meaning of its several words and the rules of syntax. (IMT 10-1)

see WORDS AND PROPOSITIONS

SENTENCES, INDICATIVE

To sum up: a sentence in the indicative "expresses" a belief; it is merely one of an indefinite multitude of acts that can express a given belief. If the sentence contains no apparent variable, it must mention only things now present to the believer; in that case it is capable of having a peculiar causal relation to these things which makes what in an earlier chapter, we called a "sentence describing an experience." If it has this peculiar relation, the sentence (and the belief which it expresses) is called "true"; if not, "false." In this case, what the sentence "expresses" and what it "indicates" are identical, unless, being false, it "indicates" nothing. (IMT 279)

SENTENCES, MOLECULAR

Sentences containing conjunctions I shall call "molecular" sentences, the "p" and "q" which are conjoined being conceived as the "atoms." Given the truth or falsehood of a set of propositions, the truth or falsehood of every molecular proposition constructed out of the set follows by syntactical rules, and requires no fresh observation of facts. We are, in fact, in the domain of logic. (HK 120)

SENTIMENT VERSUS REASON
see REASON

SERIES, CLOSED

A series is said to be "closed" *(abgeschlossen)* when every progression or regression contained in the series has a limit in the series. (IMP 103)

SERIES, DEDEKINDIAN

It was the needs of geometry, as much as anything, that led to the definition of "Dedekindian" continuity. It will be remembered that we defined a series as Dedekindian when every sub-class of the field has a boundary. (It is sufficient to assume that there is always an *upper* boundary, or that there is always a *lower* boundary. If one of these is assumed, the other can be deduced.) That is to say, a series is Dedekindian when there are no gaps. (IMP 101)

SERIES, INFINITE

An "infinite series" may be defined as a series of which the field is an infinite class. (IMP 89)

SERIES, PERFECT

A series is "perfect" when it is *condensed in itself* and *closed*, i.e. when every term is the limit of a progression or regression, and every progression or regression contained in the series has a limit in the series. (IMP 103)

SERIES, WELL-ORDERED

A "well-ordered" series is one in which every sub-class (except, of course, the null-class) has a first term. (IMP 93)

SEX

The whole conception of sex as a matter of natural delight, rising on occasion to poetry, sometimes lighthearted and gay, sometimes passionate with a tragic profundity, lies outside the purview of the pedagogic moralists, to whom sex is wicked when it is combined with delight, and virtuous only when it is drab and habitual. Poetry and joy and beauty are thrust out of life by this morality of ugliness, and something stark and rigid is brought into all human relationships. From this outlook come prudery and petty-mindedness and the death of imagination. It may be that a freer outlook also has its dangers. But they are the dangers of life, not of death. (ESO 124-5)

SEX EDUCATION

Answering questions is a major part of sex education. Two rules cover the ground. First, always give a truthful answer to a question; secondly, regard sex knowledge as exactly like any other knowledge. (EEC 213)

SEX RELATIONS, HAPPINESS IN

But I do say that the only sex relations that have real value are those in which there is no reticence and in which the whole personality of both becomes merged in a new collective personality. Of all forms of caution, caution in love is perhaps most fatal to true happiness. (CH 186)

SEXUAL INTERCOURSE

Men desire sexual intercourse, but they do not as a rule desire children strongly or often. Yet without the hope of children and its occasional realization, sexual intercourse remains for most people an isolated and separate pleasure, not uniting their personal life with the life of mankind, not continuous with the central purposes by which they live, and not capable of bringing that profound sense of fulfilment which comes from completion by children. (PSR 231)

SEXUAL MORALITY

Sexual morality, freed from superstition, is a simple matter. Fraud and deceit, assault, seduction of persons under age, are proper matters for the criminal law. Relations between adults who are free agents are a private matter, and should not be interfered with either by the law or by public opinion, because no outsider can know whether they are good or bad. When children are involved the state becomes interested to the extent of seeing that they are properly educated and cared for, and it ought to insure that the father does his duty by them in the way of maintenance. But neither the state nor public opinion ought to insist on the parents living together if they are incompatible; the spectacle of parents' quarrels is far worse for children than the separation of the parents could possibly be. (SIE 14)

SHREWDNESS

Shrewdness when it is genuine, belongs more to the unconscious than to the conscious part of our nature. It is, I suppose, the main quality required for success in business. From a moral point of view, it is a humble quality, since it is always selfish; yet it suffices to keep men from the worst crimes. (SE 21)

SIGN

see LANGUAGE

SIGNIFICANCE, PSYCHOLOGICAL THEORY OF

But there is also a purely psychological theory of significance. In this theory a spoken sentence is "significant" if its causes are of a certain kind, and a heard sentence is "significant" if its effects are of a certain kind. The psychological theory of significance consists in defining these kinds. (IMT 238-9)

SIGNIFICATION

There are, we said, two sides to signification, which we may call subjective and objective respectively. The subjective side has to do with the state of the person uttering the sentence, while the objective side has to do with what would make the sentence true or false. (HK 112)

SIMILAR

We may now state our definition of similarity as follows: One class is said to be "similar" to another when there is a one-one relation of which the one class is the domain, while the other is the converse domain. (IMP 16)

SIMULTANEITY

Thus, so far as observers on the earth are concerned, the definition of simultaneity will work well enough, so long as we are dealing with events on the surface of the earth. It gives results which are consistent with each other, and can be used for terrestrial physics in all problems in which we can ignore the fact that the earth moves. (ABCR 45)

SIN

What I do wish to do is to make people aware that there is nothing outside human desires, human beliefs, and human sins that can push the world toward disaster. (TRF 23)

The conception of sin which is bound up with Christian ethics is one that does an extraordinary amount of harm, since it affords people an outlet for their sadism which they believe to be legitimate and even noble. (RUC 8)

Those who have a scientific outlook on human behavior, moreover, find it impossible to label any action as "sin"; they realize that what we do has its origin in our heredity, our education, and our environment, and that it is by control of these causes, rather than by denunciation, that conduct injurious is to be prevented. (OSE 39)

SLAVE LABOR CAMPS

In Russia the inhumanities not unlike those of the Congo and of early British industrialism are inflicted in the forced labor camps which have become an integral part of the Soviet economy. Human

nature is not to be trusted with irresponsible power, and where irresponsible power exists, appalling cruelties are to be expected.
(BOD 16)

SOCIAL COHESION

Social cohesion, which started with loyalty to a group reinforced
by the fear of enemies, grew by processes partly natural and partly
deliberate until it reached the vast conglomerations that we now know
as nations. (AAI 16)

A creed or sentiment of some kind is essential for social cohesion, but if it is to be a source of strength it must be genuinely
and deeply felt by the great majority of the population, including
a considerable percentage of those upon whom technical efficiency
depends. Where these conditions are absent, governments may seek
to produce them by censorship and persecution; but censorship and
persecution, if they are severe, cause men to become out of touch with
reality, and ignorant or obvious of facts which it is important to
know. (P 154)

SOCIAL CONTRACT

The "social contract," in the only sense in which it is not *completely* mythical, is a contract among conquerors, which loses its
raison d'etre if they are deprived of the benefits of conquest. (P 184)

The theory that government was created by a contract is, of
course, pre-evolutionary. Government, like measles and whooping
cough, must have grown up gradually, though, like them, it could
be introduced suddenly into new regions such as the South Sea
Islands. Before men had studied anthropology they had no idea of
the psychological mechanisms involved in the beginnings of government, or of the fantastic reasons which lead men to adopt institutions
and customs that subsequently proved useful. But as a legal fiction,
to *justify* government, the theory of the social contract has *some*
measure of truth. (HWP 633)

SOCIAL PHILOSOPHY

Gradually, through the investigation of these questions, I have
come to a certain philosophy of life, guided always by the desire
to discover some way in which men, with the congenital characteristics which nature has given them, can live together in societies
without devoting themselves to making each other miserable. The
keynote of my social philosophy, from a scientific point of view, is

the emphasis upon psychology and the practice of judging social institutions by their effects upon human character. (WIBII 14-5)

SOCIALISM

Let us begin by a definition of Socialism. The definition must consist of two parts, economic and political. The economic part consists in State ownership of ultimate economic power, which involves, as a minimum, land and minerals, capital, banking, credit and foreign trade. The political part requires that the ultimate political power should be democratic. (IPI 140-1)

Socialism, like everything else that is vital, is rather a tendency than a strictly definable body of doctrine. A definition of Socialism is sure either to include some views which many would regard as not Socialistic, or to exclude others which claim to be included. But I think we shall come nearest to the essence of Socialism by defining it as the advocacy of communal ownership of land and capital. (RF 1)

Socialism from the first had aimed at certain goals: a nearer approach to equality, a greater control by wage-earners over the conditions of their work, a diminution of irresponsible power, and, as result and incentive, an ultimate immense increase in general happiness. The realization of these aims, the Socialists thought, required certain means, which were painful to the rich; fear of the means produced opposition, opposition led to bitterness and class war, and in the end there were many in whom hatred of opponents outweighed the original humanitarian motive. Marx sanctified the hatred and the strife. The gain to the wage-earner became emotionally, and even intellectually, less important than the injury to the capitalist. The present Soviet system is an externalization of Marx's liverish misanthropy. (CTR 9-10)

What do we mean by "socialism"? The word is often used very vaguely, but it is not difficult to give it a precise meaning. The definition of socialism consists of two parts, one economic and one political, one concerned with production and distribution of goods, the other with the distribution of power. (PIC 98)

As regards production, all land and capital must be the property of the state; though perhaps the state might sometimes delegate possession to some large body of producers or consumers, such as a trade-union or a co-operative society. As regards distribution, what is paid for each kind of work must be fixed by a public authority, with a minimum of what is required for bare necessaries, and a maximum of what will give the greatest incentive to efficient work. There is no need of equality of income for all as part of the definition of socialism; the fact that Chaliapin is paid more than a scene-shifter does not suffice to prove that Russia is still bourgeois. What is essential is that a man should not be able to extort profit by his possession of means of production, whether land or capital. But socialism certainly has as its ideal equality of income, subject only to such modification as may be imposed by the special needs of various classes of workers. (PIC 98-9)

SOCIALISM, GUILD

The application of this same principle of group autonomy to industry is the source of the doctrines of guild socialism. This is a subject upon which there is a considerable literature, and it would overweigh one part of our subject to enter upon its niceties. I will only say, therefore, that an industry could win autonomy, in practice, by the same methods that have been practiced by the churches, and that I believe it very desirable that all the greater industries should do so. (PIC 232-233)

SOCIALISM, POLITICS OF

On the political side, socialism is not compatible with autocracy or oligarchy, but demands that all sane adults should have an equal share of ultimate political power. Even the Bolsheviks, who oppose democracy during the time of transition, regard it as part of their ideal, and admit that socialism will not be fully realized until it is possible to restore liberal democratic institutions such as universal suffrage, free speech, and free press. (PIC 99)

SOCIETY, EVILS OF

Bolshevik theory seems to me to err by concentrating its attention upon one evil, namely, inequality of wealth, which it believes to be at the bottom of all others. I do not believe any one evil can be thus isolated, but if I had to select one as the greatest of political evils, I should select inequality of power. (PTB 167)

SOCIETY, SCIENTIFIC

If a scientific society is to survive the self-assertiveness which leads to wars will have to be curbed by authority, and spontaneity will have to be restrained in many directions. It may prove impossible to restrain it in harmful directions without diminishing it in directions that are desirable. If so, safety will have been purchased at the expense of dullness. But this is a doubtful speculation, and we may hope that it is a mistaken one.

Science may be a boon if war can be abolished and democracy and cultural liberty preserved. If this cannot be done, science will precipitate evils greater than any that mankind has ever experienced. (BOD 16)

SOCIETY, THE GOOD
see HUMAN EXCELLENCE

SOCRATES
The Platonic Socrates consistently maintains that he knows nothing, and is only wiser than others in knowing that he knows nothing; but he does not think knowledge unobtainable. On the contrary, he thinks the search for knowledge of the utmost importance. He maintains that no man sins wittingly, and therefore only knowledge is needed to make all men perfectly virtuous. (HWP 92)

SOCRATIC METHOD
The matters that are suitable for treatment by the Socratic method are those as to which we have already enough knowledge to come to a right conclusion, but have failed, through confusion of thought or lack of analysis, to make the best logical use of what we know. A question such as "what is justice?" is eminently suited for discussion in a Platonic dialogue. We all freely use the words "just" and "unjust," and, by examining the ways in which we use them, we can arrive inductively at the definition that will best suit with usage. All that is needed is knowledge of how the words in question are used. But when our inquiry is concluded, we have made only a linguistic discovery, not a discovery in ethics. (HWP 93)

SOLIPSISM
Thus I am reduced to what is called "solipsism", i.e. the theory that I alone exist. This is a view which is hard to refute, but still harder to believe. I once received a letter from a philosopher who professed to be a solipsist, but was surprised that there were no others! Yet this philosopher was by way of believing that no one else existed. This shows that solipsism is not really believed even by those who think they are convinced of its truth. (OP 291)

Thus if we cannot be sure of the independent existence of objects, we shall be left alone in a desert—it may be that the whole outer world is nothing but a dream, and that we alone exist. This is an uncomfortable possibility; but although it cannot be strictly *proved* to be false, there is not the slightest reason to suppose it is true. (PP 26-7)

We may distinguish two kinds of solipsism, which I shall call "dogmatic" and "skeptical" respectively. The dogmatic kind, in the above statement, says "There is nothing beyond data," while the skeptical kind says "There is not known to be anything beyond data." No grounds exist in favor of the dogmatic form, since it is just as difficult to disprove existence as to prove it, when what is concerned is something which is not a datum. (HK 176)
see SCEPTICISM

SOLITUDE

A certain degree of isolation both in space and time is essential to generate the independence required for the most important work; there must be something which is felt to be of more importance than the admiration of the contemporary crowd. We are suffering not from the decay of theological beliefs but from the loss of solitude. (UE 69-70)

SOME
see ALL

SOPHISTS

This explains the popularity of the Sophists with one class and their unpopularity with another. But in their own minds they served more impersonal purposes, and it is clear that many of them were genuinely concerned with philosophy. Plato devoted himself to caricaturing and vilifying them, but they must not be judged by his polemics. (HWP 75)

SORCERY

Sorcery was not, originally, considered a peculiarly feminine crime. The concentration on women began in the fifteenth century and from then until late in the seventeenth century the persecution of witches was widespread and severe. Innocent VIII, in 1484, issued a Bull against witchcraft, and appointed two inquisitors to punish it. These men, in 1489, published a book, long accepted as authoritative, called *Malleus Maleficarum*, "the hammer of female malefactors." They maintained that witchcraft is more natural to women than to men, because of the inherent wickedness of their hearts. The commonest accusation against witches, at this time, **was** that of causing bad weather. (RAS 97)

SOUL, THE

The "soul," as it first appeared in Greek thought, had a religious though not a Christian origin. It seems, so far as Greece was concerned, to have originated in the teaching of the Pythagoreans, who believed in transmigration, and aimed at an ultimate salvation which was to consist of liberation from the bondage to matter which the soul must suffer so long as it is attached to a body. The Pythagoreans influenced Plato, and Plato influenced the Fathers of the Church; in this way the doctrine of the soul as something distinct from the body became part of Christian doctrine. Other influences entered in, notably that of Aristotle and that of the Stoics; but Platonism, particularly in its later forms, was the most important pagan element in patristic philosophy. (RAS 114-5)

SOVEREIGNTY

There is no more justification for the claim to absolute sovereignty on the part of a state than there would be for a similar claim on the part of an individual. (PI 154)
see PUBLIC OPINION, INTERNATIONAL

SOVIET RUSSIA
see POWER, UNRESTRICTED

SPACE

There are two great types of spatial theory, the one represented by Newton, the other by Leibniz. These two are brought face to face in the controversy with Clarke. Both result from emphasizing one or other of the following pair of ideas. If we take two points A and B, they have (1) a distance, which is simply a relation between the two, (2) an actual length, consisting of so much space, and stretching from A to B. If we insist on the former as the essence of space, we get a relational theory; the terms A and B, whose distance is spatial, must themselves be non-spatial, since they are not relations. If we insist on the latter, the actual intervening length, we find it divisible into an infinite number of points each like the end points A and B. This alternative gives the Newtonian theory of absolute space consisting not in an assemblage of possible relations, but in an infinite collection of actual points. The objection to Newton's theory is, that it is self-contradictory; the objection to Leibniz's, that it is plainly inconsistent with the facts, and, in the end, just **as** self-contradictory as Newton's. A theory free from both these defects is much to be desired, as it will be something which philosophy has not hitherto known. (PL 112-3)

SPACE, PERSPECTIVE

Perspective space is the system of "points of view" of private spaces (perspectives), or, since "points of view" have not been defined, we may say it is the system of the private spaces themselves. (KEW 95)

SPACE, PHYSICAL AND PERCEPTUAL

It follows that the space of percepts, like the percepts, must be private; there are as many perceptual spaces as there are percipients. My percept of a table is outside my percept of my head, in my perceptual space; but it does not follow that it is outside my head as a physical object in physical space. Physical space is neutral and public: in this space, all my percepts are in my head, even the most distant star *as I see it*. Physical and perceptual space have relations, but they are not identical, and failure to grasp the difference between them is a potent source of confusion. (OP 138)

SPACE-TIME

Moreover, the space and time reckonings are no longer independent of each other. If you alter the way of reckoning position in space, you may also alter the time interval between two events. If you alter the way of reckoning time, you may also alter the distance in space between two events. Thus space and time are no longer independent, any more than the three dimensions of space are. We still need four quantities to determine the position of an event, but we cannot, as before, divide off one of the four as quite independent of the other three. (ABCR 60-1)
see RELATIVITY

SPACE-TIME, PHYSICAL

Physical space-time, as we have seen, is an inference from perceptual space and time; it contains all observed occurrences, and also all unobserved occurrences. But since it is inferential, the location of an occurrence in it is also inferential. The locating of events in physical space-time is effected by two methods. First, there is a correlation between perceptual space and time and physical space-time, though this correlation is only rough and approximate. Second, the causal laws of physics assign an order to the events concerned, and it is partly by means of them that unobserved events are located in space-time. (HK 326)

SPARTA

Sparta had a double effect on Greek thought: through the reality, and through the myth. Each is important. The reality enabled the Spartans to defeat Athens in war; the myth influenced Plato's political theory, and that of countless subsequent writers. The myth, fully developed, is to be found in Plutarch's *Life of Lycurgus*; the ideals that it favours have had a great part in framing the doctrines of Rousseau, Nietzsche, and National Socialism. (HWP 94)

SPECIALIZATION

Narrow specialization, therefore, cannot produce a philosophy which shall be of service to our age. It is necessary to embrace all life and all science—Europe, Asia, and America, physics, biology, and psychology. The task is almost super-human. All that the present author can hope to do is to make some men conscious of the problem and of the kind of directions in which solutions are to be sought. (ISP xviii-xix)

SPECTRUM

The separated colours are called a spectrum, so that a spectroscope is an instrument for seeing a spectrum. The essential feature of the spectroscope is the prism through which the light passes, which refracts different colours differently, and so makes them separately visible. The rainbow is a natural spectrum, caused by refraction of sunlight in raindrops. (ABCA 37)

When white light is passed through a gas that is not glowing, and then analysed by the spectroscope, it is found that there are dark lines, which are to a great extent (though not by any means completely) identical with the bright lines that were emitted by the glowing gas. These dark lines are called the "absorption-spectrum" of the gas, whereas the bright lines are called the "emission-spectrum." (ABCA 38)

SPEECH

We may say, generally, that speech consists, with some exceptions, of noises made by persons with a view to causing desired actions by other persons. Its indicative and assertive capacities, however, remain fundamental, since it is owing to them that, when we hear speech, it can cause us to act in a manner appropriate to some feature of the environment which is perceived by the speaker but not by the hearer, or which the speaker remembers from past perception. (IMT 30-1)

SPINOZA

Spinoza (1643-77) is the noblest and most lovable of the great philosophers. Intellectually, some others have surpassed him, but ethically, he is supreme. As a natural consequence, he was considered, during his lifetime and for a century after his death, a man of appalling wickedness. He was born a Jew, but the Jews excommunicated him. Christians abhorred him equally; although his whole philosophy is dominated by the idea of God, the orthodox accused him of atheism. (HWP 569)

We cannot accept his method, but that is because we cannot accept his metaphysic. We cannot believe that the interconnections of the parts of the universe are *logical*, because we hold that scientific laws are to be discovered by observation, not by reasoning alone. But for Spinoza the geometrical method was necessary, and was bound up with the most essential parts of his doctrine. (HWP 572)
see ETERNITY, UNDER THE ASPECT OF

SPIRIT, LIFE OF THE

The life of the spirit centers round impersonal feeling, as the life of the mind centers round impersonal thought. In this sense, all art belongs to the life of the spirit, though its greatness is derived from its being also intimately bound up with the life of instinct. (PSR 226)

STATE, FUNCTION OF THE
see CREATIVENESS; LIBERTY; ORGANIZATIONS

STATE, ORGANIC VIEW OF THE

Men who advocate what they call the "organic" view of the State always imagine that what they believe in is an antithesis to mechanism. This is a most curious delusion. A machine is essentially organic, in the sense that it has parts which co-operate to produce a single useful result, and that these separate parts have no value on their own account. A machine may not be so perfect an example of an organism as an animal is, but we can make machines and we cannot make animals. Therefore when we are exhorted to make society "organic," it is from machinery that we shall necessarily derive our imaginative models, since we do not know how to make society a living animal. (FIE 159)

STATE, THE

The State, in spite of what Anarchists urge, seems a necessary institution for certain purposes. Peace and war, tariffs, regulation of sanitary conditions and of the sale of noxious drugs, the preservation of a just system of distribution; these, among others, are functions which could hardly be performed in a community in which there was no central government. (RF 137)

STATE, THE WORLD

Apart from national cohesion within the State, which is all that State education attempts to achieve at present, international cohesion, and a sense of the whole human race as one co-operative unit, is becoming increasingly necessary, if our scientific civilization is to survive. I think this survival will demand, as a minimum condition, the establishment of a world State, and the subsequent institution of a world-wide system of education designed to produce loyalty to the world State. (ESO 26)

STATE, WITHERING AWAY OF THE

All the burning political questions of our time, according to the Communists, are questions of class conflict, and will disappear when the division of classes disappears. Accordingly the State will no longer be required, since the State is essentially an engine of power designed to give the victory to one side in the class conflict. (PTB 152)

STOICISM

The place of stoicism in life has, perhaps, been somewhat underestimated in recent times, particularly by progressive educationists. When misfortune threatens, there are two ways of dealing with the situation: we may try to avoid the misfortune, or we may decide that we will meet it with fortitude. The former method is admirable where it is available without cowardice; but the latter is necessary, sooner or later, for any one who is not prepared to be the slave of fear. This attitude constitutes stoicism. (IPI 255)

Stoicism, unlike the earlier purely Greek philosophies, is emotionally narrow, and in a certain sense fanatical; but it also contains religious elements of which the world felt the need, and which the Greeks seemed unable to supply. (HWP 252)

These passages bring out very clearly the inherent contradictions in Stoic ethics and theology. On the one hand, the universe is a rigidly deterministic single whole, in which all that happens is the result of previous causes. On the other hand, the individual will is completely autonomous, and no man can be forced to sin by outside causes. This is one contradiction, and there is a second closely connected with it. Since the will is autonomous, and the virtuous will alone is good, one man cannot do either good or harm to another; therefore benevolence is an illusion. (HWP 266)

STUFF OF THE WORLD

The stuff of the world may be called physical or mental or both or neither, as we please; in fact, the words serve no purpose. There is only one definition of the words that is unobjectionable: "Physical" is what is dealt with by physics, and "mental" is what is dealt with by psychology. When, accordingly, I speak of "physical" space, I mean the space that occurs in physics. (OP 142)

SUBJECT

The question whether all propositions are reducible to the subject-predicate form is one of fundamental importance to all philosophy which uses the notion of substance. (PL 12)

SUBJECTIVISM
see AUGUSTINE

SUBJECTIVITY

We have been using the word "objectivity" in the preceding pages, and it is time to consider exactly what we mean by it. Suppose some scene—say in a theatre—is simultaneously seen by a number of people and photographed by a number of cameras. The impression made upon a person or a camera is in some respects like that made upon other persons and cameras, in other respects different. We shall call the elements which are alike "objective" elements in the impression, and those which are peculiar we shall call "subjective." Thus those features of shapes which are considered in projective geometry will be objective whereas those considered in metrical (where lengths and angles are measured) cannot be made objective, through sight alone, but demand the use of other senses. In the photographs, a man on the stage will be longer if the camera is near the stage than if it is far off, assuming all the cameras to be alike. But if four actors are standing in a row in one photograph, they will be standing in a row in another; this is an "objective" feature of the impression. And the differences in the visual impressions of a number of spectators with normal eyesight are exactly analogous to the differences in the photographs; so also are the likenesses. Thus the "subjectivity" that we are speaking about at present is something belonging to the physical world, not to psychology. (OP 154)

In describing the world, subjectivity is a vice. Kant spoke of himself as having effected a "Copernican revolution," but he would have been more accurate if he had spoken of a "Ptolemaic counterrevolution," since he put Man back at the center from which Copernicus had dethroned him. (HK xi)

SUBMISSION, IMPULSE OF

The impulse of submission, which is just as real and just as common as the impulse to command, has its roots in fear. The most unruly gang of children ever imagined will become completely amenable to the orders of a competent adult in an alarming situation, such as a fire; when the War came, the Pankhursts made their peace with Lloyd George. Whenever there is acute danger, the impulse of most people is to seek out authority and submit to it; at such moments, few would dream of revolution. (P 19)

SUBSTANCE

If a substance is *only* defined by its predicates—and this is essential to the Identity of Indiscernibles—then it would seem to be identical with the sum of those predicates. In that case, to say that such and such a substance exists, is merely a compendious way of saying that all its predicates exist. Predicates do not *inhere* in the substance in any other sense than that in which letters inhere in the alphabet. (PL 59)

A philosophy of substance, we may say generally, should be either a monism or a monadism. A monism is necessarily pantheistic, and a monadism, when it is logical, is as necessarily atheistic. (PL 172)

SUBSTANCES

Names of substances not obviously collections of individuals, such as "milk," "wood," are apt to be learned ostensively when they denote things familiar in everyday life. The atomic theory is an attempt to identify this class of objects with the former, so that milk, for instance, is a collection of milky individuals (molecules), just as the human race is a collection of men, women, and children. (HK 69)

SUCCESS
What I do maintain is that success can only be one ingredient in happiness, and is too dearly purchased if all the other ingredients have been sacrificed to obtain it. (CH 49)

SUCCESSOR
The successor of the number of terms in the class a is the number of terms in the class consisting of a together with x, where x is any term not belonging to the class. (IMP 23)
see POSTERITY OF A GIVEN NATURAL NUMBER

SUICIDE, MORALITY OF
see CREATIVITY

SUPRALAPSARIANS
They may even find a justification of the *agent provocateur* in the theology of the supralapsarians, who held that God placed man in circumstances which made it certain that he would sin, in order that his Creator might have the opportunity of exercising the virtue of justice by punishing him. (SSI 21)

SURPLUS VALUE, CRITICISM OF MARX'S THEORY OF
He may mean either of two things. He may be giving a mere verbal definition of the word "value": when I speak of the "value" of a commodity (he may be saying), I mean the amount of labor required to produce, or rather, such quantity of other commodities as an equivalent amount of labor would produce. Or, again, he may be using "value" in an ethical sense: he may mean that goods *ought* to exchange in proportion to the labor involved, and would do so in a world ruled by economic justice. If he adopts the first of these alternatives, most of the propositions in his theory of value become trivial, while those which assert a connection between value and price become arbitrary and remain partly false. If he adopts the second alternative, he is no longer analyzing economic facts, but setting up an economic ideal . . . . Either the verbal or the ethical alternative as

the meaning of "value," therefore, reduces Marx's economic theory to a state of confusion. (FO 205)

Marx's theory of surplus value is simple in its main outline, though complicated in its details. He argues that a wage-earner produces goods equal in value to his wages in a portion of the working day, often assumed to be about half, and in the remainder of his working day produces goods which become the property of the capitalist although he has not had to make any payment for them. Thus the wage-earner produces more than he is paid for; the value of this additional product is what Marx calls "surplus value." (FO 201)

I cannot accept Marx's theory of value, nor yet, in his form, the theory of surplus value. The theory that the exchange value of a commodity is proportional to the labor involved in its production, which Marx took over from Ricardo, is shown to be false by Ricardo's theory of rent, and has long been abandoned by all non-Marxian economists. The theory of surplus value rests upon Malthus's theory of population, which Marx elsewhere rejects. Marx's economics do not form a logically coherent whole, but are built up by the alternate acceptance and rejection of older doctrines, as may suit his convenience in making out a case against the capitalists. (WNCO 133)

Marx's *magnum opus*, "Capital," added bulk and substance to the theses of the Communist Manifesto. It contributed the theory of surplus value, which professed to explain the actual mechanism of capitalist exploitation. This doctrine is very complicated and is scarcely tenable as a contribution to pure theory. It is rather to be viewed as a translation into abstract terms of the hatred with which Marx regarded the system that coins wealth out of human lives, and it is in this spirit, rather than in that of disinterested analysis, that it has been read by its admirers. (RF 18)

SYMBOL
see LANGUAGE

SYMMETRICAL RELATION
Thus a relation is symmetrical if, whenever it holds between A and B, it also holds between B and A. (KEW 50)

SYMMETRY
see ASYMMETRY

SYNCATEGORIMATIC
Sometimes it is said that some words are "syncategorimatic,"

which apparently means that they have no significance by themselves, but contribute to the significance of sentences in which they occur. According to this way of speaking, proper names are not syncategorimatic, but whether this can be a definition is a somewhat doubtful question. In any case, it is difficult to get a clear definition of the term, "syncategorimatic." (HK 73-4)

SYNDICALISM

Syndicalism stands essentially for the point of view of the producer as opposed to that of the consumer; it is concerned with reforming actual work, and the organization of industry, not *merely* with securing greater rewards for work. From this point of view its vigor and its distinctive character are derived. It aims at substituting industrial for political action, and at using Trade Union organization for purposes for which orthodox Socialism would look to Parliament. (RF 62)

SYNTHETIC

All the propositions which are not tautologies we shall call "synthetic." The simplest kinds of propositions must be synthetic, in virtue of the above argument. And if logic or pure mathematics can ever be employed in a process leading to knowledge that is not tautological, there must be sources of knowledge other than logic and pure mathematics. (AOM 173)

TAOISM

Lao-Tze's book, or rather the book attributed to him, is very short but his ideas were developed by his disciple Chuang-Tze, who is more interesting than his master. The philosophy which both advocated was one of freedom. They thought ill of government, and of all interferences with nature. They complained of the hurry of modern life, which they contrasted with the calm existence of those whom they called "the pure men of old." There is a flavor of mysticism in the doctrine of the Tao, because in spite of the multiplicity of living things the Tao is in some sense one, so that if all live according to it there will be no strife in the world. (PC 198-9)

TEACHER, FUNCTION OF THE

The function of the teacher, however, is not merely to mitigate the heat of current controversies. He has more positive tasks to perform, and he cannot be a great teacher unless he is inspired by a wish to perform these tasks. Teachers are more than any other class the guardians of civilization. They should be intimately aware of what civilization is, and desirous of imparting a civilized attitude to their pupils. (UE 117)

No man is fit to educate unless he feels each pupil an end in himself, with his own rights and his own personality, not merely a piece in a jig-saw puzzle, or a soldier in a regiment, or a citizen in a State. Reverence for human personality is the beginning of wisdom, in every social question, but above all in education. (SE 205)

I do not think that education ought to be any one's whole profession: it should be undertaken for at most two hours a day by people whose remaining hours are spent away from children. The society of the young is fatiguing, especially when strict discipline is avoided. (IPI 244)

Teachers ought to encourage intelligent disagreement on the part of their pupils, even urging them to read books having opinions opposed to those of the instructor. But this is seldom done, with the result that much education consists in the instilling of unfounded dogma in place of a spirit of inquiry. This results, not necessarily from any fault in the teacher, but from a curriculum which demands too much apparent knowledge, with a consequent need of haste and undue definiteness. (ESO 163)

TEACHERS, MARRIED

Education authorities are of the opinion that those who have to deal with the young ought always to be unhappy spinsters. This view shows gross psychological ignorance, and could not be entertained by any one who had watched closely the emotional development of young children. (MM 192-3)

TEACHERS, TRAINING

If I had to direct the training of teachers, there are two things that I should specially impress upon them: First, that a man's public duty is toward mankind as a whole, not toward any subordinate group such as a nation or a class. Secondly, that a good community is a community of good men and women—of men and women, that is to say, who live freely but not destructively or oppressively. (PIC 269)

TEACHING DIFFICULTIES
see EXAMINATIONS

TENSORS

A man punting walks along the boat, but keeps a constant position with reference to the river bed so long as he does not pick up his pole. The Lilliputians might debate endlessly whether he is walking or standing still: the debate would be as to words, not as to facts. If we choose co-ordinates fixed relatively to the boat, he is walking; if we choose co-ordinates fixed relatively to the river bed, he is standing still. We want to express physical laws in such a way that it shall be obvious when we are expressing the same law by reference to two different systems of co-ordinates, so that we shall not be misled into supposing we have different laws when we only have one law in different words. This is accomplished by the method of tensors. Some laws which seem plausible in one language cannot be translated into another; these are impossible as laws of nature. (ABCR 177-8)

The method of tensors contains the answer to a question which is rendered urgent by the arbitrary character of our co-ordinates. How can we know whether a formula expressed in terms of our co-ordinates expresses something which·describes the physical occurrences, and not merely the particular co-ordinate system which we happen to be employing? (AOM 63)

TESTS, INTELLIGENCE

This is a merit in the intelligence tests, which are too little used in England, though in America they are relied upon to an extent for which there is, to my mind, no scientific justification. Their merit is not that they are infallible—no test can be that—but that they bring out more or less correct results on the whole, and that they do not demand the exhausting and nerve-racking preparation which is required for the usual type of examination. (ESO 165)

TESTS, PSYCHOLOGICAL

Then again, there are the psychological tests of intelligence, as applied to recruits for the American army during the war. I am very sceptical of the possibility of testing anything except average intelligence by such methods, and I think that, if they were widely adopted, they would probably lead to many persons of great artistic capacity being classified as morons. The same thing would have happened to some first-rate mathematicians. Specialized ability not infrequently goes with general disability, but this would not be shown by the kind of tests which psychologists recommended to the American government. (I 52-3)

THE

see ALL

THEOCRACY

Government by a church or political party—which may be called a theocracy—is a form of oligarchy which has assumed a new importance in recent years. It had an older form, which survived in the Patrimony of St. Peter and in the Jesuit regime in Paraguay, but its modern form begins with Calvin's rule in Geneva—apart from the very brief sway of the Anabaptists in Munster. Still more modern was the Rule of the Saints, which ended in England at the Restoration, but survived for a considerable period in New England. In the eighteenth and nineteenth centuries, this type of government might have been thought permanently extinct. But it was revived by

Lenin, adopted in Italy and Germany, and seriously attempted in China. (P 187)

THEORY, DYNAMICAL

There are, speaking broadly, three great types of dynamical theory. There is the doctrine of hard extended atoms, for which the theory of impact is the appropriate weapon. There is the doctrine of the plenum, of an all-pervading fluid, for which the modern doctrine of the ether—the theory of Electricity, in fact—has at least partially forged the necessary weapons. And finally, there is the doctrine of unextended centres of force, with action at a distance, for which Newton supplied the required Mathematics. (PL 90)

THINGS

We must include in our definition of a "thing" those of its aspects, if any, which are not observed. Thus we may lay down the following definition: *Things are those series of aspects which obey the laws of physics.* That such series exist is an empirical fact, which constitutes the verifiability of physics. (KEW 117)

THIS

"This" denotes whatever, at the moment when the word is used, occupies the center of attention. With words which are not egocentric what is constant is something about the object indicated, but "this" denotes a different object on each occasion of its use: what is constant is not the object denoted, but its relation to the particular use of the word. (HK 92)

No description not involving some egocentric particular can have the peculiar property of "this," namely that it applies on each occasion of its use to only one thing, but to different things on different occasions. (IMT 137)

THOUGHT

Men fear thought as they fear nothing else on earth—more than ruin, more even than death. Thought is subversive and revolutionary, destructive and terrible; thought is merciless to privilege, established institutions, and comfortable habits; thought is anarchic and lawless, indifferent to authority; careless of the well-tried wisdom of the ages. Thought looks into the pit of hell and is not afraid. It sees man, a feeble speck, surrounded by unfathomable depths of silence; yet it bears itself proudly, as unmoved as if it were lord of the universe. Thought is great and swift and free, the light of the world, and the chief glory of man. (PSR 178-9)

THOUGHT, FUNCTION OF

The essential practical function of "consciousness" and "thought" is that they enable us to act with reference to what is distant in time or space, even though it is not at present stimulating our senses. (AM 292)

THOUGHTS

What we call our "thoughts" seem to depend upon the organization of tracks in the brain in the same sort of way in which journeys depend upon roads and railways. The energy used in thinking seems to have a chemical origin: for instance, a deficiency of iodine will turn a clever man into an idiot. (WIB 4)

TIME

see AUGUSTINE

TIME, SUBJECTIVE

The time-order of the past events in so far as I can know it by means of memory, must be connected with a quality of my recollections: some must *feel* recent and others must *feel* remote. It must be by means of this felt quality of recentness or remoteness that I place remembered events in a series when I am relying upon memory alone. In traveling from percepts toward "the dark backward and abysm of time," the present contents of my mind have an order, which I believe to be correlated, roughly at any rate, with the objective time-order of the events to which my recollections refer. This order in the present contents of my mind, which, by means of expectation, may be extended into the future, may be called "subjective" time. (HK 211-2)

TIMIDITY

Timidity depends partly upon physical health: a given child is more timid on a day when his digestion is out of order than on a day when it is functioning properly. But timidity also depends upon various mental causes: a child who is frequently punished or frequently threatened with punishment will become timid; so will, conversely, a child who is always carefully guarded against minor dangers. (SAE 90)

TOLERANCE

In the meantime, it would be well if men and women could

remember, in sexual relations, in marriage, and in divorce, to practice the ordinary virtues of tolerance, kindness, truthfulness, and
justice. Those who, by conventional standards, are sexually virtuous,
too often consider themselves thereby absolved from behaving like
decent human beings. Most moralists have been so obsessed by sex
that they have laid much too little emphasis on other more socially
useful kinds of ethically commendable conduct. (OSE 41)
see CHARITY

TOTALITARIANISM

In a totalitarian State such events as the rise of Buddhism or
Christianity are scarcely possible, and not even by the greatest heroism can a moral reformer acquire any influence whatever. This is
a new fact in human history, brought about by the much increased
control over individuals which the modern technique of government
has made possible. It is a very grave fact, and one which shows
how fatal a totalitarian regime must be to every kind of moral progress. (AAI 52)
see LIBERALISM

TRUE

What an asserted sentence expresses is a *belief*; what makes
it true or false is a *fact*, which is in general distinct from the belief.
Truth and falsehood are external relations; that is to say, no analysis
of a sentence or a belief will show whether it is true or false. (This
does not apply to logic and mathematics, where truth or falsehood,
as the case may be, follows from the form of the sentence. (HK
·111-2)
see SENTENCES, INDICATIVE

TRUTH

I conclude, therefore, that sentences containing variables may
be true in virtue of a relation to one or more unobserved facts, and
that the relation is the same as that which makes similar sentences
true when they concern observed facts, e.g., "there are men in Los
Angeles." Unobserved facts can be spoken of in general terms, but
not with the particularity that is possible where observed facts are
concerned. And there is no reason why "truth" should not be a
wider conception than "knowledge." (IMT 308)

Although the above discussion has been so far very inconclu-
sive, I find myself believing, at the end of it, that truth and knowl-

edge are different, and that a proposition may be true although no method exists of discovering that it is so. In that case, we may accept the law of excluded middle. We shall define "truth" by reference to "events" (I am speaking of non-logical truth), and "knowledge" by relation to "percepts." Thus "truth" will be a wider conception than "knowledge." (IMT 361)

My definition of truth is that a belief is true when it corresponds to a fact. But how do I get to this correspondence with fact? I answer that while we don't get as many facts as we should like, we do arrive at some: we get at our own feelings and sensations, which seem to be verifications of our previous beliefs. I think, therefore, that we can say there is such a thing as a verification of a belief by getting facts that correspond to it in certain cases, but only in certain cases; there is an enormous superstructure that goes beyond that. Perhaps in the last analysis "correspondence" comes down to expectedness. (TWW 18)

A third point, perhaps not quite so certain as our previous two, is that the truth of memory cannot be wholly practical, as pragmatists wish all truth to be. It seems clear that some of the things I remember are trivial and without any visible importance for the future, but that my memory is true (or false) in virtue of a past event, not in virtue of any future consequences of my belief. The definition of truth as the correspondence between beliefs and facts seems peculiarly evident in the case of memory, as against not only the pragmatist definition but also the idealist definition by means of coherence. (AM 165-166)

The purely formal definition of truth and falsehood offers little difficulty. What is required is a formal expression of the fact that a proposition is true when it points towards its objective, and false when it points away from it. In very simple cases we can give a very simple account of this: we can say that true propositions actually resemble their objectives in a way in which false propositions do not. (AM 273)

What we firmly believe, if it is true, is called *knowledge*, provided it is either intuitive or inferred (logically or psychologically) from intuitive knowledge from which it follows logically. What we firmly believe, if it is not true, is called *error*. What we firmly believe, if it is neither knowledge nor error, and also what we believe hesitatingly, because it is, or is derived from, something which has not the highest degree of self-evidence, may be called *probable opinion*. (PP 217)

TRUTH AND LOGIC
see LOGIC

TRUTH, CORRESPONDENCE THEORY OF
The correspondence theory of truth, according to which the truth of basic propositions depends upon their relation to some occurrence, and the truth of other propositions depends upon their syntactical relations to basic propositions. For my part, I adhere firmly to this last theory. (IMT 362-3)

TRUTH, TECHNICAL
Science thus encourages abandonment of the search for absolute truth, and the substitution of what may be called "technical" truth, which belongs to any theory that can be successfully employed in inventions or in predicting the future. "Technical" truth is a matter of degree: a theory from which more successful inventions and predictions spring is truer than one which gives rise to fewer. "Knowledge" ceases to be a mental mirror of the universe, and becomes merely a practical tool in the manipulation of matter. (RAS 11-2)

TRUTHFULNESS
Rigid truthfulness in adults towards children is, of course, absolutely indispensable if children are not to learn lying. Parents who teach that lying is a sin, and who nevertheless are known to lie by their children, naturally lose all moral authority. The idea of speaking the truth to children is entirely novel; hardly anybody did it before the present generation. I greatly doubt whether Eve told Cain and Abel the truth about apples; I am convinced that she told them she had never eaten anything that wasn't good for her. (EEC 160-1)

Truthfulness, as I mean it, is the habit of forming our opinions on the evidence, and holding them with that degree of conviction which the evidence warrants. This degree will always fall short of complete certainty, and therefore we must be always ready to admit new evidence against previous beliefs. Moreover, when we act on a belief, we must, if possible, only take such action as will be useful even if our belief is more or less inaccurate; we should avoid actions which are disastrous unless our belief is *exactly* true. (SE 201-2)

TRUTH-FUNCTION
Given the truth or falsehood of p, or of p and q (as the case

may be), we are given the truth or falsehood of the negation, disjunction, conjunction, incompatibility, or implication. A function of propositions which has this property is called a "truth-function." (IMP 147)

TRUTH-FUNCTION, THEORY OF

The theory of truth-functions is the most elementary part of mathematical logic, and concerns everything that can be said by propositions using the words "or" and "not." Thus "p and q" is the negation of "not-p and not-q." The most general relation between p and q which allows us, given p, to infer q, is "not-p or q." Or suppose you want the most general relation which, given p and q, will enable you to infer r, this will be "not-p or not-q or r." The law of excluded middle is "p or not-p"; the law of contradiction is the negation of "p and not-p." Two propositions are said to be "equivalent" when both are true or both are false, i.e., when we have "either p-and-q, or not-p-and-not-q." Two propositions which are equivalent are said to have the same "truth-value." (IMT 325)

TRUTH-VALUE
see TRUTH-FUNCTION, THEORY OF

TRUTHS, SELF-EVIDENT

But since proofs need premises, it is impossible to prove anything unless some things are accepted without proof. We must therefore ask ourselves: What sort of thing it is reasonable to believe without proof? I should reply: The facts of sense-experience and the principles of mathematics and logic—including the inductive logic employed in science. These are things which we can hardly bring ourselves to doubt and as to which there is a large measure of agreement among mankind. But in matters as to which men disagree, or as to which our own convictions are wavering, we should look for proofs, or, if proofs cannot be found, we should be content to confess ignorance. (FAR 2-3)

TWINS, IDENTICAL

Studies of identical twins have been made with a view to showing the strength of congenital elements, but unfortunately identical twins usually have a close similarity in their environment. It is to be hoped that some scientific millionaire will found a trust for separating identical twins at birth, and bringing them up in widely differing circumstances. I do not believe that, if a Queen gave birth to identical twins, one of whom was brought up in the Palace, and the other in a slum, their mental similarity at the age of twenty would be very close; but in the absence of experiment I must admit that my opinion is scarcely scientific. (ESO 44-45)

U

UNCERTAINTY, HEISENBERG'S PRINCIPLE OF

There is another result of quantum theory, about which, in my opinion, too much fuss has been made, namely, what is called Heisenberg's uncertainty principle. According to this there is a theoretical limit to the accuracy with which certain connected quantities can be simultaneously measured. In specifying the state of a physical system, there are certain pairs of connected quantities; one such pair is position and momentum (or velocity, so long as the mass is constant), another is energy and time. It is of course a commonplace that no physical quantity can be measured with complete accuracy, but it had always been supposed that there was no theoretical limit to the increase of accuracy obtainable by improved technique. According to Heisenberg's principle, this is not the case. (HK 24)

UNCONSCIOUS, CREATIVENESS OF THE

Most of the unconscious consists of what were once highly emotional conscious thoughts, which have now become buried. It is possible to do this process of burying deliberately, and in this way the unconscious can be led to do a lot of useful work. I have found, for example, that, if I have to write upon some rather difficult topic, the best plan is to think about it with great intensity—the greatest intensity of which I am capable—for a few hours or days and at the end of that time give orders, so to speak, that the work is to proceed underground. After some months I return consciously to the topic and find that the work has been done. (CH 76)

UNHAPPINESS, PSYCHOLOGICAL SOURCES OF

The psychological sources of unhappiness, which are studied by psychiatrists in their extreme forms, mostly have their source in unwise treatment during childhood. A child may be unloved, or may feel that another child is unjustly favoured at his expense; the result is almost sure to be a proneness to discontent and envy and hostility. (WIH 61)

UNIONISM, INDUSTRIAL

Industrial unionism is a product of America, and from America it has to some extent spread to Great Britain. It is the natural form of fighting organization when the union is regarded as the means of carrying on the class war with a view, not to obtaining this or that minor amelioration, but to a radical revolution in the economic system. This is the point of view adopted by the "Industrial Workers of the World," commonly known as the I.W.W. (RF 74)

UNITED NATIONS

see FOREIGN NATIONS, ATTITUDE TOWARD

UNITED STATES, THE

I have great faith in the stability of the United States. I think if that country did not exist, I should take a very much more pessimistic view of the future. (ISI 9)

UNITY

All this I profoundly believe to be possible, provided the next few years are wisely used in defensive military preparation and also— and this is equally important—in the revival of that sense of cultural unity of moral and intellectual values which united the Catholic world in the Middle Ages and the polite world in the 18th century.

Ancient enmities and rivalries within the sphere of Western Europe must be forgotten, and we must face the new world in the knowledge that we have something to defend, the loss of which will impoverish mankind for many generations to come. (HCS 12)
see DISCONTINUITY

UNIVERSAL

We speak of whatever is given in sensation, or is of the same nature as things given in sensation, as a *particular*; by opposition to this, a *universal* will be anything which may be shared by many particulars, and has those characteristics which, as we saw, distinguish justice and whiteness from just acts and white things. (PP 145)

UNIVERSALS

The less purely logical argument is derived from analysis of ordinary propositions, such as "A precedes B." Here "precedes" functions as a universal. We can, by somewhat elaborate devices, define all universals in terms of particulars and "similarity," or rather "similar," but "similar" remains a universal. The technical conclusion seems to be that every adequate minimum vocabulary must contain at least one universal word, but this word need only occur as an adjective or verb; its use as a substantive is unnecessary. (RTC 688)

In addition to our acquaintance with particular existing things, we also have acquaintance with what we shall call *universals*, that is to say, general ideas, such as *whiteness, diversity, brotherhood*, and so on. (PP 81)
see AVICENNA

UNIVERSITY, AN INTERNATIONAL

The central institution required will be an international university. This should be in some neutral territory, analogous to the District of Columbia. It should be frankly designed to serve two purposes, one the purely academic, the other that of creating and diffusing an outlook calculated to prevent war and to promote loyalty to international ideals. (EAW 195)

UNVERIFIABLES

But the word "verifiables" is capable of meaning something wider than "things that human beings experience," and does mean something wider in the ordinary usage of science. Science, when it believes itself to have established a causal law, allows itself to believe in things which cannot be observed, and so does common sense. We conclude without hesitation that so-and-so is angry when he behaves in a certain way, although we cannot observe his anger. In a sense, an entity may be said to be "verifiable" when it has been inferred in accordance with the recognized canons of scientific method. (RTC 707-8)

USEFUL, THE

Thus we find that the advocate of utility, in the sense in which his view is questionable, is a man who attaches intrinsic value only to physical satisfaction: the "useful", for him, is that which helps us to gratify the needs and desires of the body. When this is what is really meant, the advocate of utility is certainly in the wrong if he is enunciating an ultimate philosophy, though in a world where many people are starving he may be right as a politician, since the satisfaction of physical needs may be at the moment more urgent than anything else. (EEC 22)

UTILITARIANISM

At the age of fourteen I became convinced that the fundamental principle of ethics should be the promotion of human happiness, and at first this appeared to me so self-evident that I supposed it must be the universal opinion. Then I discovered, to my surprise, that it was a view regarded as unorthodox, and called Utilitarianism. (MRR 4)

The ethic based upon the greatest happiness principle, which came to be known as utilitarianism, was, when taken seriously, somewhat opposed to orthodox moral teaching. It is true that eminent divines, such as Bishop Butler, had adopted the principle, and that, until it became the watchword of the Radicals, no one found it objectionable. But any theory which judges the morality of an act by its consequences can only by a fortunate accident agree with the conventional view, according to which certain classes of acts are sinful without regard to their effects. No doubt the precept "Thou shalt not steal" is, in general, very sound, but it is easy to imagine circumstances in which a theft might further the general happiness. In a utilitarian system, all moral rules of the ordinary kind are liable to exceptions. (FO 92)
see VIRTUE

UTILITY AND CULTURE

Apart, however, from the cases in which culture and direct utility can be combined, there is indirect utility of various different kinds, in the possession of knowledge which does not contribute to technical efficiency. I think some of the worst features of the modern world could be improved by a greater encouragement of such knowledge and a less ruthless pursuit of mere professional competence. (IPI 44)

UTOPIAS
see MORE'S UTOPIA

V

VAGUENESS

Vagueness and accuracy are important notions, which it is very necessary to understand. Both are a matter of degree. All thinking is vague to some extent, and complete accuracy is a theoretical ideal not practically attainable. To understand what is meant by accuracy, it will be well to consider first instruments of measurement, such as a balance or a thermometer. These are said to be accurate when they give different results for very slightly different stimuli. A clinical thermometer is accurate when it enables us to detect very slight differences in the temperature of the blood. We may say generally that an instrument is accurate in proportion as it reacts differently to very slightly different stimuli. When a small difference of stimulus produces a great difference of reaction, the instrument is accurate; in the contrary sense it is not. (AM 180-1)

VALUE

There remains, however, a vast field, traditionally included in philosophy, where scientific methods are inadequate. This field includes ultimate questions of value; science alone, for example, cannot prove that it is bad to enjoy the infliction of cruelty. Whatever can be known, can be known by means of science; but things which are legitimately matters of feeling lie outside its province. (HWP 834)

VALUE, MARX'S THEORY OF

I cannot accept Marx's theory of value, nor yet, in his form, the theory of surplus value. The theory that the exchange value of a commodity is proportional to the labor involved in its production, which Marx took over from Ricardo, is shown to be false by Ricardo's theory of rent, and has long been abandoned by all non-Marxian economists. The theory of surplus value rests upon Malthus's theory of population, which Marx elsewhere rejects. Marx's economics do not form a logically coherent whole, but are built up by the alternate acceptance and rejection of older doctrines, as may suit his convenience in making out a case against the capitalists. (IPI 126-7)

VALUE, RICARDO'S THEORY OF

Ricardo's theory of value, while less true than his theory of rent, has had even more influence. The question of value arises in economics as follows: Suppose you have one pound to spend, you can obtain for it a certain quantity of wheat, or of beer, or of tobacco, or of pins, or of books, or what not. If a certain quantity of wheat and a certain number of pins both cost one pound, they have the same "value." What determines how many pins will have the same value as a given amount of wheat? Ricardo answered: They will have the same value if the same amount of labor has been required to produce them. The value of any commodity, he says, is measured by the work involved in making it. (FO 105)

VALUES

Questions as to "values"—that is to say, as to what is good or bad on its own account, independently of its effects—lie outside the domain of science, as the defenders of religion emphatically assert. I think that in this they are right, but I draw the further conclusion, which they do not draw, that questions as to "values" lie wholly outside the domain of knowledge. That is to say, when we assert that this or that has "value," we are giving expression to our own emotions, not to a fact which would still be true if our personal feelings were different. (RAS 242)
see SCIENCE AND VALUES

VALUES, CONSEQUENCES OF THE SUBJECTIVE THEORY OF

The consequences of this doctrine are considerable. In the first place, there can be no such thing as "sin" in any absolute sense; what one man calls "sin" another may call "virtue," and though they may dislike each other on account of this difference, neither can convict the other of intellectual error. Punishment cannot be justified on the ground that the criminal is "wicked," but only on the ground that he has behaved in a way which others wish to discourage. Hell, as a place of punishment for sinners, becomes quite irrational. (RAS 250-1)

VALUES, SUBJECTIVITY OF

Ethics, if the above analysis is correct, contains no statements, whether true or false, but consists of desires of a certain general kind, namely, such as are concerned with the desires of mankind in general—and of gods, angels, and devils, if they exist. Science can discuss the cause of desires, and the means for realizing them, but it cannot contain any genuinely ethical sentences, because it is concerned with what is true or false. The theory which I have been advocating is a form of the doctrine which is called "subjectivity" of values. (RAS 249)

VANITY

Vanity, when it passes beyond a point, kills pleasure in every activity for its own sake, and thus leads inevitably to listlessness and boredom. Often its source is diffidence, and its cure lies in the growth of self-respect. But this is only to be gained by successful activity inspired by objective interests. (CH 21)

VERACITY

Veracity, which I regard second only to kindly feeling, consists broadly in believing according to evidence and not because a belief is comfortable or a source of pleasure. In the absence of veracity, kindly feeling will often be defeated by self-deception. It used to be common for the rich to maintain either that it is pleasant to be poor or that poverty is the result of shiftlessness. Some healthy people maintain that all illness is self-indulgence. I have heard fox-hunters argue that the fox likes being hunted. (FAR 2)

VERIFIABILITY

For a proposition to be verifiable, it is not enough that it should be true, but it must also be such as we can *discover* to be true. Thus verifiability depends upon our capacity for acquiring knowledge, and not only upon the objective truth. (KEW 117)

VERIFICATION

A "verifiable" proposition is one having a certain kind of correspondence with an experience; a "true" proposition is one having exactly the same kind of correspondence with a fact—except that the simplest type of correspondence, that which occurs in judgments of perception, is impossible in the case of all other judgments, since these involve variables. Since an experience is a fact, verifiable propositions are true; but there is no reason to suppose that all true propositions are verifiable. If, however, we assert positively that there are true propositions that are not verifiable, we abandon pure empiricism. Pure empiricism, finally, is believed by no one, and if we are to retain beliefs that we all regard as valid, we must allow principles of inference which are neither demonstrative nor derivable from experience. (IMT 383)

When the statement comes first and the evidence afterwards, there is a process called "verification," which involves confrontation of the statement with the evidence. In the case of a statement in the primary language, the evidence must consist of a sensible experience or of a set of such experiences. We have already considered sentences describing experiences. Speaking broadly, the process of verification is as follows: First you hear or read or consider a sentence S; then you have an experience E; then you observe that S is a sentence which describes E. In that case you say that S is "true." I do not mean that this is a definition of the word "true," but that it is a description of the process by which you come to know that this word is applicable to a given primary sentence. (IMT 97)

Meanwhile verification remains often practically possible. And since it is sometimes possible, we can gradually discover what kinds of beliefs tend to be verified by experience, and what kinds tend to be falsified; to the former kinds we give an increased degree of assent, to the latter kinds a diminished degree. The process is not absolute or infallible, but it has been found capable of sifting beliefs and building up science. It affords no theoretical refutation of the sceptic, whose position must remain logically unassailable; but if complete scepticism is rejected, it gives the practical method by which the system of our beliefs grows gradually towards the unattainable ideal of impeccable knowledge. (AM 271)
see FALSEHOOD

VICE
see VIRTUE

VIRTUE
We defined a virtue as a habit which tends to produce a good community, and a vice as one which tends to produce a bad community. In thus judging by results, we agreed in one important respect with the utilitarian school of moralists, among whom Bentham

and the two Mills were the most eminent. The traditional view is different; it holds that certain specified classes of actions are vicious, and that abstinence from all these is virtue. (PIC 165)

VIRTUES

The fact that a virtue is good in itself is not enough; it is necessary to take account of the vices that it entails and the virtues that it excludes. (LAM 105)

VITALISM

Vitalism as a philosophy, and evolutionism, show, in this respect, a lack of sense of proportion and logical relevance. They regard the facts of life, which are personally interesting to us, as having a cosmic significance, not a significance confined to the earth's surface. (WIB 15-6)

A few words must be said about the human body as a mechanism. It is an inconceivably complicated mechanism, and some men of science think that it is not explicable in terms of physics and chemistry, but is regulated by some "vital principle" which makes its laws different from those of dead matter. These men are called "vitalists". I do not myself see any reason to accept their view, but at the same time our knowledge is not sufficient to enable us to reject it definitely. What we can say is that their case is not proved, and that the opposite view is, scientifically, a more fruitful working hypothesis. (OP 25)

VITALITY

Vitality is rather a physiological than a mental characteristic; it is presumably always present where there is perfect health, but it tends to ebb with advancing years, and gradually dwindles to nothing in old age. In vigorous children it quickly rises to a maximum before they reach school age, and then tends to be diminished by education. Where it exists, there is pleasure in feeling alive, quite apart from any specific pleasant circumstance. It heightens pleasures and diminishes pains. (EEC 61)

VOCABULARY, MINIMUM

I call a vocabulary a "minimum" one if it contains no word which is capable of a verbal definition in terms of the other words of the vocabulary. (HK 79)

VOCABULARIES, MINIMUM
see CARDINALS

W

WAR
The argument from history is very apt to be fallacious as applied to modern conditions. War is a more serious matter than it used to be. War can still settle problems, but it can only settle them the wrong way. (MRW 174)

WAR, CAUSES OF
There are two opposite forces that tend to produce great wars. On the one hand, there is the overweening ambition of the strong; on the other hand, there is the discontent of the less fortunate nations. (PPW 93)

WAR, CHANGES IN TECHNIQUE OF
Changes in the technique of war have had more influence upon the course of history than is supposed by those whose attention is mainly centred upon economic causation. There has been, since the beginning of organized fighting, an oscillation between superiority of the defensive and superiority of the offensive. Broadly speaking, when the defensive is strong civilization makes progress, and when the offensive is strong men revert towards barbarism. (WWP 16)

WAR, COMING OF
War comes only when the opposing forces are roughly equal, for if there is an obvious preponderance on either side the other side gives way. (CAN 8)

WAR, FEAR OF
If a world government is ever to succeed, fear will still be the cement holding it together, but it will be a new kind of fear—a fear of anarchy and destruction and annihilation of whole populations, not the fear of this or that group of dastardly foreigners. (KF 54)

WAR OF COLONISATION
see COLONISATION, WAR OF

WAR OF PRESTIGE

The last kind of war we have to consider is what I have called "the war of prestige." Prestige is seldom more than one element in the causes of a war, but it is often a very important element. (JWT 36)

WAR OF PRINCIPLE

The second type of war which may sometimes be justified is what may be called "the war of principle." To this kind belong the wars of Protestant and Catholic, and the English and American civil wars. In such cases, each side, or at least one side, is honestly convinced that the progress of mankind depends upon the adoption of certain beliefs or institutions, which through blindness or natural depravity, the other side will not regard as reasonable, except when presented at the point of the bayonet. (JWT 31)

Force used in defence of the law, when it is sufficiently serious, comes under the head of "wars of principle". A contest between one burglar and the whole police force can hardly be dignified with the name of war, but the suppression of an insurrection which has no general impersonal objects is essentially analogous to the suppression of an individual criminal, and may involve very serious acts of war. If an international government is ever formed, it will be very important to establish its authority, and wars waged by it against recalcitrant States will be in defence of the law. (WWP 114-5)

WAR OF SELF-DEFENCE

The next kind of war to be considered is the war of self-defence. This kind of war is almost universally admitted to be justifiable, and is condemned only by Christ and Tolstoy. The justification of wars of self-defence is very convenient, since so far as I know there has never yet been a war which was not one of self-defence. (JWT 34)

WAVE-NUMBER

In studying the connection between the different lines in the spectrum of an element, it is convenient to characterize a wave, not by its wave-length, but by its "wave-number," which means the number of waves in a centimetre. Thus if the wave-length is one ten-thousandth of a centimetre, the wave-number is 10,000; if the wave-length is one hundred-thousandth of a centimetre, the wave-number is 100,000, and so on. (ABCA 43)

WILL

It remains to say a few words about "will." There is a sense in which will is an observable phenomenon, and another in which it is a metaphysical superstition. It is obvious that I can say, "I will hold my breath for thirty seconds," and proceed to do so; that I can say, "I will go to America," and ppoceed to do so; and so on. In this sense, will is an observable phenomenon. But as a faculty, as a separate occurrence, it is, I think, a delusion. (OP 223)

WILL, HUMAN

There is no external compulsion for a man to act otherwise than as he wishes except in the obvious ways that common sense recognizes. No man can resist torture beyond a point, and a scientific tyrant can always secure obedience if his victim has not the means of suicide. A man may also be constrained by insanity to commit acts for which the law does not hold him responsible. But it is mere mythology to imagine a semipersonal pagan god or goddess regulating the lives of men or of nations in a manner independent of human will. (TRF 5)

WILL, THE GENERAL

I come now to the doctrine of the general will, which is both important and obscure. The general will is not identical with the will of the majority, or even with the will of all the citizens. It seems to be conceived as the will belonging to the body politic as such. If we take Hobbes's view, that a civil society is a person, we must suppose it is endowed with the attributes of personality, including will. But then we are faced with the difficulty of deciding what are the visible manifestations of this will, and here Rousseau leaves us in the dark. We are told that the general will is always right and always tends to the public advantage; but that it does not follow that the deliberations of the people are equally correct, for there is often a great deal of difference between the will of all and the general will. How, then, are we to know what is the general will? (HWP 697-8)

WILL-TO-DOUBT

William James used to preach the "will-to-believe." For my part, I should wish to preach the "will-to-doubt." None of our beliefs is quite true; all have at least a penumbra of vagueness and error. (FT 14)

WISDOM

I mean by wisdom a right conception of the ends of life. This is something which science in itself does not provide. Increase of science by itself, therefore, is not enough to guarantee any genuine progress, though it provides one of the ingredients which progress requires. (SO x)

WITCHCRAFT
see SORCERY

WOMEN AND WITCHCRAFT
see SORCERY

WOMEN, EMANCIPATION OF

The revolt of women against the domination of men is a movement which in its purely political sense, is practically completed, but in its wider aspects is still in its infancy. Gradually its remoter effects will work themselves out. The emotions which women are supposed to feel are still, as yet, a reflection of the interests and sentiments of men. (MM 214)

WORDS AND PROPOSITIONS

Words are not essential to propositions. The exact psychological definition of propositions is irrelevant to logic and theory of knowledge; the only thing essential to our inquiries is that sentences signify something other than themselves, which can be the same when the sentences differ. That this something must be psychological (or physiological) is made evident by the fact that propositions can be false. (IMT 237-8)

WORDS, EGOCENTRIC

There are a number of the sort that I call "egocentric," which differ in meaning according to the speaker and his position in time and space. Among these the simple ones are learned ostensively, for instance, "I," "you," "here," "now." (HK 69)

WORDS, INDICATIVE

Words that mean objects may be called "indicative" words. I include among such words not only names but words denoting qualities such as "white," "hard," "warm," and words denoting perceptible relations such as "before," "above," "in." If the sole purpose of language were to describe sensible facts, we could content ourselves with indicative words. But as we have seen, such words do not suffice to express doubt, desire, or disbelief. They also do not suffice to express logical connections, e.g., "If this is so, I'll eat my hat," or "If Wilson had been more tactful, America would have joined the League of Nations." Nor do they suffice for sentences needing such words as "all" and "some," "the" and "a." (HK 106)

WORDS, USE OF

These two ways of using words, including their occurrence in inner speech, may be spoken of together as the use of words in "thinking." If we are right, the use of words in thinking depends, at least in its origin, upon images, and cannot be fully dealt with on behaviourist lines. And that is really the most essential function of words, namely that, originally through their connection with images, they bring us into touch with what is remote in time or space. When they operate without the medium of images, this seems to be a telescoped process. Thus the problem of the meaning of words is brought into connection with the problem of the meaning of images. (AM 202-3)

WORK

The habit of viewing life as a whole is an essential part both of wisdom and of true morality, and is one of the things which ought to be encouraged in education. Consistent purpose is not enough to make life happy, but it is an almost indispensable condition of a happy life. And consistent purpose embodies itself mainly in work. (CH 219)

WORK, ETHICS OF

Let us, for a moment, consider the ethics of work frankly, without superstition. Every human being, of necessity, consumes, in the course of his life, a certain amount of the produce of human labor. Assuming, as we may, that labor is on the whole disagreeable, it is unjust that a man should consume more than he produces. Of course he may provide services rather than commodities, like a medical man, for example; but he should provide something in return for his board and lodging. To this extent, the duty of work must be admitted, but to this extent only. (IPI 21-2)

WORLD, A NEW

A new world is needed, and the battle of the democracies must be inspired by the hope of creating it. Our battle must not be purely defensive: it must be inspired by a new hope and a new vision. No hope has much chance of realization, in our technically unified but politically divided planet, unless through the creation of an international authority, strong enough and resolute enough to prevent the recurrence of world wars. The creation of such an authority, for the first time in history, is now a practical possibility. When once it exists, the men who serve it will see new opportunities of progress. Philosophers, historians, economists, men of science will be liberated from the nightmare oppressions that have impeded their creativeness. Our times of darkness may be succeeded by a great age, in which a new productiveness will be generated by new hopes and wider loyalties. (EAW 203)

WORLD ARMY

In order that the loyalty of the armed forces may be above suspicion, it will be necessary that they should be composed, not of large national contingents, but of units of mixed nationality; every regiment, every battleship, every air squadron will have to contain members of different national origins, all of whom will have to be trained from the moment of their recruitment in a new loyalty superseding the old national loyalty. (STGS 57)

WORLD, BEST OF ALL POSSIBLE

Whenever Leibniz is not thinking of theological objections, he regards God's action on the world as entirely limited to creation. God's goodness, he says, led him to desire to create the good, his wisdom showed him the best possible, and his power enabled him to create it. (PL 184)

WORLD GOVERNMENT

It is as clear as noonday that only one thing can make world peace secure, and that is the establishment of a world government with a monopoly of all the more serious weapons of war. (STGS 57)

WORLD-STATE

The only ultimate cure for war is the creation of a world-state or superstate, strong enough to decide by law all disputes between nations. And a world-state is only conceivable after the different parts of the world have become so intimately related that no part can be indifferent to what happens in any other part. (PIC 4-5)

WORLD STRUCTURE
see LANGUAGE

WORLD, THE
see DISCONTINUITY

WORLD, THE PHYSICAL

But we have found it necessary to emphasize the extremely abstract character of physical knowledge, and the fact that physics leaves open all kinds of possibilities as to the intrinsic character of the world to which its equations apply. There is nothing in physics to prove that the physical world is radically different in character from the mental world. I do not myself believe that the philosophical arguments for the view that all reality must be mental are valid. But I also do not believe that any valid arguments against this view are to be derived from physics. The only legitimate attitude about the physical world seems to be one of complete agnosticism as regards all but its mathematical properties. (AOM 270-1)

X

X-RAYS

Everybody knows something about X-rays, because of their use in medicine. Everybody knows that they can take a photograph of the skeleton of a living person, and show the exact position of a bullet lodged in the brain. But not everybody knows why this is so. The reason is that the capacity of ordinary matter for stopping the rays varies approximately as the fourth power of the atomic number of the elements concerned . . . . . The human body consists mainly of carbon, oxygen, nitrogen and hydrogen, but the bones consist mainly of calcium. Consequently X-rays which go through the rest of the body easily are stopped by the bones with the result that we get a photograph of the skeleton. (ABCA 97-8)

Z

ZENO'S PARADOX

We may therefore escape from his paradoxes either by maintaining that, though space and time do consist of points and instants, the number of them in any finite interval is infinite; or by denying that space and time consist of points and instants at all; or lastly, by denying the reality of space and time altogether. (KEW 193-4)

ZERO

0 is the class whose only member is the null-class. (IMP 23)

CHRONOLOGICAL LIST OF WORKS FROM WHICH
SELECTIONS ARE TAKEN

1900 A Critical Examination of the Philosophy of Leibniz. Cambridge at the University Press; George Allen & Unwin, Ltd., 1937.

1904 On History. Independent Review, July 1904.

1912 The Problems of Philosophy. Williams & Norgate. Henry Holt & Company.

When Should Marriage be Dissolved? The English Review, August 1912.

The Essence of Religion. The Hibbert Journal, October 1912.

1914 Our Knowledge of the External World as a Field for Scientific Method in Philosophy. George Allen & Unwin, Ltd. W. W. Norton & Company, Inc.

1916 Principles of Social Reconstruction (Why Men Fight). George Allen & Unwin, Ltd. Liveright Corporation.

Justice in War-Time. George Allen & Unwin, Ltd. The Open Court Publishing Co.

Marriage and the Population Question. International Journal of Ethics, July 1916.

1917 Political Ideals. The Century Co.

Roads to Freedom: Socialism, Anarchism and Syndicalism (Proposed Roads to Freedom). George Allen & Unwin, Ltd. Henry Holt & Co.

1918 Mysticism and Logic. George Allen & Unwin, Ltd. W. W. Norton & Company, Inc.

1919 Introduction to Mathematical Philosophy. George Allen & Unwin, Ltd. The Macmillan Company.

1920 The Practice and Theory of Bolshevism (Bolshevism: Practice and Theory). George Allen & Unwin, Ltd. Harcourt, Brace & Co.

1921 The Analysis of Mind. George Allen & Unwin, Ltd. The Macmillan Company.

1922 The Problem of China. George Allen & Unwin, Ltd. The Century Co.
Free Thought and Official Propaganda. George Allen & Unwin, Ltd.
B. W. Huebsch, Inc. (The Viking Press).
Hopes and Fears as Regards America. The New Republic, March 30,
1922. (Reprinted in New Republic Anthology. Dodge Publishing
Company.)

1923 The Prospects of Industrial Civilization (With Dora Russell). George
Allen & Unwin, Ltd. The Century Co.
The ABC of Atoms. Routledge and Kegan Paul, Ltd. E. P. Dutton
& Co.
Leisure and Mechanism. Dial, August 1923.
Where is Industrialism Going? Century Magazine, November 1923.
Freedom in Education: A Protest against Mechanism. Dial, Febru-
ary 1923.

1924 Styles in Ethics. In Our Changing Morality, edited by Freda Kirch-
wey. Liveright Corporation.
Government by Propaganda In These Eventful Years. The Encyclo-
pedia Britannica Company, Ltd.
Icarus, or the Future of Science. Routledge and Kegan Paul, Ltd
E. P. Dutton & Co.
How to be Free and Happy. The Rand School of Social Science.
Logical Atomism. In Contemporary British Philosophy, First Series.
George Allen & Unwin, Ltd. The Macmillan Company.
Bolshevism and the West (Debate with Scott Nearing). George Allen
& Unwin, Ltd.
If We are to Prevent the Next War. Century Magazine, November
1924.

1925 The ABC of Relativity. Routledge and Kegan Paul, Ltd. Harper &
Bros.
What I Believe. Routledge and Kegan Paul, Ltd. E. P. Dutton &
Co.
Life in the Middle Ages. Dial, April 1925.

1926 On Education Especially in Early Childhood (Education and the
Good Life). George Allen & Unwin, Ltd. Liveright Corporation.

1927 Why I am Not a Christian. Watts & Co., Ltd. American Association
for the Advancement of Atheism, Inc.
The Analysis of Matter. Routledge and Kegan Paul, Ltd. Harcourt,
Brace & Co., Inc.
An Outline of Philosophy (Philosophy) George Allen & Unwin, Ltd.
W. W. Norton & Company, Inc.

Introduction to Selected Papers of Bertrand Russell. Modern Library, Inc.

1928 Science. In Whither Mankind, edited by Charles A. Beard. Longmans, Green & Co.

Sceptical Essays. George Allen & Unwin, Ltd. W. W. Norton & Company, Inc.

Science and Education. St. Louis Post-Dispatch, December 9, 1928. (Reprinted in Drift of Civilization, George Allen & Unwin, Ltd., 1930).

1929 Marriage and Morals. George Allen & Unwin, Ltd. Liveright Corporation.

Three Ways to the World. Edited by Baker Brownell. D. Van Nostrand, Inc.

On the Evils Due to Fear. In If I Could Preach Just Once. Harper & Brothers.

What I Believe. Forum, September 1929. (Reprinted in Living Philosophies, Simon & Schuster, Inc., 1931).

1930 The Conquest of Happiness. George Allen & Unwin, Ltd. Liveright Corporation.

Introduction to The New Generation. Edited by Calverton and Schmallhausen. The Macaulay Co.

Has Religion Made Useful Contributions to Civilization? Watts & Co., Ltd.

Divorce by Mutual Consent. In Divorce (Divorce as I See It). Douglas. The John Day Company.

1931 The Scientific Outlook. George Allen & Unwin, Ltd. W. W. Norton & Company, Inc.

1932 Education and the Social Order (Education and the Modern World). George Allen & Unwin, Ltd. W. W. Norton & Company, Inc.

1934 Freedom and Organization (Freedom versus Organization). George Allen & Unwin, Ltd. W. W. Norton & Company, Inc.

Why I Am Not a Communist. In The Meaning of Marx. Farrar & Rinehart, Inc.

1935 In Praise of Idleness. George Allen & Unwin, Ltd. W. W. Norton & Company, Inc.

Religion and Science. T. Butterworth-Nelson. Henry Holt & Co., Inc.

1936 Which Way to Peace? Michael Joseph Ltd.

Why Radicals are Unpopular. Common Sense, March 1936.

Our Sexual Ethics. The American Mercury, May 1936.

1937 The Amberley Papers. (With Patricia Russell). Hogarth. W. W. Norton & Company, Inc.
The Future of Democracy. The New Republic, May 5, 1937.

1938 Science and Social Institutions. In Dare We Look Ahead. George Allen & Unwin, Ltd. The Macmillan Company.
Power: A New Social Analysis. George Allen & Unwin, Ltd. W. W. Norton & Company, Inc.
My Religious Reminiscences. Rationalist Annual, 1938. Rationalist Press Association.
Taming Economic Power. University of Chicago Round Table, November 13, 1938.

1939 What is Happiness? In What is Happiness, H. C. Kinsey & Co., Inc.
Living Philosophy Revised. In I Believe, edited by Clifton Fadiman. Simon & Schuster, Inc.
Dewey's New Logic. In The Philosophy of John Dewey, edited by Paul A. Schilpp. Northwestern University. Library of Living Philosophers. Democracy and Economics. In Calling America. Survey Graphic, February 1939. Harper & Brothers.
Is Security Increasing? University of Chicago Round Table, January 15, 1939.
Munich Rather than War. Must Democracy Use Force? The Nation, February 11, 1939.
If War Comes—Can America Stay Neutral? Common Sense, symposium, March 1939.

1940 Freedom and Government. In Freedom: Its Meaning, edited by Ruth N. Anshen. Harcourt, Brace & Co.
An Inquiry into Meaning and Truth. George Allen & Unwin, Ltd. W. W. Norton & Company, Inc.
The Philosophy of Santayana. In The Philosophy of Santayana, edited by Paul A. Schilpp. Northwestern University. The Library of Living Philosophers.
Letter on the Bertrand Russell Case. New York Times, April 26, 1940.

1941 Hegel's Philosophy of History. Dialogue. Invitation to Learning. Random House.
A World Federation. New Leader, September 27, 1941.
A Philosophy for You in These Times. Reader's Digest, October 1941.

1942 Descartes' Discourse on Method. Dialogue in The New Invitation to Learning. Random House.

Spinoza's Ethics. Dialogue in The New Invitation to Learning. Random House.

Carroll's Alice in Wonderland. Dialogue in The New Invitation to Learning. Random House.

1943 The International Significance of the Indian Problem (India Looms Up). With Patricia Russell. Free World, January 1943. Reprinted in Treasury for the Free World. Arco Publishing Company.

Some Problems of the Post-War World. Free World, April 1943. Reprinted in Treasury for the Free World. Arco Publishing Company. (Problems We Will Face).

Zionism and the Peace Settlement. Zionist Organization of America.

Education after the War. The American Mercury, August 1943.

Citizenship in a Great State. Fortune, December 1943.

1944 My Mental Development. In The Philosophy of Bertrand Russell, edited by Paul A. Schilpp. Northwestern University. Library of Living Philosophers.

Reply to Criticisms. In The Philosophy of Bertrand Russell, edited by Paul A. Schilpp. Northwestern University. Library of Living Philosophers.

Education in International Understanding. Tomorrow, June 1944.

The Future of Pacifism. The American Scholar, January 1944.

Can Americans and Britains be Friends? Saturday Evening Post, June 3, 1944.

1945 A History of Western Philosophy. George Allen & Unwin, Ltd. Simon & Schuster, Inc.

1947 Still Time for Good Sense. Magazine '47, November 1947.

The Faith of a Rationalist. Rationalist Press Association.

1948 Human Knowledge: Its Scope and Limits. George Allen & Unwin, Ltd. Simon & Schuster, Inc.

Boredom or Doom in a Scientific World. United Nations World, September 1948.

Social Cohesion and Human Nature. The Listener, December 30, 1948.

Replies in Last Chance, edited by Clara Urquhart. Beacon Press, Boston.

1949 Authority and the Individual. George Allen & Unwin, Ltd. Simon & Schuster, Inc.

The High Cost of Survival. This Week, The New York Herald Tribune, December 18, 1949.

A Guide for Living in the Atomic Age. United Nations World, November 1949.

1950 Letter in The World's Best, edited by Whit Burnett. The Dial Press.

Is a Third War Inevitable? United Nations World, March 1950.

The Science to Save Us from Science. New York Times Magazine, March 19, 1950.

Came the Revolution. . . Saturday Review of Literature, March 25, 1950.

Can We Afford to Keep Open Minds? New York Times Magazine, June 11, 1950.

Americans are. . .The Impact of America upon European Culture. Vogue. February 1950.

If We are to Survive This Dark Time. New York Times Magazine, September, 1950.

The Kind of Fear We Sorely Need. New York Times Magazine, October 29, 1950.

To Replace our Fears with Hope. New York Times Magazine, December 31, 1950.

1951 To Face Danger without Hysteria. New York Times Magazine, January 21, 1951.

Unpopular Essays. George Allen & Unwin, Ltd. Simon & Schuster, Inc.

The Impact of Science on Society. Columbia University Press.

The Political and Cultural Influence. In The Impact of America on European Culture. Beacon Press.

ACKNOWLEDGEMENTS

Acknowledgements are due primarily to Lord Russell for his kind permission to make the extensive selections from his works represented here. The choices were that of the editor and the fault resultant from the annoying, though necessary, foreshortening of exposition and argument is entirely his; so, too, are the errors of omission, though space was a contributing factor. The editor is deeply grateful for the generous consent and the interest expressed by Lord Russell as this volume grew.

Our thanks are also due to Lord Russell's publishers:

George Allen & Unwin, Ltd.: A Critical Exposition of the Philosophy of Leibniz; Our Knowledge of the External World, Principles of Social Reconstruction, Justice in War-Time, Roads to Freedom, Introduction to Mathematical Philosophy, Practice and Theory of Bolshevism, The Analysis of Mind, The Problem of China, Free Thought and Official Propaganda, Prospects of Industrial Civilization, Logical Atomism, Science and Social Institutions, Science and Education, Mysticism and Logic, In Praise of Idleness, An Outline of Philosophy, On Education Especially in Early Childhood, The Conquest of Happiness, Education and the Social Order, Sceptical Essays, Inquiry into Meaning and Truth, The Scientific Outlook, Power, Human Knowledge, Marriage and Morals, Authority and the Individual, Freedom versus Organization, History of Western Philosophy, Unpopular Essays, Bolshevism and the West, Bolshevism in Theory and Practice.

The American Mercury: Our Sexual Ethics, Freedom and the College, Education after the War.

The American Scholar: The Future of Pacifism.

Appleton-Century-Crofts, Inc.: Letter in "The World's Best." Political Ideals, Prospects of Industrial Civilization.

Arco Publishing Company: Some Problems of the Post War World, The International Significance of the Indian Problem.

The Beacon Press: The Political and Cultural Influence; Last Chance.

The Century Magazine: Where is Industrialism Going?, If We are to Prevent the Next War.

The University of Chicago Round Table: Taming Economic Power, Is Security Increasing?

The Citadel Press: Introduction to "The New Generation."

Columbia University Press: The Impact of Science on Society.

Common Sense: Why Radicals are Unpopular, If War Comes—Can America Stay Neutral?

The John Day Company: Divorce by Mutual Consent.

The Dial Magazine: Leisure and Mechanism, Freedom in Education: A Protest against Mechanism, Life in the Middle Ages.

E. P. Dutton & Co.: The ABC of Atoms, Icarus or the Future of Science, What I Believe.

The Encyclopedia Britannica Company, Ltd.: Government by Propaganda.

The English Review: When Should Marriage be Dissolved?

Fortune Magazine: Citizenship in a Great State.

Magazine '47: Still Time For Good Sense.

Haldeman-Julius Company: An Outline of Intellectual Rubbish, Ideas that Have Harmed Mankind, Ideas that Have Helped Mankind.

Harcourt, Brace & Co.: Bolshevism: Practice and Theory, Freedom and Government, The Analysis of Matter.

Harper & Brothers: ABC of Relativity, On the Evils Due to Fear, Foreword to Feibleman's An Introduction to Pierce's Philosophy, Democracy and Education.

Harper's Magazine: The Functions of a Teacher.

The New York Herald Tribune (This Week): The High Cost of Survival.

The Hibbert Journal: The Essence of Religion.

Hogarth Press: The Amberley Papers.

Independent Review: On History.

International Journal of Ethics: Marriage and the Population Question.

Michael Joseph, Ltd.: Which Way to Peace?

The New Leader: A World Federation.

Library of Living Philosophers, Inc.: My Mental Development, Reply to Criticisms, Dewey's New Logic, The Philosophy of Santayana.

The Listener (The British Broadcasting Corporation): Social Cohesion and Human Nature.

Liveright Publishing Corporation: Why Men Fight, Styles in Ethics,

Education and the Good Life, The Conquest of Happiness, Marriage and Morals.

Longmans, Green & Co.: Science.

The Macmillan Company: Introduction to Mathematical Philosophy, The Analysis of Mind, Logical Atomism, Science and Social Institutions.

The Modern Library (Random House, Inc.): Introduction to Selected Papers of Bertrand Russell, Hegel's Philosophy of History, Descartes' Discourse on Method, Spinoza's Ethics, Carroll's Alice in Wonderland.

Modern Monthly: Why I am not a Communist.

The Nation: Munich Rather than War: Must Democracy Use Force?, The Superior Virtue of the Oppressed.

National Book League: Philosophy and Politics.

The New Palestine: Zionism and the Peace Settlement.

The New Republic: Hopes and Fears as Regards America; The Future of Democracy.

The New York Times: Letter on the Bertrand Russell Case.

The New York Times Magazine: The Science to Save Us from Science, Can We Afford to Keep Open Minds?, If We are to Survive This Dark Time, The Kind of Fear We Sorely Need, To Replace Our Hopes with Fears, To Face Danger without Hysteria.

W. W. Norton & Company, Inc.: Our Knowledge of the External World, Mysticism and Logic, Philosophy, In Praise of Idleness, Education and the Modern World, Sceptical Essays, Inquiry into Meaning and Truth, The Scientific Outlook, Power, The Amberley Papers, Freedom versus Organization.

Open Court Publishing Company: Justice in War-Time.

Oxford University Press: Religion and Science, Problems of Philosophy.

G. P. Putnam's Sons: What is Happiness?

Rand School of Social Science: How to be Free and Happy.

Rationalist Press Association: The Faith of a Rationalist, Why I am not a Christian.

The Reader's Digest: A Philosophy for You in These Times.

Routledge and Kegan Paul, Ltd.: ABC of Atoms, Icarus, ABC of Relativity, What I Believe, Analysis of Matter.

St. Louis Post Dispatch: Science and Education.

Saturday Evening Post: Can Americans and British be Friends?

Saturday Review of Literature: Came the Revolution.

Simon & Schuster, Inc.: What I Believe, Living Philosophy Revised,

Human Knowledge, Authority and the Individual, Unpopular Essays, History of Western Philosophy.

Survey Graphic (Survey Associates, Inc.): Democracy and Economics.

Tomorrow: Education in International Understanding.

United Nations World (Free World): Boredom or Doom in a Scientific World, A Guide for Living in the Atomic Age, Is a Third War Inevitable?, Some Problems of a Post War World, The International Significance of the Indian Problem.

D. Van Nostrand Company, Inc.: Three Ways to the World.

The Viking Press (Successor to B. W. Huebsch): Free Thought and Official Propaganda.

Vogue (The Conde Nast Publications, Inc.): The Impact of America upon European Culture.

C. A. Watts & Co., Ltd.: My Religious Reminiscences, Has Religion Made Useful Contributions to Civilization?

Ordering Information For
Philosophy Books
From Carol Publishing Group

Thank you for choosing this book.

Carol Publishing Group offers many additional books from some of the great philosophical and theological thinkers of all time, including Sartre, Paine, Einstein and Buber.

Ask for the titles listed below at your bookstore. Or to order direct from the publisher call 1-800-447-BOOK (MasterCard or Visa) or send a check or money order for the books purchased (plus $3.00 shipping and handling for the first book ordered and 50¢ for each additional book) to Carol Publishing Group, 120 Enterprise Avenue, Distribution Center BR, Secaucus, NJ 07094

The Age of Reason by Thomas Paine, paperback $7.95 (#50549)

The Bertrand Russell Dictionary of Mind, Matter & Morals, paperback $9.95 (#51400)

The Christ by Charles Guignebert, paperback $9.95 (#51143)

The Creative Mind: An Introduction to Metaphysics by Henri Bergson, paperback $8.95 (#50421)

Deceptions and Myths of the Bible by Lloyd M. Graham, paperback $14.95 (#51124)

The Diary of Soren Kierkegaard, paperback $7.95 (#50251)

The Emotions: Outline of a Theory by Jean-Paul Sartre, paperback $5.95 (#50904)

Essays in Existentialism, by Jean-Paul Sartre, paperback $9.95 (#50162)

The Ethics of Ambiguity by Simone de Beauvoir, paperback $7.95 (#50160)

The Ethics of Spinoza, paperback $8.95 (#50536)

Existentalism and Human Emotions by Jean-Paul Sartre, paperback $6.95 (#50902)

The Great Secret by Maurice Maeterlinck, paperback $7.95 (#51155)

The Life and Major Writings of Thomas Paine, paperback $15.95 (#50414)

Literature & Existentialism by Jean-Paul Sartre, paperback $4.95 (#50105)

The Mystery-Religions and Christianity by Samuel Angus, paperback $9.95 (#51142)

Out of My Later Years by Dr. Albert Einstein, paperback $9.95 (#50357)

Philosophers of China: Classical and Contemporary by Clarence Burton Day, paperback $5.95 (#50622)

The Philosophy of Existentialism by Dr. Gabriel Marcel, paperback $5.95 (#50901)

The Psychology of Imagination by Jean-Paul Sartre, paperback $8.95 (#50305)

Rights of Man by Thomas Paine, paperback $9.95 (#50548)

The Sayings of Muhammad by Allama Sir-Abdullah Al-Mamum Al-Suhrawardy, paperback $6.95 (#51169)

The Unfinished Dialogue: Martin Buber and the Christian Way by John M. Oesterreicher, paperback $5.95 (#51050)

The World As I See It by Dr. Albert Einstein, paperback $7.95 (#50711)

Prices subject to change. Books subject to availability.